C000055397

Business Studies
CLASS–XII (2020-21)

Theory: 80 Marks
Project: 20 Marks

3 Hours

Units		Periods	Marks
Part A	**Principles and Functions of Management**		
1.	Nature and Significance of Management	12	16
2	Principles of Management	14	
3	Business Environment	12	
4	Planning	14	14
5	Organising	15	
6	Staffing	16	20
7	Directing	15	
8	Controlling	12	
	Total	**110**	**50**
Part B	**Business Finance and Marketing**		
9	Financial Management	20	15
10	Financial Markets	18	
11	Marketing Management	30	15
12	Consumer Protection	12	
	Total	**80**	**30**
Part C	**Project Work (One)**	**30**	**20**

Part A: Principles and Functions of Management

Unit 1: Nature and Significance of Management

Concept	After going through this unit, the student/ learner would be able to:
Management - concept, objectives, and importance	<ul><li>Understand the concept of management.</li><li>Explain the meaning of 'Effectiveness and Efficiency.</li><li>Discuss the objectives of management.</li><li>Describe the importance of management.</li></ul>
Management as Science, Art and Profession	<ul><li>Examine the nature of management as a science, art and profession.</li></ul>
Levels of Management	<ul><li>Understand the role of top, middle and lower levels of management</li></ul>
Management functions-planning, organizing, staffing, directing and controlling	<ul><li>Explain the functions of management</li></ul>
Coordination- concept and importance	Discuss the concept and characteristics of coordination. <ul><li>Explain the importance of coordination.</li></ul>

Unit 2: Principles of Management

Principles of Management- concept and significance	• Understand the concept of principles of management. • Explain the significance of management principles.
Fayol's principles of management	• Discuss the principles of management developed by Fayol.
Taylor's Scientific management- principles and techniques	• Explain the principles and techniques of 'Scientific Management'. • Compare the contributions of Fayol and Taylor.

Unit 3: Business Environment

Business Environment- concept and importance	• Understand the concept of 'Business Environment'. • Describe the importance of business environment
Dimensions of Business Environment- Economic, Social, Technological, Political and Legal Demonetization - concept and features	• Describe the various dimensions of 'Business Environment'. • Understand the concept of demonetization
Impact of Government policy changes on business with special reference to liberalization, privatization and globalization in India	• Examine the impact of government policy changes on business in India with reference to liberalisation, privatization and globalisation since 1991. • Discuss the managerial response to changes in business environment.

Unit 4: Planning

Concept, importance and limitation	• Understand the concept of planning. • Describe the importance of planning. • Understand the limitations of planning.
Planning process	• Describe the steps in the process of planning.
Single use and standing plans. Objectives, Strategy, Policy, Procedure, method Rule, budget and Programme	• Develop an understanding of single use and standing plans • Describe objectives, policies, strategy, procedure, method, rule, budget and programme as types of plans

Unit 5: Organising

Concept and importance	• Understand the concept of organizing as a structure and as a process. • Explain the importance of organising.
Organising Process	• Describe the steps in the process of organizing
Structure of organisation- functional and divisional concept. Formal and informal organisation- concept	• Describe functional and divisional structures of organisation. • Explain the advantages, disadvantages and suitability of functional and divisional structure. • Understand the concept of formal and informal organisation. • Discuss the advantages, disadvantages of formal and informal organisation.
Delegation: concept, elements and importance	• Understand the concept of delegation. • Describe the elements of delegation. • Appreciate the importance of Delegation.
Decentralization: concept and importance	• Understand the concept of decentralisation. • Explain the importance of decentralisation. • Differentiate between delegation and decentralisation.

Unit 6: Staffing

Concept and importance of staffing	• Understand the concept of staffing. • Explain the importance of staffing
Staffing as a part of Human Resource Management concept	• Understand the specialized duties and activities performed by Human Resource Management
Staffing process	• Describe the steps in the process of staffing
Recruitment process	• Understand the meaning of recruitment. • Discuss the sources of recruitment. • Explain the merits and demerits of internal and external sources of recruitment.

Selection - process	<ul><li>Understand the meaning of selection.</li><li>Describe the steps involved in the process of selection.</li></ul>
Training and Development - Concept and importance, Methods of training - on the job and off the job - vestibule training, apprenticeship training and internship training	<ul><li>Understand the concept of training and development.</li><li>Appreciate the importance of training to the organisation and to the employees.</li><li>Discuss the meaning of induction training, vestibule training, apprenticeship training and internship training.</li><li>Differentiate between training and development.</li><li>Discuss on the job and off the job methods of training.</li></ul>

Unit 7: Directing

Concept and importance	<ul><li>Describe the concept of directing.</li><li>Discuss the importance of directing</li></ul>
Elements of Directing	<ul><li>Describe the various elements of directing</li></ul>
Motivation - concept, Maslow's hierarchy of needs, Financial and non-financial incentives	<ul><li>Understand the concept of motivation.</li><li>Develop an understanding of Maslow's Hierarchy of needs.</li><li>Discuss the various financial and non-financial incentives.</li></ul>
Leadership - concept, styles - authoritative, democratic and laissez faire	<ul><li>Understand the concept of leadership.</li><li>Understand the various styles of leadership.</li></ul>
Communication - concept, formal and informal communication; barriers to effective communication, how to overcome the barriers	<ul><li>Understand the concept of communication</li><li>Understand the elements of the communication process.</li><li>Discuss the concept of formal and informal communication.</li><li>Discuss the various barriers to effective communication.</li><li>Suggest measures to overcome barriers to communication.</li></ul>

A to Z Business Studies

As Per the New syllabus of C.B.S.E New Delhi
For Class XII

Aakash Tiwari

NOTION PRESS

A to Z Business Studies

As Per the New syllabus of C.B.S.E New Delhi

Publisher:

NOTION PRESS

Old No. 38, New No. 6, Mc Nichols Road,
Chetpet, Chennai, Tamil Nadu 600031

India. Singapore. Malaysia.

ISBN- 9798602625806

.First Edition

NOTICE: This book has been published with all reasonable efforts taken to make the material error-free after the consent of the author. No part of this book shall be used, reproduced in any manner whatsoever without written permission from the author, except in the case of brief quotations embodied in critical articles and reviews

Price: ₹ 450.00

Unit 8: Controlling

Controlling - Concept and importance	<ul><li>Understand the concept of controlling.</li><li>Explain the importance of controlling.</li></ul>
Relationship between planning and controlling	<ul><li>Describe the relationship between planning and controlling</li></ul>
Steps in process of control	<ul><li>Discuss the steps in the process of controlling.</li></ul>

Part B: Business Finance and Marketing

Unit 9: Financial Management

Concept, role and objectives of Financial Management	<ul><li>Understand the concept of financial management.</li><li>Explain the role of financial management in an organisation.</li><li>Discuss the objectives of financial management</li></ul>
Financial decisions: investment, financing and dividend- Meaning and factors affecting	<ul><li>Discuss the three financial decisions and the factors affecting them.</li></ul>
Financial Planning - concept and importance	<ul><li>Describe the concept of financial planning and its objectives.</li><li>Explain the importance of financial planning.</li></ul>
Capital Structure – concept and factors affecting capital structure	<ul><li>Understand the concept of capital structure.</li><li>Describe the factors determining the choice of an appropriate capital structure of a company.</li></ul>
Fixed and Working Capital - Concept and factors affecting their requirements	<ul><li>Understand the concept of fixed and working capital.</li><li>Describe the factors determining the requirements of fixed and working capital.</li></ul>

Unit 10: Financial Markets

Financial Markets: Concept, Functions and types	<ul><li>Understand the concept of financial market.</li><li>Explain the functions of financial market.</li><li>Understand capital market and money market as types of financial markets</li></ul>
Money market and its instruments	<ul><li>Understand the concept of money market.</li><li>Describe the various money market instruments.</li></ul>

Capital market and its types (primary and secondary), methods of floatation in the primary market	<ul><li>Discuss the concept of capital market.</li><li>Explain primary and secondary markets as types of capital market.</li><li>Differentiate between capital market and money market.</li><li>Discuss the methods of floating new issues in the primary market.</li><li>Distinguish between primary and secondary markets.</li></ul>
Stock Exchange - Functions and trading procedure	<ul><li>Give the meaning of a stock exchange.</li><li>Explain the functions of a stock exchange.</li><li>Discuss the trading procedure in a stock exchange.</li><li>Give the meaning of depository services and demat account as used in the trading procedure of securities.</li></ul>
Securities and Exchange Board of India (SEBI) - objectives and functions	<ul><li>State the objectives of SEBI.</li><li>Explain the functions of SEBI.</li></ul>

Unit 11: Marketing

Marketing – Concept, functions and philosophies	<ul><li>Understand the concept of marketing.</li><li>Explain the features of marketing.</li><li>Discuss the functions of marketing.</li><li>Explain the marketing philosophies.</li></ul>
Marketing Mix – Concept and elements	<ul><li>Understand the concept of marketing mix.</li><li>Describe the elements of marketing mix.</li></ul>
Product - branding, labelling and packaging – Concept	<ul><li>Understand the concept of product as an element of marketing mix.</li><li>Understand the concept of branding, labelling and packaging.</li></ul>
Price - Concept, Factors determining price	<ul><li>Understand the concept of price as an element of marketing mix.</li><li>Describe the factors determining price of a product.</li></ul>
Physical Distribution – concept, components and channels of distribution	<ul><li>Understand the concept of physical distribution.</li><li>Explain the components of physical distribution.</li><li>Describe the various channels of distribution.</li></ul>

Promotion – Concept and elements; Advertising, Personal Selling, Sales Promotion and Public Relations	<ul><li>Understand the concept of promotion as an element of marketing mix.</li><li>Describe the elements of promotion mix.</li><li>Understand the concept of advertising.</li><li>Understand the concept of sales promotion.</li><li>Discuss the concept of public relations.</li></ul>

Unit 12: Consumer Protection

Concept and importance of consumer protection	<ul><li>Understand the concept of consumer protection.</li><li>Describe the importance of consumer protection.</li><li>Discuss the scope of Consumer Protection Act, 1986</li></ul>
Consumer Protection Act 1986: Meaning of consumer Rights and responsibilities of consumers Who can file a complaint? Redressal machinery Remedies available	<ul><li>Understand the concept of a consumer according to the Consumer protection Act 1986.</li><li>Explain the consumer rights</li><li>Understand the responsibilities of consumers</li><li>Understand who can file a complaint and against whom?</li><li>Discuss the legal redressal machinery under Consumer protection Act 1986.</li><li>Examine the remedies available to the consumer under Consumer protection Act 1986.</li></ul>
Consumer awareness - Role of consumer organizations and Non-Governmental Organizations (NGOs)	<ul><li>Describe the role of consumer organizations and NGOs in protecting consumers' interests.</li></ul>

Unit 13: Project Work

Question Paper Design
Business Studies (Code No. 054)
Class XII (2020-21)
March 2021 Examination

Marks: 80   **Duration: 3 hrs.**

SN	Typology of Questions	Objective Type/ MCQ 1 Mark	Short Answer I 3 Marks	Short Answer II 4 Marks	Long Answer I 5 Marks	Long Answer II 6 Marks	Marks
1	**Remembering**: Exhibit memory of previously learned material by recalling facts, terms, basic concepts, and answers.	5	1	1	1	1	23
2	**Understanding**: Demonstrate understanding of facts and ideas by organizing, comparing, translating, interpreting, giving descriptions, and stating main ideas	5	2	1	-	1	21
3	**Applying**: Solve problems to new situations by applying acquired knowledge, facts, techniques and rules in a different way.	5	1	-	1	1	19
4	**Analysing and Evaluating:** Examine and break information into parts by identifying motives or causes. Make inferences and find evidence to support generalizations. Present and defend opinions by making judgments about information, validity of ideas, or quality of work based on a set of criteria. **Creating**: Compile information together in a different way by combining elements in a new pattern or proposing alternative solutions.	5	1	1	1	-	17
	Total	20x1=20	5x3=15	3x4=12	3x5=15	3x6=18	80 (34)

There will be **Internal Choice** in questions of 3 marks (1 choice), 4 marks (1 choice), 5 marks (2 choices) and 6 marks (2 choices). In all, total 6 internal choices.

BUSINESS STUDIES
Contents

Part -A:Principles and Functions of Management

Part-B: Business Finance and Marketing

Part-C: Project Work

Part-D: EXAMINATION ZONE

Part A:
Principles and Functions of Management

NATURE AND SIGNIFICANCE OF MANAGEMENT

CONTENT

☞ **Introduction :**

To Traditional Viewpoint of management is considered inappropriate in the present day environment where workers are educated and have higher level of aspirations. In present day environment it is not possible direct the efforts of employees by force. It is necessary to create an environment so that employee perform in desired manager; on the other hand, traditional definition does not define functions of management.

☞ **Concept of Management**

1. Process.   2. Effective and efficient performance

☞ **Characteristics of Management**

1. Management is goal oriented process.   2. Management is Pervasive.
3. Management is Multidimensional.
   (a) Management of work
   (b) Management of People.
   (c) Management of Operations.
4. Management is Continuous process.   5. Management is Group Activity.
6. Management is a dynamic function.   7. Management is an intangible force.
8. Management is a composite process..

☞ **Objectives of Management**

1. Organisational Objectives.
2. Social Objectives.
3. Personal Objectives.

☞ **Importance of Management**

1. Management helps in achieving group goal.
2. Management improves efficiency.
3. Management creates a dynamic organisation.
4. Management brings harmony in work.
5. Management helps in achieving personal objectives.
6. Management helps in development of society.

☞ **Nature of Management**

1. Management is an Art.
2. Management as a Science.
3. Management as a Profession.

☞ **Levels of Management**

1. Top Level Management.
2. Middle Level Management.
3. Supervisory Level Management.

☞ **Functions of Management**

1. Planning.
2. Organising.
3. Staffing.

4.   Directing.
5.   Controlling

☞ **Co-ordination**
Co-ordination: The Essence of Management.
Nature/Features of Co-ordination
1.   Coordination Integrate Group Efforts.
2.   Ensure Unity of efforts.
3.   Continuous process.
4.   Coordination is a pervasive function.
5.   Coordination is the responsibility of all managers.
6.   Coordination is a deliberate function.

☞ **Importance of Co-ordination**
1.   Size of organisation.
2.   Functional differentiation.
3.   Specialization.

WEIGHTAGE

Units	Very Short Answer	Short Answer I & II	Long Answer I & II	Total
Unit-1(5)	………	………	5(1)	5(1)

---

1.   NATURE AND SIGNIFICANCE OF MANAGEMENT

☞ **MEANING OF MANAGEMENT**
Every organisation represents group of people whose efforts are directed towards certain common objectives. These objectives are not achieved by chance, but through a process called 'management'. Management process refers/includes series of functions like planning, organizing, staffing, directing & controlling their activities to attain common organisational goal.

☞ **CONCEPT OF MANAGEMENT**
Traditional Concept of Management
Defined as - **"Management is the art of getting things done through others"**.

Mary Parker Follett

Modern concept of Management
Defined as - **"Management is a process of getting things done with the aim of achieving goals effectively and efficiently"**.

Modern definition insists on:
1.   **Process :** Process refers to the series of steps or basic functions necessary to get the things done. These steps are planning, organizing, staffing, directing and controlling.
2.   **Effectiveness and Efficiency: -**

Effectiveness means doing the right task and completing it within the given time period.
"Doing the Right things"

Efficiency means doing the task correctly, using resources wisely and in cost effective manner.

"Doing Things Right"

DIFFERENCE BETWEEN EFFICIENCY AND EFFECTIVENESS

Basis of Difference	Efficiency	Effectiveness
1. Orientation	Input-Output Orientation	Goal – achievement orientation
2. Emphasis	Doing things rightly	Doing right things
3. Focus	Means	Ends
4. Determining Factors	Internal	External

☞ **Characteristics or Features Management**

1. **Management is goal oriented process:** Management always aims at achieving the organisational objectives. The functions and activities of manager lead to the achievement of organisational objectives; for example, if the objective of a company is to sell 1000 computers then manager will plan the course of action, motivate all the employees and organise all the resources keeping in mind the main target of selling 1000 computers. .

2. **Management is all pervasive :** Anything m1nus management is nothing or zero. Here by anything we mean all types of activities – business and non – business. If we deduct management out of these activities, the result will be failure or zero. It means management is necessary to conduct any type of activities. Hence, it is pervasive or universal.

3. **Management is multidimensional:** Management does not mean one single activity but it includes three main activities:

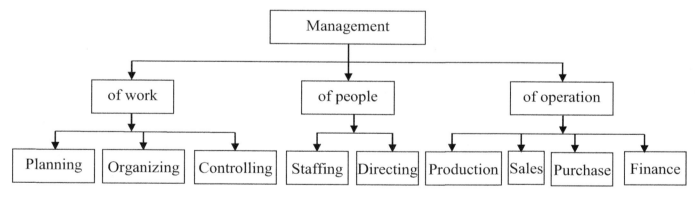

(a) **Management of Work:** Every organisation is established for doing some work, like a school provides education a hospital treats patients, a factory produces some product etc. **"Management make sure that work is accomplished effectively and efficiently".**

(b) **Management of People :** People refers to Human resources and Human resources are the most important assets of an organisation. Two organisation can easily acquire same type of physical and financial resources but what helps organisation to win over the other is the efficient staff. **"Management of people means reinforcing their strength and eliminating their weakness."**

(c)   **Management of Operations :** Operations refers to activities of production cycle such as buying inputs, converting them into semi-finished goods, finished goods or This process involves transform input into desired output for customer. Management of operations concentrates on mixing management of work with management of people i.e., deciding what work has to be done, how it has to be done and who will do it.

4.   **Management is a continuous process :** Management is a continuous or never ending function. All the functions of management are performed continuously, for example planning, organising, staffing, directing and controlling are performed by all the managers all the time. Sometimes, they are doing planning, then staffing or organising etc. Managers performs ongoing series of functions continuously in the organisation.

5.   **Management is a group activity:** It means that it is not a single person who consummates all the activities of an organisation. An organisation is a group of different individuals who work together in team spirit and coordination to achieve the goals of the organisation.

6.   **Management is a dynamic function :** In order to be successful, an organisation must change itself and its goals according to the needs of the environment, which consists of various economic, social, technological, legal and political factors. For example, McDonald's, the fast food restaurant, made major changes in its menu to be able to survive in the Indian market.

7.   **Management is an intangible force:** Management is that power which cannot be seen. It can only be felt. If any organisation is leading toward higher levels of achievement, it signifies the existence of good management and vice versa. In other words, achievement reflects the quality of management and its effectiveness.

8.   **Management is a composite process:** Management consists of series of functions which must be performed in a proper sequence. These functions are not independent of each other. They are interdependent on each other. As the main functions of management are planning, organising, staffing, directing and controlling; organizing cannot be done without planning, similarly directing function cannot be executed without staffing and planning and it is difficult to control the activities of employees without knowing the plan. All the functions inter-dependent on each other that is why management is considered as a composite process of all these functions.

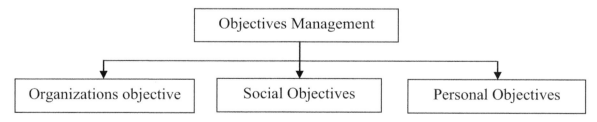

☞   **Objectives of Management**

1.   **Organisational objectives :** The main objective of any organization should be to utilize human and material resources to the maximum possible advantage, i.e., to fulfill the economic objectives of a business. These are survival, profit and growth.

A.   **Survival :** The basic purpose of every organisation is to survive and exist in the competition market for a long period of time and it is possible only when it is able to cover its cost and earn profit.

B.   **Profit:** The most important objective of every organisation is earning adequate amount of profit. Profit is essential for survival, growth and expansion of business. Profit is the reward given to businessman for bearing risk.

C.   **Growth:** Every Business want to grow management must ensure growth of business. Growth can be measured (a) increase in sales turnover, (b) increase in the number of product and employee, (c) increase in capital investment, etc.

2.   **Social Objectives :** It refers to the consideration of the interest of the society during managerial activities. An organisation is established in a society. It runs through the resources made available by the society. That is why it become the responsibility of every organisation to account for social benefits. These are :-
(a)   To supply quality goods and services at reasonable prices.
(b)   Pollution free methods of production.
(c)   Increasing employment opportunities especially for the economically weaker sections of the society and back ward classes.
(d)   Providing basic facilities to the employees like medical facilities, schools etc.

3.   **Personal Objectives :** Individual objectives are related to the employees of the organization. As employees are most important resources of every company and satisfied and motivated employees contribute maximum for the organisations.
Main objectives of management towards employees are as follows:
(i)   To give deserving remuneration.
(ii)   To provide good working environment.
(iii) To provide a share in profit.

☞ **IMPORTANCE OF MANAGEMENT**
Anything — Management = Zero/Failure/Nothing

The above mentioned mathematical equation highlights the significance of management very well.

1. **Management helps in the achieving group goal:** Management tries to integrate the objective of individuals along with organisational goal. Management directs the efforts of all the individuals in the common direction of achieving organisational goal.

2. **Management improves efficiency:** Manager try to reduce the cost and improve productivity with minimum wastage of resources. Management insists on efficiency and effectiveness in the work through function of Management.

3. **Management creates a dynamic organisation :** Every organisation works in an ever changing environment. To face the changing environment, many changes need to be made in the organisation as well. But people resist changes. Manager creates a favourable environment through introducing employees to the benefits of adapting to changes.

4. **Management brings harmony in work :** In an organisation employees come from different background, they have different attitudes and different styles of working and every one start following his own style, it can lead to chaos and confusion in the organisation. By giving direction manager bring uniformity and harmony in the action of employees.

5. **Management helps in achieving personal objective :** Efficient managers read the people in such a manner that along with organisational goal individual goal of employees is also achieved. As organisational and individual goal are in one direction employees can earn more by producing more. This will fulfill the objectives of both groups.

6. **Management helps in the development of society :** Management has some responsibility towards society. Managers by fulfilling their social responsibilities help in the development of society. These responsibilities include providing employment opportunities, preventing environment from getting polluted, making available good quality products at a reasonable price, etc.

☞ **NATURE OF MANA&EMENT**

A. **Management is an Art:**
An art requires application of personal skills and knowledge to achieve the desired results. It involves continuous practice and creativity. It can be attained with the help of study, observation and experience.

Following are main features of art :
(i) **Existence of theoretical knowledge :** Art is always based on certain theoretical knowledge. On the basis of this knowledge one can understand how a particular work can be accomplished. For example Music, Singing, Acting etc.

In this context management is an art as a lot of literature is available in various areas of management like Marketing, Finance and Human Resources. Thus, management possesses this feature of art.

(ii) **Personalised application :** The use of available theoretical knowledge is found in varying degree among different persons. For example, two teachers, two players, or two goldsmiths will always differ in performing their jobs. Management possesses this feature of art too. There are various principles of management as developed by management experts. Managers apply these principles differently depending on their level of knowledge. Sometimes they may get exactly opposite results while applying the same principles.

(iii)   **Based on Practice and creativity :** Just as art can be embellished with the help of practice, in the same way managerial skill also improves with practice. Every manager has a desire to become a complete expert in his field. They can fulfill their desire by continuous practice. A fully developed manager not only moulds the organisation according to the changing circumstances but also has the capacity to change the outward circumstances according to his will. Thus, management possesses this feature of art too.

B.   **Management as a Science :** Science refer to that systematic body of knowledge which comprises of exact principles which is acquired on the basis of observation and experiments and verification of this knowledge is possible.

Following are the main features of science:

(i)   **Systematic body of knowledge :** In science organised and systematic study material is available which is used to acquire the knowledge of science. Like science in management also there is systematic body of knowledge because it has its own theory and principles which are developed by the management experts after years of research like Henry Fayol & F.W. Taylor.

(ii)   **Principles are based on repeated experiments :** Before developing scientific principles scientists test these principles under different conditions and places. Similarly, managers also test and experiment managerial principles under different conditions in different organisations. But, since management deals with human beings and human behavior, the results of these experiments are not so exact. Thus management may be called as inexact science.

(iii)   **Universal Validity:** Scientific principles are based on truth and they can be applied at every time and in every situation. Thus, its universal application is possible. In the field of management too, managerial knowledge and principles of management are considered to be based on truth and they, too, can be applied anywhere and in every situation. But the principles of management are not as exact as the principles of science as their application may not yield the desired results always.

Conclusion:- The management cannot be treated as a perfect science, but as its principles are subject to change with time, situation and human nature, it is better to call it Applied Science or Inexact Science. Ernest Dale has called management a soft science because its principles are not very rigid.

Why Management is not considered as pure science?
                 OR
Why Management is called as Inxact Science?
The absence of two main features of science viz 'Principle based on experimentation' and 'Universal Validity', management cannot be considered as a perfect science, rather it is a social science. The principle and theories of Management are situational i.e. their results vary depending upon the situation. That is why it is regarded as 'Soft Science' and sometime it is also called as 'Inexact science'. The main reasons for the inexactness of science of management are:

    (a)   As in perfect science like chemistry, it is difficult to establish cause and effect relationship in management.

    (b)   Many of the principles of Management are not the outcome of research.

    (c)   Situation factors affect the application of management principles.

    (d)   Management deals with human beings, whose behaviour is very difficult to predict accurately.

C.   **Management as a Profession:** Profession refers to that economic activity which is conducted by a person having some special knowledge and skill which is acquired through training and instruction & follows ethical standards to serve various sections of society.

Following are the main features of profession

    (i)   **Well defined body of Knowledge :** The foremost quality of a professional is the possession of specialized knowledge which is acquired through training and instruction. Management has its own principles based on experiments. It requires special competence to bring them into use. On this basis management can be accepted as a profession.

    (ii)   **Restricted Entry :** The entry to a profession is restricted through acquiring educational degree. For example a degree in law is essential for joining the law profession but as far as the management is concerned there is no such condition for being a manager. Hence on this basis management cannot be accepted as a profession.

    (iii)   **Professional Association :** All professions are affiliated to a professional association which regulates entry, grants certificate of practice and formulates & enforce a code of conduct. For example:- Bar council of India for Lawyer, Medical council of India for Doctors etc. for managers All India Management Association (AIMA) has been established. But it is not essential to be a member of the AIMA in order to a manager. Therefore on this basis cannot be accepted as a profession.

    (iv)   **Ethical code of Conduct:** Members of a profession are bound to follow a code of conduct which means the rules and regulations framed to guide the behaviour of professionals. In case of management AIMA has devised a code of conduct for Indian managers. But its membership is not compulsory for all managers. Here also management cannot be accepted as a profession.

    (v)   **Service Motive:** The basic motive of a profession is to serve their client's. So they keep social interest in their mind while charging fee for their professional's services. Thus for professionals, clients interest is the first priority and not their fees. So in order to survive in a dynamic environment an organisation has to fulfill its social obligation such as good quality product at reasonable prices etc. along with its objective of maximizing profit. So here we can accept management as a profession.

Conclusion: Management is not a full fielded profession like legal or medical profession because it does not fulfill all the characteristics of a profession.

LEVELS OF MANAGEMENT

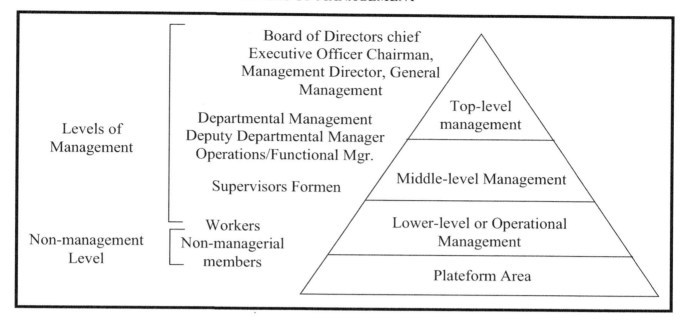

1. **Top Level Management**

    Top Level Management consists of the senior – most executives of the organisation. It is a team consisting of managers from different functional levels.

    IT CONSIST OF
    - ✓ Chairman,
    - ✓ Managing Director,
    - ✓ Board of Directors,
    - ✓ Chief Executive Officer.
    - ✓ Chief Operating Officer,
    - ✓ Chief Marketing Officer,
    - ✓ Chief Financial Officer
    - ✓ Joint Managing Director
    - ✓ President,
    - ✓ Vice President
    - ✓ General Manager etc.

    Top management has all the management authorities and because of these authorities officers of these levels are accountable to owners or share holders of the company.

Following Functions are included in the list for Top Level Management :—

(i) **Determining Objectives :** Top –level management sets objectives for the organisation. For example, an objective can be set that in the following year the sales of the company has to cross Rs.1,000 Crore.

(ii) **Determining Policies :** Only at this level policies related to the realization of objectives are formed. For example, it can be a sales policy of a company to just make cash sales.

(iii) **Determining Activities:** Different activities to be performed for the fulfillment of an objective are fixed, such as sales, purchase, advertisement, production, research, etc.

(iv) **Assembling Resources:** Needed resources are assembled (arranged) for the realization of an objective, like capital, raw material, fixed assets, etc.

(v) **Controlling the Work Performance :** The work – in – progress is closely monitored in a company to get the desired results.

(vi) **Approving Budgets :** Budgets prepared by different managers are given final shape, i.e., approval is given to the budgets.

2. **Middle Level Management :**
Middle level management lies between top level and lower level management.
IT CONSIST OF
- ✓ Divisional heads
- ✓ Branch Manager
- ✓ Departmental heads
- ✓ Functional head (Production, Marketing,
- ✓ Deputy Departmental heads Finance Manager etc)
- ✓ Plant Superintendents
- ✓ Executive Officer
- ✓ Human resources Manager
- ✓ Functional Vice President
- ✓ Assistant vice president
- ✓ Project Manager
- ✓ Operations Manager (Functional Manager)
- ✓ Factory Manager, etc

Main Following are the man Functions of Middle

(i) **Interpreting Policies :** At this level, policies framed by top level managers are interpreted. Like the marketing manager introduces his salesman to the sales policy of the company that at no cost credit sales will be made.

(ii) **Preparing Organisational Set – up :** Every middle – level managers prepares outline of his respective department in accordance with the objectives of the organsiation.

(iii) **Appointing Employees :** Every department manager appoints employees to fulfill the activities of his department.

(iv) **Issuing Instruction :** Departmental managers direct their subordinates about what to do and how they have to do it. Needful resources are made available to subordinates so that they can do the assigned jobs uninterrupted.

(v) **Motivating Employees :** Middle – Level managers motivate their employees by various means so that they work most efficiently to achieve organisational objectives.

(vi) **Creating Cooperation :** Cooperation among different divisions is required to successfully achieve company's objectives and this is done by middle level managers.

3. **Lower/Supervisory/Operational Level Management :** It is also known as supervisory management.
It consist of

- ✓ Supervisors
- ✓ File man
- ✓ Foreman
- ✓ Section officer
- ✓ Inspector
- ✓ Superintendent
- ✓ Charge Man etc.

They are also called first line Managers.

Their authority and responsibility is limited according to the plans drawn by the top management. But their importance cannot be overlooked. The quality and quantity of output depends upon this level.

☞ **Main Following are the main Functions of middle Level Management :**

(i) **Submitting Workers' Grievances :** Lower – level managers are in direct contact with the workmen who are directly engaged in the completion of work. They themselves sort out the ordinary problems of the workmen and submit workers' serious grievances to the middle level managers.

(ii) **Ensuring Proper Working Environment:** Lower – level managers ensure that proper arrangement of water, electricity, ventilation, cleanliness, etc. is made at the workplace. This increases efficiency.

(iii) **Ensuring Safety of Workers:** They look after safety of workers, avoiding accidents and providing them safe and secure working environment.

(iv) **Helping Middle – level Management :** They help middle – level managers in recruiting, training and promoting employees.

(v) **Inviting Suggestions :** They invite suggestions from their subordinates, as to how the quality of work can be improved.

(vi) **Creating Better Human Relations :** They create better human relations so that conflict/dispute can be avoided at the workplace.

Functions of Management

1. **Planning:** Planning is the primary function of management. It is concerned with both ends and means, i.e., what to do and how to do it. **Therefore, planning means setting objectives and targets and formulating an action plan to achieve them effectively and efficiently.**
   Planning cannot prevent problems, but it can predict them and prepare contingency plans to deal with them.

2. **Organising :** Once a specific plan has been established for the accomplishment of an organisational goal, the organizing function determines what activities and resources are required. It decides who will do a particular task, where it will be done and when it will be done.
   Thus, **organizing is the management function of assigning duties, grouping tasks, establishing authority and allocating resources required to carry out a specific plan.**

3. **Staffing :** A very important aspect of management is to make sure that the right people with the right qualifications are available at the right places and times to accomplish the goals of the organisation.
   Finding the right people for the right job is known as staffing.

Staffing function of management pertains to recruitment, selection, placement and training of personnel. Staffing function of management is also known as the human resource function.

4.   **Directing** : Directing is telling people what to do and seeing that they do it to the best of their ability. **Directing involves leading, influencing and motivating employees to perform the tasks assigned to them.**
There are four elements of directing, viz. (i) Supervision, (ii) Motivation, (iii) Leadership and (iv) Communication.

5.   **Controlling** : Controlling is the management function of monitoring organisational performance towards the attainment of organisational goals. It involves establishing standards of performance, measuring actual performance, comparing it with standards and taking corrective action where any significant deviation is found.
Managerial control implies the measurement, of accomplishment against the standard and the correction of deviations to assure attainment of objectives according to plans.

☞   **Coordination**
Concept of Coordination
Coordination means synchronizing the efforts by unifying, integrating and harmonizing the activities of different departments and individuals for the achievement of objectives.
It is through the process of coordination that a manager ensures the orderly arrangement of individuals and group efforts to ensure unity of action in the realization of common objectives.

☞   **Co-ordination : The Essence of Management**
Coordination is not a separate function of management, it is the essence of management.
Coordination is the force that binds all the other functions of management Coordination is implicit and inherent in all functions of management.
(i)   Coordination is required in **planning**
   ✓   The objective and available resources.
   ✓   The master plan and plans of different departments and divisions.
      e.g., 'coordination between production department plans and sales department targets.
(ii)   Coordination is required in **organizing**
   ✓   For resources of an organisation and activities to be performed.
   ✓   For assigning authority, responsibility and accountability.
      e.g., if the finance manager is given authority to raise funds, he/she should also be given the responsibility to manager funds efficiently.
(iii)   Coordination in **staffing** is needed
   ✓   between skill of workers and jobs assigned to them.
   ✓   between efficiency of workers and the compensation.
      e.g., a CA should generally be given work of financial nature.

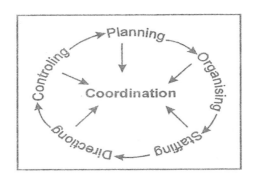

(iv)   Coordination in **directing** is required
- ✓   among orders, instructions and suggestions.
- ✓   among superiors and subordinates

e.g., a manager instructs the subordinates, motivates them and also supervises their work.

(v)   Coordination in **controlling** is required
- ✓   between planned standards and actual performance.
- ✓   between correction of deviation and achievement of objective.

e.g., if the planned target is 100 units of output and the actual output is 80 units, then corrective action is taken to ensure that plans coordinate with actual performance.

☞ **Nature/Features of Co-ordination**

1. **Coordination Integrate Group Efforts :** The concept of co-ordination always applies to group efforts. There is no need for co-ordination when only single individual is working. The need for orderliness, integration arises only when more individuals are working as different individuals come from different backgrounds, have different styles of working so there is need to unify their efforts in common direction.

2. **Ensure Unity of efforts :** Co-ordination always emphasizes on unifying the efforts of different individuals because conflicting efforts may cause damage to organisation. The main aim of every manager is to co-ordinate the activities and functions of all individuals to common goal.

3. **Continuous process :** Co-ordination is a non-ending function. It is a continuous function although its degree may vary. The managers work continuously to achieve co-ordination and maintain coordination because without co-ordination companies cannot function efficiently.

4. **Coordination is a pervasive function :** Co-ordination is a universal function, it is required at all the levels, in all the departments and to perform all the functions due to interdependence of various activities on each other. For example if low quality inputs are purchased by purchase department, it will result in production of low quality product which further result in low sale, low revenue and so on.

5. **Coordination is the responsibility of all managers :** Coordination is not the task of only top level managers but managers working at different levels try to coordinate the activities of organisation. The top level try to coordinate the overall plans and policies of organisation, middle level try to coordinate departmental activities and lower level coordinate the activities of workers.

6. **Coordination is a deliberate function :** Every manager tries to coordinate the activities or organisation to avoid confusion and chaos. Without coordination efforts of individuals cannot be united and integrated; that is why while performing various activities in the organisation managers deliberately performs coordination function.

☞ **Importance of Co-ordination**

The need and importance of coordination can be more clear by the following points:

1. **Size of organisation :** The need of coordination increases with the increase in size of organisation because in large organisation there are more number of persons working each individual has his own needs and objectives, so there is more need to bring together or synchronies the efforts of these employees towards common goal. Employees may have their individual objectives. For

organisational efficiency it is important to harmonies individual goals and organisational goals through coordination.

2. **Functional differentiation :** The functions of an organisation are divided into different departments, sections or divisions and each department works in isolation by giving more importance to its objective. But in actual practice these departments are interlinked and interdependent. So there is more need to relate and bring together the activities of different sections as they are part of one organisation only. The coordination is needed to minimize the differences among departments.

3. **Specialization :** In large and modern organisation these is high degree of specialization and the specialists or experts feel that they are the only qualified people and they always take right decision in right direction. There are number of specialists working in the organisation. If all of them work in their own way it will result in chaos and confusion. So there is need to coordinate the activities of all the specialists in a common direction and get maximum benefit of these specialists.

Difference Between Co-ordination and Co-operation

	Basis	Co-ordination	Co-operation
1.	Meaning	Co-ordination refers to bringing together the activities of an organisation.	Co-operation refers to voluntary efforts of in individuals is to work together and help each other.
2.	Nature	Co-ordination is a conscious and deliberate action of manager.	It is a voluntary effort of employees.
3.	Interdependence	Co-ordination is interdependent upon co-operation as it is incomplete without it.	Co-operation is also dependent upon co-operation as it is meaningless without it.
4.	Relations	It includes co-operation and hence has a wider scope.	Co-operation arises out of informal relations.
5.	Scope	It includes co-operation and hence has a wider scope.	It has a narrow scope as it is towards establishing coordination.
6.	Requirement	Co-ordination is essential for achievement of organisational goal, where a group of people work together.	Co-operation is voluntary in nature, it arises only when people desire to work together.

EXERCISE — 1

Very Short Answer Questions:

Q 1.   'In an organisation employees are happy and satisfied, there is no chaos and the effect of management is noticeable.' Which characteristic of management is highlighted by this statement?

Ans.   Management is an intangible force.

Q 2.   'The management principles can be applied to all types of activities.' Which characteristic of management is highlighted by this statement?

Ans.   Management is all-pervasive.

Q 3.   Name the process of designing and maintaining an environment in which individuals working together in groups, efficiently accomplish selected aims.

Ans.   Management.

Q 4.   Why is it said that management is a goal-oriented process?

Ans.   Management is said to be goal-oriented process as it helps in getting goals by coordinating the efforts of various individuals.

Q 5.   Why is "management called a group activity"?

Ans.   It means that it is not a single person (manager) who consummates the whole process of management but it is conducted by a group of persons (managers).

Q 6.   Volvo Ltd.'s target is to produce 10,000 shirts per month at a cost of Rs. 100 per shirt. The Production Manager achieved this target at a cost of Rs. 90 per shirt. Do you think the Production Manager is effective? Give one reason in support of your answer.

Ans.   Yes, because he has achieved the target.

Q 7.   Hero Ltd's target is to produce 10,000 shirts per month at a cost of' 150 per shirt. The Production Manager could achieve this target at a cost of Rs. 160 per shirt. Do you think the Production Manager is effective? Give reason in support of your answer.

Ans.   Yes, he is an effective manager as he has achieved the target.

Q 8.   Hero Ltd.'s target is to produce 20,000 shirts per month at a cost of Rs. 150 per shirt. The Production Manager could achieve this target at a cost or Rs. 170 per shirt. Do you think the Production Manager is efficient? Give reason in support of your answer.

Ans.   No, he is not 'efficient because he has achieved the target but not in a cost-effective manner.

Q 9.   What is meant by 'effectiveness' in management?

Ans.   It means accomplishing the given task within a given time framework, no matter whatever is the cost.

Q 10.   'Management is a soft science.' How?

Ans.   Management is a soft science as its principles are not very rigid.

Q 11.   Name any two main management institutes of India.

Ans.   (i)   TIM, Ahmedabad   (ii)   IIM, Bengaluru.

Q 12.   Which are the two main categories of levels of organ isation.

Ans.   (i)   Managerial level   (ii)   Non-managerial level.

13.   Your grandfather has retired as the Director of a manufacturing company. At which level of management was he working? Different types of functions are performed at this level. State any one function

Ans.   →   Top-level Management   →   Determining Objectives

Q 14.   Your grandfather has retired from an organisation in which he is responsible for implementing the plans developed by the top management. At which level of management was he working? State one more function performed at this level.

Ans.   →   Middle-ltve 1 Management   →   **Interpreting Policies**

Q 15.   Your grandfather has retired from an organisation in which he is responsible for overseeing the efforts of the workforce. At which level of management was he working? State one more function performed at the level.

Ans. —* Lower-level Management Ensuring Safety of Workers

Q 16. Raman is working as 'Plant Superintendent' in TIFCO Ltd.

Name the managerial level at which he is working? State any four functions he will perform as 'Plant Superintendent' in this company.

Ans. He is working at Middle-level Management. Refer to any four functions of Middle-level Management.

Q 17. Deeraj is working as Operations Manager in TIFCO Ltd.

Name the managerial level at which he is working. State any four functions he will perform as Operations Manager in this company.

Ans. He is working at Middle-level Management. Refer to any four functions of Middle-level Management.

Multiple Choice Questions:

Q 18.   Which is not a Function of Management of the following?
   (A) Planning   (B) Staffing
   (C) Co-operating   (D) Controlling

Q 19.   Management is:
   (A) an Art   (B) a Science
   (C) Both (A) and (B)   (D) None of these

Q 20.   The following is NOT an Objective of Management.
   (A) Earning Profits   (B) Growth of the Organization
   (C) Providing Employment   (D) Policy Making

Q 21.   Policy Formulation is the function of:
   (A) Top Level Managers   (B) Middle Level managers
   (C) Operational Management   (D) All of these

Q 22.   Co-ordination is:
   (A) Function of Management   (B) The Essence of Management
   (C) An Objective of Management   (D) None of these.

EXERCISE – 2

Q 1.   How Management is a 'Goal Oriented Process'?

Q 2.   How is management a "Continuous Process'?

Q 3.   State why management is not a Pure Science?

Q 4.   Explain 'Management as a Science'.

Q 5.   Explain 'Management as an art'.

Q 6.   Write names and two functions each of the levels or tenets of management engaged in:
   (a)   Overseeing the activities of the workers
   (b)   Taking key decisions.

Q 7.   Name any two designations and two functions given to the First Line Managers.

Q 8.   Name the levels of management engaged in:
(i)   Determining Policies
(ii)   Assembling Resources
(iii)   Interpreting Policies.

EXERCISE – 3

Q 1.   Explain the objectives of management.

Q 2.   'Anything minus management is zero.' Explain the importance of management in the light of this statement.

Q 3.   'Management is the art of getting things done through others.' Explain the importance of management in the light of this statement.

Q 4.   'Lack of proper management results in wastage of time, money and efforts.' Do you agree with this statement? Give reasons in support of your answer.

Q 5.   'In the absence of management, the productive resources will remain resources and shall never become production.' Explain the importance of management in the light of the above statement.

Q 6.   'Success of an organisation largely depends upon its management.' Explain any five reasons to justify the above statement.

Q 7.   "Management is a science like physics or chemistry." Do you agree with this statement? Give reasons in support of your answer.

Q 8.   "Management is regarded as an Art by some, as Science or as an inexact Science by others. The truth seems to be somewhere in between." In the right of this statement explain the true nature of management.

Q 9.   'Coordination is the essence of management.' Do you agree? Give reasons.

Q 10.   'Management is considered to be both an art and science.' Explain.

EXERCISE – 4

Case Study

Q 1.   A Company X is facing a lot of problems these days. It manufactures White Goods like Washing Machines, Microwave Ovens, Refrigerators and Air Conditioners. The Company's margins are under pressure and the Profits and Market Share are Declining. The Production Department blames Marketing for not meeting Sales Targets and Marketing blames Production Department for producing goods which are not of good quality meeting Customers expectations. The Finance Department blames both the Production and Marketing for declining returns on Investment and Bad Marketing.

What Quality of Management do you think the company is lacking ? Explain briefly. What steps should the Company Management take to bring the company back on track?

Q 2.   A Company wants to modify the existing product in the market due to Decreasing Sales. You can imagine any product about which you are familiar. What decisions/steps should each Level of Management take to give effect to this decision?

Q 3.   A Firm plans in advance and has a sound organization structure with efficient Supervisory Staff and Control System. On Several occasion it finds that Plans are not being adhered to. It leads to confusion and duplication of work. Advise remedy.

PRINCIPLES OF MANAGEMENT

CONTENT

☞ **Nature**
1. Universal Application
2. General guidelines
3. Formed by practice and experiments/Evolutionary
4. Flexibility
5. Behavioural in nature
6. Based on cause and effect relationship
7. Contingent

☞ **Significance**
1. Increase the management efficiency and insight
2. Optimum utilization of resources
3. Scientific Decisions
4. Meeting changing environment requirement
5. Effective administration
6. Fulfilling Social responsibilities
7. Providing Base for Management Development, Research and Education.

☞ **Fayol's Principles of Management**
1. Background and History of Fayol
2. Why is Henry Fayol called as the father of Management thought?

☞ **Principles of Management Developed by Fayol**
1. Principle of Division of Work
2. Principle of Authority and Responsibility
3. Principle of Discipline
4. Principle of Unity of Command
5. Unity of Direction
6. Subordination of Individual Interest to General Interest
7. Principle of remuneration of persons
8. Principle of centralisation and decentralisation
9. Principle of scalar chain
10. Principle of order
11. Principle of Equity
12. Stability of tenure of personnel
13. Principle of Initiative
14. Principle of Esprit De Corps

☞ **Scientific Principles of Management**
1. Science, not rule of thumb
2. Harmony, not discord
3. Co-operation, not individualism
4. Development of workers to their greatest efficiency and prosperity

☞ **Scientific Techniques of Taylor**
1. Functional Foremanship

2. Standardization and simplification of work

3. Fatigue Study

4. Method Study

5. Time Study

6. Motion Study

7. Differential Piece Wage System

WEIGHTAGE

Units	Very Short Answer	Short Answer I & II	Long Answer I & II	Total
Unit - 2(6)	-----	3(2)	-----	6(2)

PRINCIPLES OF MANAGEMENT

☞ **Meaning of Principle of Management**
"Principle is a fundamental statement or truth providing a guide to the thought or action."
G.R. Terry

The principles of management act as guidelines for the practice of management. They help in predicting What would happen if the principles were applied. For example, application of the principle of 'discipline' leads to smooth and systematic functioning of the business and helps in improving efficiency. Without proper understanding of management principles, a person cannot perform managerial functions efficiency.

☞ **Nature/Features/Characteristics of Management**

1. **Universal Application :** Principles of management have universal applicability. It implies that principles of management can be applied in all types of organisations: business or non – business, public sector or private sector, manufacturing sector or service sector and small or large throughout the world.

2. **General guidelines :** Principles of management just provide general guidelines to managerial actions; they do not provide readymade solutions to the problems. This is so because organisations have to work in a dynamic environment having complex factors and business realities may not completely match with the prescriptions of principles of management principles.

3. **Formed by practice and experiments/Evolutionary :** The management principles are developed only after deep and thorough research work. They are not developed overnight or they are not the personal feelings of any person. Proper observations and experiments are conducted before developing them. These are the expressions of deep experiences of the leaders of management thoughts. Therefore they are evolutionary in nature.

4. **Flexibility :** Principles of management are not rigid but flexible. This is so because principles of management are situation bound and these principles are modified according to situational requirements. Thus, a manager may modify principles of management according to his own needs.

5. **Behavioural in nature :** Management principles are formed to guide and influence the behaviour of employees. These principles insist on improving relationship between superior, Subordinates and all the members of organisation. They also establish relations between human and material resources. For example, principle of Discipline improve commitment of employees towards the organisation and principle of Espirit de Corps mould the behaviour of employees towards team spirit. **Based on cause and effect relationship :** Principle of management establish relationship between cause and effect by prescribing "what effect will result if a particular principle of management is applied in a given situation." However, this cause-effect relationship is in a probable way because these are applied on human being.

7. **Contingent :** Management Principles are contingent or dependent upon the situations prevailing in organisation. Their application and effect depend upon the nature of organisation. The application of principle has to be changed according to the nature, size and type of organisation.

☞ **Significance/Importance of Management**

1. **Increase the management efficiency and insight :** Management principles act as guidelines for the managers. These principles improve knowledge, ability and understanding of managers under various managerial situations. The effects of these principles help the managers to learn from their mistakes. These principles guide managers to take right decision at the right time.

2. **Optimum utilization of resources :** The management principles insist on planned activities and systematic organisation of men and materials in the organisation. Principles are designed to get maximum benefits from the human efforts and other resources.
    For example, principle of fair remuneration, order, stability of personnel etc.

3. **Scientific Decisions :** Understanding of principles of management leads to scientific decisions. Scientific decisions are those which are based on rational criteria. In scientific decision various alternatives are evaluated on the basis of rational criteria rather than on the basis of personal preferences. Knowledge of principles of management helps in identifying rational criteria. As a result, there are scientific decisions.

4. **Meeting changing environment requirement :** Management principles train the managers to adopt the changes in technology in right direction and at right level in the organization. Thus, although the management principles are general guidelines, yet they are modified by the managers to meet changing requirements of the environment.

5. **Effective administration :** Management principles act as guidelines for top level management to formulate various administrative plans and policies for smooth and systematic functions of the organization. For example, the principle of Unity of Command avoid dual subordination and Unity of Direction unifies the efforts of all the employees in common direction and hence removes confusion from the minds of the employees.

6. **Fulfilling Social responsibilities :** Management Principle not only act as a guidelines for achieving organizational objectives but these principle also guide the managers for perform social responsibilities.
    For example the principle of "Fair Remuneration" insists on adequate salary to employees.

7. **Providing Base for Management development, Research and Education :**
    Management development- it involves developing relevant skills in managers which are developed through training involving understanding of various principles of management and their applications.
    Research - For undertaking research in management, the researcher should have through knowledge of existing principles.
    Education - Professional courses such as BBA, MBA also teach these principles as part of their curriculum. All the management institute take aptitude test and these tests are based on management principles only.

☞ **Fayol's Principles of Management**

1. **Background and History of Fayol** : Henry Fayol was born in France in 1841. He got degree in Mining Engineering in 1860 and started working as engineer in a Coal Mining Company. In 1888 he was promoted as the managing director of the company. At that time the company was in the situation of insolvency. He accepted the challenge and applied his managerial techniques to bring out the company from this situation and he succeeded. When he retired after 30 years the company was a leading coal-steel company with strong financial background.

2. **Why is Henry Fayol called as the father of Management thought?**
   Henry Fayol is called as the Father of Management Thought because he made the following three significant contributions to the theory of management.

   I. **Distinction between various skills** - He made a clear distinction between technical and managerial skills.

   II. **Identification of Functions of Management** - He identified the main steps in the process of management which are considered the major functions of management – planning, organizing, staffing, directing, controlling.

   III. **Development of 14 Principles of Management** - He developed principles of management that provided a basis for developing a prescriptive approach to categorizing management knowledge.

According to Fayol, principles of management are flexible and not absolute. These must be utilized in the light of changing and special conditions.

☞ **Fayol's Principles of Management**

1. **Principle of Division of Work :**
   According to this principle the whole work must be divided into small tasks or units and instead of assigning the whole work to one person one task or unit of work should be assigned to one person according to the capability, qualification and experience of the person. When a person is performing a part of job again and again he will become perfect and specialized in doing that and the efficiency level will improve. Fayol said not only the factory work but technical, managerial and skill jobs should also be divided into small segments for specialization.

   For example, in a furniture manufacturing company one person can be asked to cut the wood pieces, one to join them, one to polish, one to give finishing touch to furniture. With this division each person will become specialised in his part of job and his effectiveness and efficiency improves.
   Positive Effect:
   (a) Specialization   (b) Improve efficiency

   Consequences of violation of this principle:
   (a) Lack of efficiency   (b) No Specialization
   (c) Duplication of work.

2. **Principle of Authority and Responsibility :**
   Authority means power to take decision. Responsibility means obligation to complete the job assigned on time. According to this principle there must be balance between the authority and responsibility. Excess of authority without matching responsibility may bring negative results and

excess of responsibility without matching authority will not allow the worker to complete his job on time. There is need to bring balance between both for best results.

For example, if a person is given responsibility to produce 100 units in one week time but he is not given authority to purchase the raw materials. If there is no raw material available in the store-room as a result he could not complete the target of producing 100 units on time. The worker cannot be blamed for not completing on time because he was given only the responsibility and not the matching authority to carry on the work. Excess of responsibility with less authority results in non-completion of job.

Positive Effect:

(a) no misuse of authority   (b) Meeting responsibility on time

Consequences of violation of this principle:

(a) Delay in work   (b) Misuse of Authority

3.   **Principle of Discipline :**

Discipline refers to general rules, regulations for systematic working in an organisation. Discipline does not mean only rules and regulations but it also mean developing commitment in the employees towards organisation as well as towards each other. Fayol insists that discipline is required at superior as well as subordinate level. The disciplinary rules shall not be applicable only on subordinates but discipline requires goods superiors at every level, clear and fair agreement between superior and subordinates.

For example, the employees must honour their commitments towards the organisation by working effectively and efficiently. On the other hand, superiors must also meet their commitments by meeting their promises of increments, promotions, wage revisions etc.

Positive Effect:

(a) Systematic working   (b) Meeting responsibility on time

Consequences of violation of this principle:

(a) Disorder, Confusion and chaos   (c) Delay in work

4.   **Principle of Unity of Command :**

According to this principle an employee should receive orders from one boss only because if he is receiving orders from more than one boss then he will get confused and will not be able to understand that whose orders must be executed first and on the other hand, if employees is receiving orders from more bosses he gets chance to give excuses by saying that he was busy in executing the orders of other boss. To avoid confusion and to give no chance of excuse to employee, the orders must come from one boss only. If there are more bosses it can create problem of ego-clash among the superiors as every superior will want his order must be executed by the employee.

For example, if employees of production department is asked to go slow in production to maintain quality standard by the production in charge and sales in charge instructs the employee to fasten the production to meet the pending orders. In this situation employee will get confused as to whose instructions must be followed by him.

Positive Effect:

(a) No Confusion   (b) No ego

(c) Improve effectiveness

Consequences of violation of this principle:

(a) Confusion

(b) Subordinates escape responsibilities by giving excuses.

(c) Ego clashes

5. **Unity of Direction :**

According to this principle 'one unit means one plan", that is the efforts of all the members and employees of organisation must be directed towards one direction that is the achievement of common goal. If this principle is applied it leads to coordination. Each department and a group having common objectives must have one head and one plan only.

For example, if an organisation is producing different lines of products - cosmetics, medicines and confectionery items each product has its own market and its own environment. Each division must plan its target and every employee of that division must put his efforts towards the achievement of plan of their division under the direction of one head only.

Positive Effect:

(a) achievement of organizational goal.

(b) Effort get unified in one direction.

Consequences of violation of this principle:

(a) Lack of coordination

(b) Wastage of efforts and resources

(c) Difficult to achieve organizational goal.

6. **Subordination of Individual Interest to General Interest :**

According to this principle the interest of organisation must supersede the interest of individuals or employees. In the organisation all the employees are working with some objective and there is always an objective of organisation. If the objectives of individual are in the same direction of organisation then there is no problem but if the objectives of both the groups are in different directions then manager must try to reconcile individual interest with organisational goal and if it is not possible then individual goal must be sacrificed for achieving organisational goal.

The goal of organisation must not be sacrificed because individuals will be able to achieve their objectives only when organisation prospers.

For example, if individual's objective is to earn more remuneration and organisation is going through the situation of financial crisis and has the objective of cutting down the expenses. In this situation the individual must sacrifice his interest as when organisation will come out from financial crisis then he can achieve his objective.

Positive effect:

(a) Achievement of organizational goal.

(b) Coortlinaon between individual and organizational goal.

Consequences of violation of this principle:

(a) No achievement of organizational goal.

(b) Even employees will also suffer in long run.

7. **Principle of remuneration of persons :**

According to this principle employees in the organisation must be paid fairly adequately give them maximum satisfaction. The remuneration must be just and fair because if employees are underpaid they will not be satisfied and an unsatisfied person can never contribute his maximum. Dissatisfaction will lead to increase in employee's turn-over. So to have stability in organisation and to maximum efforts from employees, the employees must be paid fairly. The fair wage is determined according to

(a) financial capacity of the concern

(b) by keeping in mind the Minimum Wage Act of govt.

(c) the wages and salaries paid by the competitors.

For example, if in a particular year the organisation has earned more profits then apart from giving extra profit to shareholders and owners, some part of profit must be given to employees also in the form of bonus. This will encourage and motivate to put more efforts and increase the profit of the company.

Positive effect:

(a) Employees get motivated.

(b) Devotion and commitment of employees improves.

Consequences of violation of this principle:

(a) Increase in turnover of employees.

(b) Dissatisfaction and de-motivation of employees.

8. **Principle of centralisation and decentralisation :**

Centralisation refers to concentration of authority or power in few hands at the top level. Decentralisation means evenly distribution of power at every level of management. According to Fayol a company must not be completely centralised or completely decentralised but there must be combination of both depending upon the nature and size of the organisation. A small organisation can be well-organised and managed with centralised technique but in large organisation there is need for decentralisation. Secondly, if employees are not fully developed and are less in number then there must be centralisation. Fayol advised not to have complete centralisation or complete decentralisation but a combination of both.

For example, the major decisions and activities of setting up organisational goals, plans, policies, and strategies can be centralised but there can be policy of decentralisation for the activities of routine work such as purchase of raw materials, fixing targets of workers etc.

Positive effect:

(a) Benefits and centralization as well as decenrtalisation.

(b) Fast decision at operational level and strict control by top level.

Consequences of violation of this principle:

(a) Complete centralization will result in delay in decision.

(b) Complete decentralization will result in misuse of authority.

9 **Principle of scalar chain :**

Scalar chain means line of authority or chain of superiors from highest to lowest rank. Fayol insists that this chain must be followed strictly in the organisation. Every information must pass through every key of this chain, no skipping of any one key should be allowed.

Figure 2.1 explains the principle

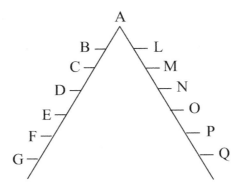

Figure: 2.1

According to scalar chain principle if E wants to contact 0 he has to move through E → D → C → B → A → L → M → N and then 0. If this chain is broken then there are chances of communication gap in the organisation but sometimes following scalar chain becomes a long process and if some important information has to be passed, it gets delayed so in case of emergency and urgent information, Fayol permitted a short cut in the chain which is called "Gang-Plank". Gang plank permits direct communication between the employees working at the same level of authority without following the scalar chain.

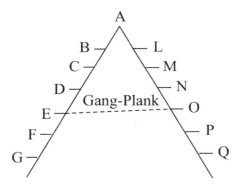

Figure : 2.2 Figure with Gang-Plank

For example, if E wants to pass some urgent information to 0 then instead of following the long route of scalar chain, he can directly communicate with 0 by constructing a gang-plank, but no gang plank can be constructed between the people working at different levels, i.e., no gang plank between D and L.

Positive effect:
(a) Systematic flow of information. (b) No communication gap in the organization.

Consequences of violation of this principle:
(a) There may be communication gap.
(b) No clarity in authority — responsibility relationship.

10   **Principle of order :**

In this principle order does not mean command but it refers to orderly arrangement of men and material that is a fixed place for everything and everyone in the organisation. Fayol insists that there must be a fixed place to keep every material and thing used in the organisation and fixed place or seat or cabin for every employee of the organisation so that no time and energy is wasted in search of any material or any person.

For example, if a worker is in need of a tool he must known in which box or tool-room it will be found and if he needs guidance from supervisor he must know the fixed cabin of supervisor. If no fixed place is given   then worker will waste his time and energy in search of tools or supervisor.

Positive effect:

(a) No wastage of time in search of men or material.

(b)Smooth and systematic working of organization.

Consequences of violation of this principle:

(a) wastage of time and energy in search of men and material.

(b) Not able to contact the people at the right time.

11.   **Principle of Equity**

Equity refers to kind, fair and just treatment to employees. Employees will put their maximum efforts when they are treated with kindness and justice. If a manager is biased in dealing with employees then employees will get dissatisfied and will not contribute to their maximum capacity. Equity does not mean equal salary to a peon and supervisor but equity means application of same disciplinary rules, leave rules in the same way irrespective of their grade, position and gender.

For example, the rules for granting medical leave to an employee should be same irrespective of their position, grade or gender.

Positive effect:

(a) Employees get satisfied.

(b) Motivate the employees and boost up the moral of the employees.

Consequences of violation of this principle:

(a) dissatisfaction in employees

(b) Increase in turnover

(c) Unhealthy relation between superior and subordinates.

12.   **Stability of tenure of personnel :**

It refers to no frequent termination and transfer. According to this principle the management must provide the feeling of job security among the employees because with the feeling of insecurity for the job, the employees cannot contribute their maximum. Frequent turnover of employees is bad for organisation and such decision must be taken when they are almost unavoidable.

Not only turnover but frequent transfer or rotation should also be avoided because it takes some time to a person to learn and get settled on a job and by the time he gets settled and he receives transfer order then it will be wastage of resources and employee will not be able to contribute his best for organisation.

Positive effect:
(a) Improves efficiency level of employees.
(b) No Wastage of time and resources.

Consequences of violation of this principle:
(a) Wastage of resources in learning the new job.
(b) Frustration and dissatisfaction among employees.

13. **Principle of Initiative :**
Initiative refers to chalking out the plan and then implementing the same. Fayol suggested that employees in the organisation must be given an opportunity to take some initiative in making and executing a plan. It gives immense satisfaction to employees. So managers must welcome the suggestions and ideas of employees before framing the plan. The initiative does not mean disobedience i.e., once decisions are taken by management then every employee must follow it whether it is according to employee's suggestion or not.

For example, before setting up of plan the manager must welcome the suggestions and ideas of employees to allow their maximum participation. But once the plan is made every employee must follow it and implement it.

Positive effect:
(a) Develops feeling of belongingness in employees.
(b) Employees achieve the target on time if they are set up with their consultation.

Consequences of violation of this principle:
(a) Employees will not work to the best of their ability.
(b) De-motivation among employees.

14. **Principle of Esprit be Corps :**
Esprit De Corps means union is strength. Fayol emphasized on the team work. He suggested that every employee in the organisation must consider him as a part or member of a team and try to achieve the team goal because team contribution is always better and more than individual contribution. Management must develop a feeling of belongingness among the employees as they must feel themselves as members of organisation's team and contribute maximum to achieve team's goal.

For example, if the production manager assigned a target of manufacturing 100 units to a group of 10 members, members divided the target among themselves to produce 10 units each, principles of team spirit says that each member of the group should not concentrate only on achieving his individual target of 10 units but they must concentrate on achieving group target of 100 units so if two workers of that group fall sick, then the other eight members must divide their individual target among themselves and try to achieve the target of their group.

Positive effect:
(a) Develops team spirit.
(b) Achievement of group goal.

Consequences of violation of this principle:
(a) Team goal may not be achieved.
(b) No Team spirit and more stress on individualism.

☞ **Scientific Management**
Background History of F.W. Taylor:-
Frederic W. Taylor was a mechanical engineer employed in Midvale Steel Company in USA. He is as 'Father of Scientific Management because he made the following significant contributions to the management thought.

1. **Principles of Scientific Management** — He developed the principles of scientific management.
2. **Techniques of Scientific Management** – He developed various techniques of scientific management through various experiments.

He advocated a detailed scientific study of each job to determine the best way of doing it. His primary emphasis was on adoption of scientific methods to the problems of management.

☞ **Meaning of Scientific Management**
Scientific Management can be defined as "Application of science for each and every element of management". in general language it means apply scientific tools, methods and trained personnel in order to increase the output. Scientific management insists on replacement of rule of thumb by science that means decisions in the organisation should not be taken on the basis of wills and wishes of manager but decisions must be based on scientific studies conducted by using scientific tools.

Definition of Scientific Management
"Scientific Management means knowing exactly what you want men to do and seeing that they do it in the best cheapest way."
Taylor   -

☞ **Scientific Principles of Management**
1. **Science, not rule of thumb :**
   According to this principle Taylor insists that each job performed in the orpanisation should be based on scientific enquiry and not on intuition, experience and hit and miss methods. He says that there must be thinking before doing which is not in case of rule of thumb. Rule of thumb dictatorship of manager whereas scientific decisions are based on cause and effect and scientific measurement of methods and ways of production.

   For example, in rule of thumb the standard time required to do a particular job is decided by the managers on the basis of his past experience. Taylor insists that standard time for a job should be set up scientifically by performing time study in the organisation and then the day's target should be fixed.

2. **Harmony, not discord:**
   According to this principle those who work together in an organisation must work in harmony that is with mutual give and take and proper understanding. Generally in every organisation there are two groups of people - workers group and management group and both the groups work as rivals of each other as workers always feel that they are underpaid and are over burdened with the work and management always feels that workers are good for nothing. In this principle Taylor insists that there is need for both the groups to change their attitudes for each other. He insists on mental revolution which means complete change of attitude and outlook for each other. They must develop positive thinking for each other and work with harmony and avoid discord as their objectives are in one direction only.

   For example, the main objective of workers is to earn more and the objective of management is to maximise production; instead of discord for each other's objective workers can earn more by producing more which will help in maxirnising the production also. Management should share the gains of the company with workers at the same time workers must contribute to their best level. Taylor feels that prosperity of organisation depends upon prosperity of employer as well as employees.

3. **Co-operation, not individualism**
   According to this principle work must be carried on in co-operation between Workers and management. instead of individualism. This 'Principle cooperation, not individualism' is an extension of 'principle of harmony, not discord' because cooperation leads to harmony and individualism leads to conflict (discord) thus Workers and managers must work with mutual confidence and understanding for each other. The management must take workers in confidence

before setting up the standard task for them because when standards or targets are set up in consultation of workers, then they will try their best to achieve it. For example, while assigning job to workers if management asks them about their interest and then work is assigned according to their interest, definitely the workers will perform it more efficiently.

4. **Development of workers to their greatest efficiency of prosperity :**
Industrial efficiency depends upon the efficiency of workers. Workers efficiency depends upon proper training and their selection. Taylor insisted due care should be taken while selecting the employees and after selecting they must be given job according to their qualification. Employees must be sent for training from time to time to update their knowledge. This will ensure greatest efficiency and prosperity for both company and workers.

☞ **Scientific Techniques of Taylor**
Along with scientific principles Taylor developed some scientific techniques by conducting various experiments at his work place.
The common techniques are:

1. **Function & Foremanship :**
Functional foremanship is an extension of the principle of division of work or specialization to the shop floor. Each worker will have to take orders from eight foremen in the process of production. Foremen should have intelligence, education, tact, judgement, special knowledge, energy, honesty and good health. All these qualities cannot always be found in a single foreman. So, Taylor proposed eight specialists.

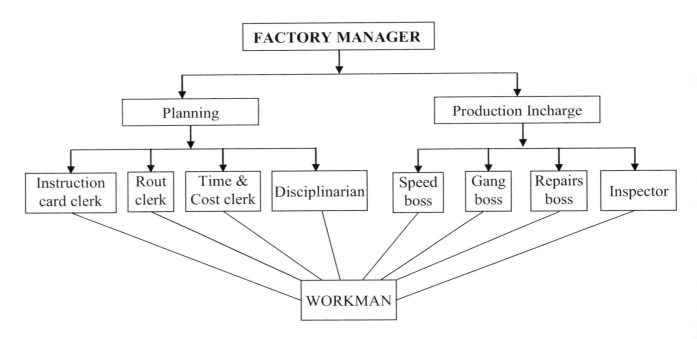

FUNCTIONAL FOREMANSHIP

Role in Foremen under planning incharge
- Instruction card – Drafting instructions for workers.
- Route clerk – Specifying the route of production.
- Time and cost clerk – Preparing time and cost sheet.
- Disciplinarian – Ensuring discipline.

Role of Foremen under production incharge
- Speed boss – Timely and accurate completion of job.
- Gang boss Keeping machines and tools, etc. ready for operation by workers.
- Repairs boss – Ensuring proper working condition of machines and tools.
- Inspectors – Checking the quality of work.

  Objective : Taylor developed the concept of functional foremanship to improve the quality of the supervision where worker is supervised by several specialist to improve operational efficiency.

2. **Standardization and Simplification of work :**

Scientific management always emphasises on maintaining standards relating to every step of business operations. Standardization of output is possible if standard is maintained right from selection of tools, equipment and machine to use maximize the output by keeping in mind the quality standards Standardisation does not mean only quality standard but it refers to setting up standard for size, type, weights, measures and quality of product.

Objective of standardisation of work are :
- To reduce a given line of product to fixed types, sizes and characteristics.
- To establish standards of excellence and quality in materials.
- To establish standards of performance of men and machines.
- To establish interchangeability of manufactured parts and products.

Simplification emphasizes on elimination of unnecessary diversity of products, size and types. As more varieties means more inventory, more type of machinery, more labour cost etc: by simplifying the task there can be economy in use of machine, labour, inventory maintenance etc. It wili also help in improving the quality and reduction of cost.

For example; A paper Manufacturing Co. in USA reduced its varieties from 2000 to 200 which brought positive results for the company.

A fruit can Manufacturing Co. reduced varieties from 200 to 32 and got efficient and effective results.

Objective : It aim at setting standards for every organisation activity to maximize outputs and making work as simple as possible by eliminating unnecess diversity of products.

3. **Fatigue Study :**

This technique of scientific management is conducted to find out:

(a) The Frequency of Rest intervals (b) The Duration of Rest intervals (c) The No. of Rest intervals. It is human tendency that a person feels physically and mentally tired if she/he is made to work continuously without any rest. The rest period enables one to regain the stamina and to work again with same capacity. Fatigue study intends to find out the number and frequency of rest intervals that must be provided to a worker in completing a job efficiently. Workers cannot work at a stretch. After putting in work for a certain period of time they feel tired which affects their performance. If they are allowed rest intervals, they will regain their stamina and will resume their work greater energy. For example, if workers are involved in heavy manual labour such as brick layering or poor working conditions then small pauses must be given to them and after each interval they resume their work with greater enthusiasm.

4. **Method Study :**

The method study technique of scientific management is conducted to find out the one best method or way of performing the job which keeps production cost minimum and makes maximum use of resources of the organisation.

Taylor suggested that method of production should not be decided by rule of thumb method but all the methods must be tried in the organisation and the one which brings maximum benefits with minimum cost must be selected.

For example, for production of shoes there can be labour intensive method and machine intensive method. To find out which is best management must evaluate the cost of production with both the methods and compare both the methods with the available resources of the company. The method which involves minimum cost and exploits maximum resources must be selected as the best method of production.

5. **Time Study :**
The technique of time study is conducted to determine or the objectives of time study are:
(a) The standard time required to perform a job.
(b) Setting up the standard target for workers.
(c) Determining the number of workers required to perform a job.
(d) Categorizing the workers in efficient and inefficient categories.

Taylor suggested that the time required to perform the job should not be decided by intuition, will and wish of manager, but Time Study must be conducted to determine the standard time scientifically. To conduct Time Study Taylor suggested to observe an average worker when he is performing the job with a stop watch in hand and note down the average time taken by the worker in completion of job. Taylor suggested to repeat the same observations for 100 times and then taken out the average time. This time should be considered the average time for performance of the job. Keeping this time in mind the targets for workers should be fixed and the workers who are able to achieve their targets in standard time are average workers. If the worker is able to achieve target before standard time then he is an efficient worker and if the worker failed to achieve target in standard time then he is an inefficient worker.

6. **Motion Study**
The scientific technique of motion study is conducted : or the objectives of motion study are
(a)   To determine the movements of workers when they are performing the job.
(b)   To differentiate between productive and unproductive movements.
(c)   For cutting down unproductive and wasteful movements.
(d)   To design suitable equipments and tools to minimise the unproductive movements of workers.

To conduct motion study Taylor suggested to observe an average worker when he is performing the job and note down all the movements he is doing. How many times he is getting up from his place, how many times he is bending down etc. Repeat it for 100 times with different workers. After writing all the movements classify them in productive and unproductive movements and make the strategy to cut down or minimise the unproductive movements.

For example, while observing an average worker, if it is observed that worker has to bend frequently to pick up the tools box placed under his table, then a stool can be placed near his seat to keep the tool box so that worker does not waste his energy in bending again and again. Same energy he can use for improving his production capacity or efficiency level.

7. **Differential Piece Wage System**
The Scientific technique of differential piece rate system emphasizes on paying different rate of wage for efficient and inefficient employees. The technique of differential wage rate system insists on:
(a)   Paying different rate of wage to efficient and inefficient employees.
(b)   Extra wages paid to efficient employees will motivate them to remain efficient.
(c)   Extra wages paid to efficient employees will motivate inefficient employees to come in the category of efficient employees.
(d)   When payment is given according to no. of units produced automatically the production will be maximised.

To conduct or adopt differential wage system Taylor suggested that the company must fix a standard rate of wage for workers producing standard output or their target. The workers who produce more than the standard-target must be paid with a higher rate of wage and those who are producing less than standard output must be paid with a rate less than standard rate.

For example, if the standard target if 10 units per day and standard rate is Rs.50 per unit:
The worker who is producing 10 units must be paid Rs.500 (Standard Rate x Standard Output).
The worker who is producing more than standard output must be rewarded by paying more than standard rate say Rs.60 per unit.

So he will receive Rs. $12 \times 60 = $ Rs.720 (Higher Output $\times$ Higher Rate).
The worker who is producing less than standard output must be taxed and penalised by paying less than standard rate say Rs.40 per unit.
So he will receive Rs.$8 \times 40 = $ Rs.320 (Lower Output $\times$ Lower Rate).
This difference in wages will motivate the workers to become efficient and earn more.

☞ **Management Principles Vs Pure Science Principles**
Management principles differ from pure science principles in the following ways:
1. Management principles are quite flexible whereas pure science principles are rigid.

2. Application of management principles requires assessment of situations in which these are applied because of involvement of human beings who differ considerably whereas pure science principles are not situation – bound.

3. Management principles keep on changing with changes in situational factors whereas pure science principles do not change with time.

4. Management principles are evolved out of personal experiences, observations and experiments whereas pure science principles are evolved only through experiments.

☞ **Management Principles Vs Management Techniques**
Management principles differ from management techniques in the following ways:
1. Management principles provide guidelines for managerial actions whereas management techniques prescribe methods and procedures involving a series of steps in performing a work.

2. Management principles have flexibility in their applications whereas management techniques are of definite nature in their applications.

☞ **Management - Principles Vs Values**
1. Management Principles are guidelines for managerial actions whereas values are rules for behaviour of individual in society.

2. Management Principles are technical in nature where as values are ethical in nature.

3. Management Principles insist on fulfilling of values and ethics of society.

Difference between unity of command and unity of direction

Basis	Unity of Command	Unity of Direction
1.Meaning	One subordinate should receive orders from one should be responsible to only one superior.	Each group of activities having same objective must have one head and one plan.
2. Aim	It prevents dual subordination.	It prevents overlapping of activities.
3. Implication	It affects an individual employee.	It affects the entire organization.

Difference between time study and motion study

Basis	Time Study	Motion Study
1. Meaning	Time study is conducted to find out the standard time for performing a task.	Motion study is conducted to find out total movements of workers while they are performing the task.
2. Purpose	The purpose of time study is to find out standard time to fix a fair days work for the workers.	The purpose of motion study is to eliminate wasteful and unproductive movements of workers to increase their efficiency level.
3. Method of conducting	It is conducted with the help of a stop watch.	It is conducted with the help of a movie camera which keeps eye on workers movements.

Comparison between Taylor & Fayol

	Point of Difference	Taylor	Fayol
1	Concern	Taylor's techniques and principles are concerned with worker's efficiency.	Fayol's principles are concerned with management efficiency.
2	Level Perspective	Taylor started his studies and approach from lowest level in the organisation	Fayol started his studies and approach from the highest level in the organisation
3	Emphasis	Taylor laid great emphasis on standardisation of work	Fayol laid great emphasis on functions of managers
4	Focus	Taylor laid focus on eliminating wasteful movements and saving energy of workers. It forces on increase in productivity,	Fayol's focus was on development of principles for better management. It focus on improving overall achieve station.
5	Major contribution	Taylor's main contribution was development of scientific techniques and scientific principles,	Fayol's main contribution was development of fourteen principles of general management.
6	Personally	Taylor developed a personality of scientist and became famous as father of scientific management	Fayol developed the personality of a researcher and practitioner. He became famous as father of general management.
7	Unity of Command	Did not follow this principle as Taylor insisted on minimum 8 bosses.	Strictly followed this principle i.e., only one boss for one employee.
8	Expression	Taylor's techniques are expressed as scientific management.	Fayol's techniques are expressed as general theory of administration.
9	Applicability	Applicable to specialised situation.	Applicable universally.

EXERCISE — 1

Q 1.   What is meant by principles of management?

Q 2.   Give any one reason of why the principles of management are called contingent,

Q 3.   Give any two points of the nature of principles of management.

Q 4.   State how the management principles are flexible.

Q 5. How have the management principles been derived?

Q 6. The Principles of management are different form house of pure science. "State any one difference.

Q 7. Why is it said that management principles are universal?

Q 8. Give any one reason of why principles of management do not provide readymade solution to all managerial problems?

Q 9. Give any one reason of why principles of management are not rigid prescriptions.

Q 10. What is mean by ' Universal applicability' of principles of management?

Q 11. State one violating effect of the principle of management - namely the "Division" of Work

Q 12. State one positive effect of the principle of Management - Namely the 'Authority and Responsibility'

Q 13. State one violating effect of the principle of management - namely the' Discipline'

Q 14. State one positive effect of the principle of management - namely the 'Unity of Command'

Q 15. State one violating effect of the principle of management - namely the 'Unity of Direction'

Q 16. State one positive effect of the principle of management - namely the 'Remuneration to employees.

Q 17. Why did Fayol introduce the concept of 'Gang Plank' in the principle of 'Scalar Chain?

Q 18. What is the job of 'Speed Boss' under functional foremanship?

Q 19. As a technique of scientific management what is the meaning of' Standardization of Work?

Q 20. As a technique of scientific management what is the meaning of 'Simplification?

Q 21. What is meant by' Method Study?

Q 22. State the objective of 'Motion Study?

Q 23. What is meant by" Time Study"

Q 24. What is meant by" Fatigue Study"

Q 25. Give the meaning of" Mental Revolution" as suggested by F.W Taylor.

Q 26. What is the main objective of" Method - Study?

Q 27. State the objective of" Time - Study?

Q 28. Different techniques were developed by Taylor to facilitate principles of scientific management One of them is" Fatigue Study What is the objective of this Study?

Q 29. What is the main objective of fatigue study?

Q 30. What is the main objectives of simplification in scientific management?

EXERCISE – 2

Q 1.   The production manager of ABC Ltd. instructs a salesman to go slow in selling the product, whereas the marketing manager is insisting on fast selling to reach the target

Which principle of management is being violated in this case? State any two consequences of tne violation of this principle.

Q 2.   Hina and Harish are typists in a company having the same education qualification Hina is getting Rs.3,000 per month and Harish Rs. 4,000 per month as salary for the same working hours

Which principle of management is violated in this case? Name and explain the principle.

Q 3.   The production Manger of Bharat Ltd. instructs a salesman to go slow in selling the product, whereas the Marketing Manager is insisting on fast selling to achieve the target

Which principle of management is being violated in the case State any one of the consequences of violation of this principle

Q 4.   Mohan a manager, does not distribute the work amongst his subordinates either according to capability or proportionately:

which principle of management is being overlooked any why Give one violating effect.

Q 5.   Mohan the manger of ab business undertaking is very lax with his fellow employees and subordinates He does not give them parameters or rules for reporting to work and completion of assignments.

Which principle of management is being over looked and why? Give one violating effect.

Q 6.   Mohan, a manager, very often speaks to people at all levels passing on instructions regarding his department and also the other departments.

Which principle of management is being overlooked and why Give one violating effect,

Q 7.   Mohan a manger expects his subordinates to work for the happiness and pleasure of being in the organisation

Which principal of management is being overlooked and why? Give one violating effect.

Q 8.   Mohan a manger expects his subordinates to adapt to the new environment and working conditions without giving them time to settle down.

Which principle of management is being overlooked and why? Give one violating effect.

Q 9.   The subordinates in a company receive orders regarding their work form different operative heads for the same task.

Which principal of management is being overlooked and why? Give one violating effect.

Q 10.   In a particular company no importance had been attached to the suggestions given by the subordinaties In 2007 the company appointed Mr. Lotus is its Chief Executive Officer He was an MBA degree - holder from IIM Ahmedabad with and experience of a suggesting form every big or small employee of the company In a very short time there were implemented in different fields This campaign fetched the company an additional profit Rs. 50 Crore.
    (i)   What principle of management will have been working behind Mr. Lotus.'s thinking?
    (ii)   What will be the effect of implementing these suggestions on the employees?

EXERCISE – 3

Q 1.   In an arrogations Ashok and Sheela are working at the same posts but being male employee Ashok has more rights then Sheela. Which value is violated here?

Q 2.   A firm has taken the decision to employ more male employees than female employees because they can work overtime in case of excess work, Which values are being affected here?

Q 3.   An organisation proposes the use of CFL's and LED's which consumes less electricity than normal bulbus for its listing arrangements, Which value is attained by the organisation ?

Q 4.   An organisation has bone plantation around its factory premises and only after purifying the wastes, it throws it into the drains Which values are being followed by the organisation?

Q 5.   An entrepreneur wants to start his business in backward area because government gives many incentives and rebates in taxes Which results in low cost and he will be able to sell the product at low prices, There be will be able to get large area by deforestation which are being affected hare?

ANSWERS
EXERCISE – 1

Q 1.   Principles of management are those basic truths which have the ability to predict the results of managerial activities.

Q 2.   Because principles of management are affected by situations

Q 3.   (A) Universal Applicability   (B) General Guidelines

Q 4.   They are not in the form of final truth and can be changed any time

Q 5.   On the basis of observation and experimental studies.

Q 6.   The principles of management are not definite like the principles of pure science.

Q 7.   Because these are applicable in both business and non - business spheres in a similar manner

Q 8.   It is seas business situations are dynamic

Q 9.   Because they are directly concerned with human behaviour and behaviour of human beings is always uncertain

Q 10.   It means that the principles of management are intended to apply to all types of organizations at all places.

Q 11.   Benefits of specialization will not be available.

Q 12.   Helpful in achieving the target.

Q 13.   Height of disorder.

Q 14.   The efficiency of the subordinates increases.

Q 15   Decrease in the efficiency of the organization

Q 16.   Decline in the labour turnover rate.

Q 17   This concept was developed to contact with the employees of equal rank in case of emergency to avoid delay in communication

Q 18.   He ensures that all the workers are performing their job at the required speed.

Q 19.   It refers to set the standards for different factors, after due deliberation

Q 20.   It means putting an end to unnecessary types, qualities, size / weight. etc.

Q 21.   It refer to identify the most suitable way to do a particular activity

Q 22. The main objective of this study is to eliminate the necessary motions.

Q 23.   It refers to determine the standard time required to complete a particular activity.

Q 24.   It refers determine the duration and frequency of rest intervals to complete a particular jab.

Q 25.   It refers to the change in the attitude of management and workers towards one another form competition to cooperation.

Q 26.   It main objective is o minimise ne cost of production and maximise the quality and level of consumer satisfaction

Q 27.   The Main objective of time - study is to get the estimated figure of labour costs. to determine the number of required workers and to decide about the suitable incentive plan.

Q 28.   The main objective of this study is to maintain the efficiency level of workers.

Q 29.   The main objective of this study is to maintain the efficiency level of workers.

Q 30.   Effecting economy in the use of machines.

EXERCISE – 2

Q 1.   The principle of Unity of Command is violated in this case, The following are the violating effects of it :
(i)   It creates a confused situation for the subordinates.
(ii)   It reduces the efficiency of the subordinates.

Q 2.   The principle of Equity is violated Hence explain this principle

Q 3.   The principle of Unity of Command is being violated. As per this principle an individual employee should receive orders form only one superior at a time and that employee should be answerable only to that superior, The violation of this principle reduces the efficiency of the subordinates.

Q 4.   The principle of Equity is violated as the manager is not impartial as far as the distribution of work among the employees is concerned It creates dissatisfaction for the skilled workers.

Q 5.   The principle of Discipline is violated as the manger's behaviour is not disciplined at all It creates an atmosphere of doubt and suspicion.

Q 6.   The Principle of Scalar Chain is violated as during communication the various steps of Scalar Chain are overlooked It creates flow of information

Q 7.   The principle of Remuneration of Employees is violated as the mangers expectation has no use without providing fair remuneration to the employees It increase the labour turnover rate

Q 8.   The principle being overlooked is Stability of Personal as the manger is not providing so much opportunity to the employees so that they get settled It increases the recruitment and training expenses.

Q 9.   The Principle being overlooked is Unity of Command as at the same time there are many spurious giving orders to the same employee. It reduces the efficiency of the subordinates.

Q 10.   (i)   Principal of initiative
        (ii)   Their attachment with the company will increase and they will offer new and useful ideas.

EXERCISE – 3

Q 1.   Gender baseness.

Q 2.   (i)   Gender banishes   (ii)   Conservatism
        (iii)   Effect of male dominating society   (iv)   Inequality of rights for same work

Q 3.   (i)   Save Electricity   (ii)   Reduction in Cost
        (iii)   Protection of environment

Q 4.   (i)   Safety form Water and Air Pollution (ii)   Protection of Environment
        (iii)   Fulfilling the Social responsibility

Q 5.   (i)   Deprivation of environment form deforestation
        (ii)   Availability of goods at low cost
        (iii)   Development of backward areas
        (iv)   Employment opportunities increase in backward area

BUSINESS ENVIRONMENT

CONTENT

☞ **INTRODUCTION :**
Every business enterprise owes its existence to society. It draws its inputs from society, converts them into output and supplies it to society. It operates in association with various groups in society such as customers, suppliers, competitors, banks and financial institutions, trade unions etc. They constitute the environment of business as they influence the functioning of business.

☞ **FEATURES/CHARACTERISTICS**
1. All the external forces.
2. Specific and general forces.
3. Inter-relation.
4. Uncertainty.
5. Dynamic.
6. Complex.
7. Relativity.

☞ **IMPORTANCE**
1. Enabling the identification of opportunities and getting the first mover advantages.
2. Helping in the identification of threats and early warning signals or Radar effect.
3. Tapping useful resources.
4. Coping with the rapid changes.
5. Assisting in planning and policy formulation. 6. Improvement in performance.
7. Image building.

☞ **DIMENSIONS OF BUSINESS ENVIRONMENT**
1. Economic Environment.
2. Social Environment.
3. Political Environment.
4. Legal Environment.
5. Technological Environment.

☞ **Government Policy Changes**
The major changes or impacts of the new economic policy 1991 are:
1. Liberalisation.
2. Privatisation.
3. Globalisation.

☞ **Impact of Govt. Policy changes on Business and Industry**
1. Increasing Competition.
2. More demanding customers.
3. Rapidly changing Technological environment.
4. Necessity for change.
5. Need for developing human resources.
6. Market orientation.
7. Loss of Budgeting Support to the Public Sector.
8. Enhanced Focus on Exports.

WEIGHTAGE

Units	Very Short Answer	Short Answer I & II	Long Answer I & II	Total
Unit – 3 (5)	---	---	5(1)	5(1)

3. BUSINESS ENVIRONMENT

☞ **Meaning of Business Environment**

Business Environment refers to all individuals or institutions (Supplier, Customers, Competitors etc) and other forces (economic, social, political etc) which are external to a business and beyond its control but that may affect its performance.

A few examples of external forces having influence on a business are as follows:

Changes in Business Environment	Effect on Performance of Business Enterprises
1. Increasing taxes by government.	Increased cost of production, hence things become expensive to buy
2. Increased competition in the market	Reduction in profit margins
3. Changes in fashions and tastes of consumers	Shift in Market demand from existing products to new ones
4.Technological improvements and innovations	Render existing Products obsolete, e.g. LCD TVs become obsolete with introduction of LED TVs
5. Political uncertainty	Creates fear in the minds of investors to invest in long - term projects

Business Environment consists of the external forces which affect the functioning of a business enterprise. These forces may be

(i)   General Environment

(ii)   Specific Environment

It should be noted that every business unit also has internal environment which includes production, financial, marketing, personal aspects etc.

General external environment forces exercise their influence on a business unit in an indirect manner i.e. by influencing the specific external forces. These include economic, social, political technological etc.

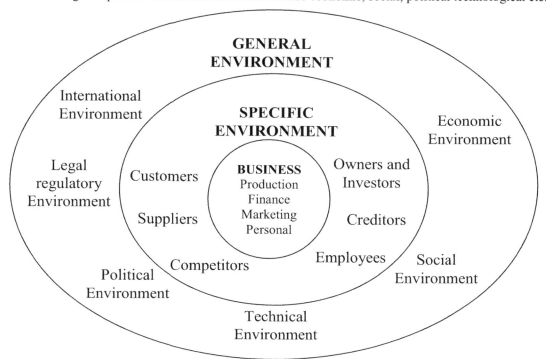

Specific or operating external environment forces influence the working of a business firm in an direct manner. Those include customers, owners and investors, suppliers, creditors, employees etc.

☞ Features/Characteristics/Nature of Business Environment

1. **All the external forces :** Business Environment includes all the forces, institutions and factors which directly or indirectly affect the Business Organisations.

2. **General and Specific Forces :** Business environment covers both general and specific forces Genera forces include economic, social, political legal and technological conditions and they have general or indirect impact on the environment. Specific forces include invertors customers, suppliers, competitors etc. and they have a direct impact on the business

3. **Interrelated Elements :** All the forces or factor of business environment are interrelated to each other. For example, political environment affects economic environment and social environment affects both political and economic environment. Similarly, specific environment forces have relation with the general environment forces.

4. **Uncertainty :** It is very difficult to predict the changes of Business Environment. As environment is changing very fast for example in IT, fashion industry frequent and fast changes are taking place.

5. **Dynamic :** Business environment is highly flexible and keep changing, It is not static or rigid that s why it is essential to monitor and scan the business environment continuously.

6. **Complex :** It is very difficult to understand the impact of Business environment on the companies Although it is easy to scan the environment but it is very difficult to know how these changes will influence Business decisions. Some-time change may be minor but it might have large impact. For example, a change in government policy to increase the tax rate by 5% may affect the income of company by large amount.

7. **Relativity :** The impact of Business Environment may differ from company to company or country D country. For example, when consumer organisation CES published the report of finding pesticides in cold drinks, resulted in decrease in sale of old drinks, on the other hand it increased the sale of juice and other drinks.

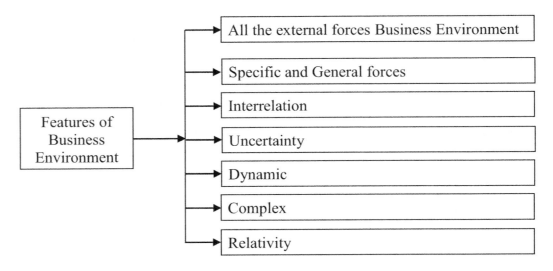

☞ **Importance of Business Environment**

'The complete awareness and understanding of business environment is known as 'Environment Scanning'. **Signification of understanding environment in shaping the future of business can be appreciated if we consider the following facts.**

1. **It enables the firm to identify opportunities and getting the first mover advantage :**
   'Opportunities' refer to the positive external environment trends and changes that will help a firm to improve its performance. By keeping in touch with the changes in the external environment, an enterprise can identify opportunities and find strategies to capitalise on the opportunities at the earliest. For example, Maruti Udyog became the leader in the small car market because it was the first to recognise the need for small cars in an environment of rising petroleum prices and a large middle-class population in India

2. **It helps the firm to identify threats and early warning signals :**
   'Threats' refer to the external environment trends and changes that will hamper a firm's performance. Environmental scanning helps to identify possible threats in future. For example if an Indian firm finds that an MNC is entering the Indian market with new substitutes, this should work as a warning signal for the Indian firm. Based on this information, the Indian firm can improve the quality of its products, reduce cost of production, engage in aggressive advertisements, etc.

3. **It helps in assisting in planning and policy formulation :**
   Environment analysis helps in identifying threats and opportunities in the market. These can serve as the basis for deciding the future course of action (planning) or training guidelines for decision-making (policy).

4. **It helps in tapping useful resources :**
   A business firm is an open system which gets resources such as capital, labour, machines and equipment, materials, etc. from the environment, converts them into goods and services desired by the customers and then supplies its output to the environment. Thus, a business firm depends on its external environment for tapping various resources and for the sale of its output.

5. **It helps in coping with rapid changes :**
   Managers must understand and examine the business environment and develop suitable courses of action to cope with turbulent market conditions, rapid changes in technology, intense global competition, etc.

6. **It helps in improving performance :**
   The enterprises which continuously monitor their environment and adopt suitable business practices not only improve their present performance, but also continue to succeed in the market for a longer period. For example, if a firm is sensitive to the external environment, it will come out with new products and services to meet the future requirements of the customers.

7. **Image building :**
   If a firm is sensitive to the external environment, it will come out with new products and services to meet the requirements of the customers. This would build the image or reputation of the firm in the eyes of the customers and the general public. Because of sensitivity to Indian consumers' requirements, LG was able to enhance its brand image in the Indian market in a short span of time.

☞ **Dimensions of Business Environment**

The Dimensions or the factors constituting the business environment include political, social, technological, legal and economic factors which are considered important for taking decisions and for improving the operations of a firm. These are a part of general environment which influences the performance of many firms at the same time.

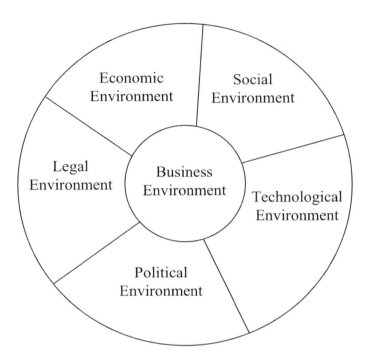

1. **Economic Environment :**

    Economic Environment consists of factors like inflation rates, interest rates, consumer's incomes, economic policies, market conditions etc. which affect the performance of a business firm.

    Example of Impact of Economic Environment on Business: -
    (1) In case of construction companies and automobile manufactures, low long-term interest rates are beneficial because they result in increased spending by consumers for buying homes and cars.
    (2) Increase in the incomes of the consumers leads to increase in their purchasing power. Hence, demand for goods and services rises.
    (3) High inflation-rates generally result in constraints on business enterprise because they increase the costs of raw materials or machinery and payment of wages & salaries to employees.

2. **Social Environment :** Business originates and develops in society. Therefore, the effect of various social factors on business is but natural. Social factors include customs, fashions, traditions, wishes, hopes, level of education, population. Standard of living of the people, religious values, distribution of incomes corruption, family set-up, consumers' consciousness, etc.

For example :
(i)   The celebration of Diwali, Eid, Christmas and Guru Parv in India provides significant financial opportunities for greetings card companies, sweets or confectionery manufactures, tailoring outlets and many other related business.
(ii)   Social trends present various opportunities to business enterprises. For example, the health-and- fitness trends has created a demand for products like diet soft drinks, gyms, bottled (mineral) water and food supplements.

3. **Political Environment :** Political environment constitutes all the factors related to government aflars such as type of government in power, attitude of government towards different groups of societies, policy changes implemented by different governments etc. The political environment has immediate and great impact on the business transactions so businessman must scan this environment very carefully. The businessman has to make changes in his organisation according to the changing factor of political environment. For example, in 1977 when Janta Government came in power they made the policy of sending back all the foreign companies. As a result the Coca Cola company had to close its business and leave the country.

The common factors and forces which influenced the Indian political environment are:
(a)   The government in Hyderabad is taking keen interest in boosting LT. industry, as a result the state is more commonly known as Hyderabad instead of Hyderabad.
(b)   After the economic policy of liberalisation and globalisation, the foreign companies got easy entry in India. As a result the Coca Cola which was sent back in 1977 came back to India. Along with Coca Cola, Pepsi Cola and many other foreign companies are establishing their business in India.

4. **Legal Environment :** Legal environment constitutes the laws and various legislations passed in the parliament. The businessman cannot overlook the legislations because he has to perform his business transactions within the framework of legal environment. The common legislation passed which has affected the business transactions are Trade Mark Act. Essential Commodity Act, Weights and Measures Ac etc. Most of the time legal environments put constraints on the businessman but sometimes they prove opportunities also. An adequate knowledge of rules and regulations framed by the Govt. is a precize for better business performance. non-compliance of laws can land the business enterprise into legal problems. For example, the advertisement of alcoholic beverages is prohibited. Advertisements of cigarettes carry the statutory warning 'Cigarette smoking is injurious to health.

5. **Technological Environment:** Technological environment refers to changes taking place in the method of production, use-of new equipments and machineries to improve the quality of product. The businessman must closely monitor the technological changes taking place in his industry because he will have to implement these changes to remain the competitive market. Technological changes always bring quality improvement and more benefits for customers.

The recent technological changes of Indian market are;
I.   Digital watches have killed the prospects and the business of traditional watches.
II.   Colour T.V. technology has closed the business of black and while T.V.
III.   Artificial fabric has taken the market of traditional cotton and silk fabrics.
IV.   Photo copier and Xerox machines have led to the closure of carbon paper business.
V.   Shift in Demand from vacuum tubes to transistors.

☞ **Government Policy Charges**

As a part of economic reforms, the Government of India announced a new industrial policy in July, 1991.

1. **Liberalisation :** Liberalisation means – **"freeing the Indian business and industry from all unnecessary government controls and restrictions."**

    Liberailsation of the Indian industry has taken place with respect to:

    (i)   abolishing licensing requirement in most of the industries except a short list,

    (ii)   freedom in deciding the scale of business activities, i.e., no restrictions on expansion or contraction of business activities,

    (iii) removal of restrictions on the movement of goods and services,

    (iv)   freedom in fixing the prices of goods and services,

    (v)   simplifying procedures for imports and exports, and

    (vi)   making it easier to attract foreign capital and technology to India.

2. **Privatisation:** Privatisation means – **"giving greater role to the private sector in the nation building, process and drastically reducing the role of the public sector."**

    To achieve this, the government adopted the policy of planned disinvestments', which means transferring the public sector enterprises to the private sector. It results in dilution of stake of the Government in the public enterprise. If there is dilution of Government ownership beyond 51%, it would result in transfer of ownership and management of the enterprise to the private sector.

3. **Globalisation :** 'Globlisation' means the integration of our economy with the world economy. Till 1991, the government's regulations were with respect to (a) licensing of imports, (b) tariff restrictions and (c) quantitative restrictions. The main purpose of globalisation is to promote export and import with different countries.

    Accordingly, new trade policy was adopted during 1991 to liberalise the exports and imports of the country from restrictions mentioned earlier. Globalisation has increased the level of interaction and interdependent among different countries of the world. Physical and political boundaries are no longer a barrier in the way of business enterprises to serve the customers in different markets of the world.

☞ **Impact of Government Policy Changes on Business**

The policy of Liberalisation, Privatisation and Globalisation of the government has made a significant impact on the working of Indian business and industry.

1. **Increasing competition:** Firms now face competition not only from Indian firms, but also from multinational companies (MNCs), especially in service industries like telecommunications, airlines, banking, insurance, etc.

2. **More demanding customers:** Customers today have become more demanding because increased competition in the market gives the customers wider choice in purchasing better quality of goods and services.

3. **Market orientation:** Earlier firms had production-oriented marketing operations. But in the present scenario, there is a shift to market orientation, where the firms have to study and analyse the market first to identify customer needs and produce goods accordingly. Marketing research, educational advertising, after-sales services, etc. have become more significant.

4. **Rapidly changing technological environment:** Technology is changing very fast, which creates tough challenges before smaller firms. The rapidly changing technological environment requires

improvement in machines, processes, products and services. Business firms have to develop new products and technologies to survive and grow in the market.

5. **Necessity for change:** After 1991, the market forces have become turbulent as a result of which the enterprises have to continuously modify their operations. Investments in R&D and innovations schemes have become a must.

6. **Need for developing human resource:** The new market conditions require people with higher competence and greater commitment. So, there is a need for developing human resources. As a result, compensation levels for managerial and technical services have sharply increased.

7. **Loss of budgetary support to the public sector:** The Central Government's budgetary support for financing the public sector outlays has declined. So, Public Sector Units will have to be more efficient and generate their own resources to survive.

8. **Enhanced Focus on Exports :** The new trade policy has helped Indian business firms to boost exports and hence earn precious foreign exchange required for improving according to their requirements.

EXERCISE – 1

Q.1   What do you mean by business environment?

Q.2   What is economic environment?

Q.3   Define social environment.

Q.4   What is political environment?

Q.5   Define legal-regulatory environment.

Q.6 Explain the meaning of globalisation.

Q.7   Which policy of the Government has moved India towards globailsation?
Hint: The New Industrial Policy, 1991.

Q.8   What do you mean by disinvestment?
Hint: When the share capital of a public sector unit is sold over to private sector it is called disinvestment.

Q.9   Which sector of the Indian economy was given greater importance after independence?
Hint: Public sector.

Q.10   What is the name of the economy where both public and private sectors coexist?
Hint: Mixed economy.

Q.11   "The understanding of business environment enables the firm to identify opportunities." What is meant by opportunities' here?

Q.12   Business environment includes both 'specific and general forces'. List any four general forces.

EXERCISE – 2

Q.1   Briefly explain the characteristics of environment of a business.

Q.2   Give any two examples of the impact on business organisations due to changes in economic environment.

Q.3   Give any two examples of the impact on business organisations of changes in social environment.

Q.4   Define the terms 'liberalisation' and 'globalisation.'

Q.5   Briefly explain the importance of business environment.

Q.6   Explain 'increasing competition' and 'more demanding customers' as impact of Government policy changes in business and industry.

EXERCISE – 3

Q.1   Explain the term 'business environment' and discuss the impact of economic environment on business.

Q.2   Explain the dimensions of business environment.

Q.3   What is the impact of political environment on business? Discuss.

Q.4   How is a business firm influenced by political and legal environment?

Q.5   Discuss the influence of economic environment on business.

Q.6   How does social environment influence the working of a business?

Q.7   Explain the impact of government's industrial policy on business.

Q.8   How is a business influenced by the legal-regulatory environment? Discuss.

PLANNING

CONTENT

☞ **MEANING:**

Planning means setting objectives and targets and formulating an action plan to achieve them. It is concerned with both ends and means i.e., what is to done and how it is to be done.

☞ **FEATUES OF PLANNING**
1. Focus on objectives.
2. Primary function of management
3. Pervasive.
4. Continuous.
5. Futuristic/forward looking.
6. Involve decision making.
7. Planning is a mental exercise.

☞ **IMPORTANCE OF PLANNNG:**
1. Planning Provides Direction.
2. Planning Reduces the risk of uncertainties.
3. Planning Facilities Decision Making.
4. Planning reduces over lapping and wasteful activities.
5. Planning Promotes innovative ideas.
6. Planning establishes standard for controlling.

☞ **LIMITATIONS OF PLANNING:**
1. Planning leads to rigidity.
2. Planning may not work in dynamic environment.
3. It reduces creatively.
4. Planning involves huge costs.
5. It is a time consuming process.
6. Planning does not guarantee success.

☞ **PLANNING PROCESS:**
1. Setting up of the objectives.
2. Developing premises.
3. Identifying alternative courses of actions.
4. Evaluation of alternative courses.
5. Selecting an alternative.
6. Implement the plan.
7. Follow up.

☞ **Types of Plans**
(A) **Standing Plans**
   (i) Objectives
   (ii) Strategy
   (iii) Policies.
   (iv) Procedures

(v)   Rules
(vi)   Method

(B)   Single Use Plans
(i)   Programmes
(ii)   Budget

(C)   Differences

WEIGHTAGE

Units	Very Short Answer	Short Answer I & II	Long Answer I & II	Total
Unit – 4 (6)	----	3(2)	----	6(2)

4.   PLANNING

☞ **MEANING OF PLANNING :**
Planning means setting objectives and targets and formulating an action plan to achieve them. it is concerned with both ends and means i.e., what is to done and how it is to be done.
"Planning seeks to bridge the gap between where we are and where we want to go".

☞ **FEATURES/NATURE/CHARACTERISTICS OF PLANNING :**
1.   **Focus on objectives:** Planning puts focus on objectives. This is done in two forms. First, planning specifies the objectives which are to be achieved within a specified time. Second. planning also specifies how these objectives may be achieved.

2.   **Primary function of Management:** Planning is a primary function of management as it lays down base for other functions of management All other functions of management are performed within the framework of the plans drawn by planning process. This is the reason that planning is also referred to as primacy of planning.

3.   **Pervasive:** Planning is pervasive and extends throughout the organisation. Thus, every manager at every level of management performs planning function. This is why an organisation has plans at different levels: overall organisational plan, divisional plan, departmental plan and sectional plan

4.   **Continuous:** Planning is a continuous process for the following reasons:
(a)   Plans are prepared for a particular period. Hence, there is need for a new plan after the expire of that period.
(b)   In case of any discrepancy plans are to be revised.
(c)   In case of rapid changes in the business environment plans are to be revised.

5.   **Futuristic/Forward looking :** Planning decides the plan of action – what is to be done, how it is to be done, when it to be done, by whom is it to be done – all these questions are related to future. Under planning, answers to these questions are found out. While an effort is made to find out these answers, the possibility of social, economic, technical and changes in legal framework are kept in mind. Since planning is concerned with future activities, it is called futuristic.

6.   **Involve decision making :** Planning becomes a necessity when there are many afternatives to do a job. A planner chooses the most appropriate alternative. Therefore, it can be arrested that planning

is a process of selecting the best and rejecting the inappropriate. It is, therefore, observed that planning involves decision making.

7. **Planning is a mental exercise:** Planning is a mental process which requires higher thinking:
    (i)   For making assumptions and predictions regarding future by scanning the environment.
    (ii) For evaluating various alternatives and selecting the most appropriate. So it right to called an intellectual process.

☞ **Importance/Significance of Planning**
    "The manager who acts without planning must learn to live without profit".
    "If you fail to plan, you plan to fail".

1. **Planning Provides Direction :** By stating in advance how work is to be done, planning direction for action. Since under planning objectives are well defined, employees are aware of what to do and how to do etc. So this leads to unity of Direction and Coordination in work.

    "Planning keeps the organisation on right path"

2. **Planning Reduces the risk of uncertainties:** Business enterprises operate in an uncertain environment. Planning enables a manager to look ahead and anticipate changes and uncertain events so that he/she may take appropriate steps to deal with them, Thus, planning helps to reduce the risks of uncertainty.

3. **Planning Facilitates Decision Making:** Planning helps the manager to look into the future and make a choice from amongst various alternative courses of action. The manager has to evaluate the positive and negative aspects of each alternative and select the most feasible and profitable plan, with least negative consequences. Planning involves setting targets and predicting future conditions, thus helping in taking rational decisions.

4. **Planning reduces over lapping and wasteful activities:** Planning reduces overlapping and wasteful activities by prescribing what is to be done and how this can be done. Because of this prescription, only necessary activities are performed, unnecessary activities are avoided and there is no duplication of activities.

5. **Planning Promotes innovative ideas:** It is clear that planning selects the best alternative out of the many available. All these alternatives do not come to the manager on their own, but they have to be discovered, While making such as effort of discovery, many new ideas emerge and they are studied intensively in order to determine the best out of them. In this way, planning imparts a real power of thinking in the managers. It leads to the birth of innovative and creative ideas.

6. **Planning establishes standard for controlling :** Planning provides the goals or standards against which actual performance is measured. A comparison of actual performance with the standards helps managers to identify the deviations and to take corrective action. Planning makes control meaningful and effective. Control is blind without planning.' Thus, planning is the basis for controlling.

☞ **LIMITATION O PLANNING**
    "Though planning is an important tool of management,
    yet it is not a remedy for all types of problems."

1. **Planning leads to rigidity:** The existence of a plan puts managerial activities in a rigid framework. One of the limitations is rigidity. Programmes are carried out according to the plan and deviations are considered to be highly undesirable. This attitude makes managers and employees inflexible in their operations. They become more concerned with observance of rules and procedures as laid down in the plan rather than achieving the goals.

2. **Planning may not work in dynamic environment:** Business environment is very dynamic as there are continuously changes taking place in economic, political and legal environment. It become very difficult to fore-cast these future changes. Plans may fail if the changes are very frequent. The environment consists of number of segments and it becomes very difficult for a manager to assess future changes in the environment. For example there may be change in economic policy, change in fashion and trend or change in competitor's policy. A manager fore see these changes accurately and plan may fail if many such changes take place in environment.

3. **It reduces creativity :** With the planning the managers of the organisation start working rigidly and they become the blind followers of the plan only. The managers do not take any initiative to make changes in the plan according to the changes prevailing in the business environment. They stop giving suggestions and new ideas to bring improvement in working because the guidelines for working are given in planning only.

4. **Planning involves huge cost:** Planning is a costly process. There are two types of costs involved in planning process. First, cost is involved in paying salaries and other financial benefits to those persons who are involved in planning process. Second, planning process requires lot of information collection and processing, keeping records, etc., which involve lot of cost. If the benefits of planning are not, more than its cost than it should not carry on.

5. **It is a time consuming process:** Planning process is a time-consuming process because it takes long time to evaluate the alternative and select the best one. Lot of time is needed in developing planning premises. So, because of this, the action gets delayed. And whenever there is a need for prompt and immediate decision then we have to avoid planning.

6. **Planning does not guarantee success :** Sometimes managers have false sense of security that plans have worked successfully in past so these will be working in future also. There is a tendency in managers to rely on pretested plans. It is not true that if a plan has worked successfully in past, it will bring success in future also as there are so many unknown factors which may lead to failure. Planning only provides a base for analyzing future. It is not a solution for future course of action.

☞ **PLANNING PROCESS**

1. **Setting up of the objectives:** The first and foremost step in the planning process is setting organisationa objectives or goals which specify what the organisation wants to achieve. For example, an increase in sale by 20% could be the objective of the organisation.

2. **Developing premises:** Planning is concerned with the future, which is uncertain. Therefore, the manager is required to make certain assumptions about the future. These assumptions are called premises. Assumptions are made in the form of forecasts about the demand for a particular product, government policy, interest rates, tax rates, etc. Therefore, accurate forecasts become essential for successful plans.

3. **Identifying alternative courses of actions :** Once objectives are set and assumptions are made, then the next step is to identify all possible alternative courses of action. For action, in order to achieve the organisational objectives of increasing profit, the alternatives may be:

    (a)   Increase the sales of an existing product, or

    (b)   Produce and sell a completely new product.

4. **Evaluation of alternative courses:** The positive and negative aspects of each proposal need to be evaluated in the light of the objective to be achieved, its feasibility and consequences. For example, the more risky the investment, the higher is the possibility of returns. To evaluate such proposals, detailed calculations of earnings, earnings per share, interest, taxes, dividends are made.

5. **Selecting an alternative:** This is the real point of decision making. The best/ideal plan has to be adopted, which must be the most feasible, profitable and with least negative consequences.

    The manager must apply permutations and combinations and select the best possible course of action. Sometimes, a combination of plans may be selected instead of one best plan.

6. **Implement the plan :** Once the plans are developed, they are put into action. For this, the managers communicate the plans to all the employees very clearly and allocate them resources (money, machinery, etc.).

7. **Follow-up:** Planning is a continuous process so the manager's job does not get over simply by putting the plan into action. The managers monitor the plan carefully while it is implemented. The monitoring of plan is very important because it helps to verify whether the conditions and predictions assumed in plan are holding true in present situation or not. if these are not coming true then immediately changes are made in the plan. During follow up many adjustments are made in the plan.

☞   **Types of Plans**

Planning's a pervasive function which means it is not the task of top level managers only but managers working at different levels perform planning function. The plans formed by top level manager may differ from the plans formed by middle and lower managers. There are several types of plan in an organisation. Based on the nature of usage of these plans, these are divided into two broad categories.

(A)   **Single Use Plans :** These plans are concerned with some special problem. These plans end the moment the problems are solved. After having been used once there is no importance of these plans and, in future, whenever they are needed they are re-created. These plans include (i) Budget, and (ii) Programme.

(B)   **Standing Plans :** As their name indicates that these plans are formulated once and they are repeatedly used. These plans continuously guide the managers. That is why it is said that a standing plan is a standing guide to recurring problems. These plans include (i) Objectives, (ii) Strategies, (iii) Policies, (iv) Procedures, (v) Methods and (vi) Rules.

Difference between Standing and Single-use Plans

Basis of Difference	Standing Plans	Single-Use Plans
1. Period	These plans are formulated for a long period.	These plans are for a short period and are repeatedly formulated in case of need.
2. Object	These plans are formulated to bring about informity in the decisions.	These plans are designed to run successfully some particular activities.
3. Types	They are six types: (i) Objectives, (ii) Strategies, (iii) Policies, (iv) Procedures, (v) Methods and (vi) Rules.	They are of two types: (i) Budget and (ii) Programme.
4. Scope	They guide the managers in particular matters like price policy and sales policy,	These plans guide in matters of daily routine.
5. Basis	They are based on the main objectives of the organisation.	They are based on the standing plans of the organisation.

(A)   **Standing Plans**

1.   **Objectives : "Objective is the end which an organisation seeks to achieve by its operations."**
       For example: increase in sale by 10% achieving 20% growth on yearly basis.
       ➢   Objectives are the end result of every activity. It defines desired future position which the organisation would like to realize.
       ➢   Objectives are usually set by top management of the organisation. They serve as a guide for overall business planning and all other managerial activities.
       ➢   Objective need to be expressed in specific terms i.e., they should be measurable in quantitative terms, desired results to be achieved within a given time period.

2.   **Strategy : "Strategy defines the future decisions regarding the organisations directions and scope in the long run".**
       Strategy formulation is the task of top level management.
       For example: a company's marketing strategy may include: (i) choice of channels of distribution, (ii) pricing strategy, (iii) choice of advertising media, (iv) choice of sales promotion techniques, etc.
       Therefore, a strategy is a comprehensive plan which includes three dimensions:
       (i)   Determining long-term objectives of the enterprise,
       (ii)   Adopting a particular course of action, and
       (iii)   Allocating resources necessary to achieve the objectives.
       Whenever a strategy is formulated, the business environment needs to be taken into consideration because the changes in the economic, political, social, legal and technological environment will affect an organisation's strategy.

3.   **Policies: "Policy is general statements or understandings which guide thinking in decision-making".**
       For example, different business firms may follow different sales policies as stated below:
                            "We don't sell on credit".
              "It is our policy to deal with wholesalers only".

➤ A policy is based on the objectives of the enterprise. While objectives provide the ends which a manager should try to achieve, the policies provide broad guidelines as to how the objectives of the enterprise are to be achieved.

➤ Policies are guides to managerial action and decisions in the implementation of strategy.

➤ There are policies for all levels and departments in the organisation ranging from company's major policies to minor policies.

- Company's major policies are for all, e.g., customers, clients, competitors, etc.

- Whereas minor policies are meant for insiders.

➤ Policies define the broad parameters, within which a manager may function.

4. **Procedures:** Procedures are sequence of routine steps on how to carry out activities.

In business procedures are generally established for purchase of raw materials, processing of order, selection of employees, redressed of grievances etc.

➤ Procedures are generally meant for insiders to follow.

➤ Policies and procedures are inter-linked with each other; Procedures are steps to be carried out within a broad policy framework.

For example, the recovery of money from the debtors can be made in the following order:

(i)   Writing letters,

(ii)   Contacting on telephone,

(iii) Meeting Personally,

(iv)   Taking legal action

This is the procedure of collecting money from all the debtors. There is a difference between policies and procedures. There can be two policies of the organisation regarding the recovery of money from the debtors.:

(i) Tight Collection Policy, and (ii) Lenient Collection Policy. Under the first policy an effort is made to recover money from the debtor by treating him harshly. Under the second policy, the debtor will be given enough time for the payment of money while treating him leniently. In both these policies the above- mentioned procedures will remain the same.

5. **Rules: "Rules are specific statements that inform what is to be done. A 'rule' reflect-s a managerial decision that a certain action must or must not be taken"**

Example: Rule of 'No smoking' inside the office premises.

Rules are usually the simplest type of plans because they allow no flexibility / discretion / compromise in their application. They are to be enforced rigidly and there is generally a fine or penalty for violation of rules.

There is a difference between rule and policy. Policy only guides arid gives an authority to the officer to take decision within a certain limit. For example, goods can be sold on credit is a question of policy. But who is to be given goods on credit or who is not be given this facility depends on the sales managers. In other words, he shall have to make use of his reasoning. On the other hand, rules are static and there no reasoning involved. For example, a definite percentage of interest will be charged on the amount money payable on account of credit sales after the lapse often days. This is a rule which is applicable to all customers without distinction. There is difference between rule and procedure. Rules tell us what should be done and what should not be done. On the other hand, procedures lay down the manner to complete a particular work. For example, it is a rule that no interest will be charged if the payment is received within ten days of the sale. But after ten days, writing letters, contacting through telephone, having personal meeting and taking legal action is a procedure through which balance amount is sought to be collected.

6.   **Methods :** Methods can be defined as formalized or systematic way of doing routine or repetitive jobs. The managers decide in advance the common way of doing a job. So, that

(a) There is no doubt in the minds of employees;

(b) There can be uniformity in actions of the employees;

(c) These help in applying the techniques of standardisation and simplification;

(d) Act as guide for employees.

If the common way of doing the job is not decided in advance then there will be confusion and comparison will not be possible. For example, for the valuation of stock, the organisation must decide in advance what method has to be adopted (lifo or fifo). So that everyone follows the same method and comparison with the past value of stock can be done.

1.   **Programmes :** A programme means a single-use comprehensive plan laying down the 'what', 'how', 'who' and 'when' of accomplishing a specific job. Through programme the managers are informed are informed in advance about various needs so that there is no problem in future. The programmes can be of different types, e.g., production programme, training programme, sales promotion programme, management development programme, etc. In case of sales promotion programme, the 'what', 'how', 'who', 'when' of everything right from the purchase of the raw material to the manufacturing of the product is defined.

The moment a work is completed for which the programme has been designed, its utility ends. In order words, a new programme is designed for every new work. Programmes are made to get a systematic working in the organisation.

2.   **Budget :** Budget is the statement of expected result expressed in numerical terms. In budgets the results are always measurable and most of the time these are financial in nature but it does not mean that company prepares only financial budget. Financial budget is also known as profit plan of the company because it includes the expected income and related expenditures with that income and the profit which the company will earn in the coming year. Along with financial budget capital budget is prepared to find out the expected capital requirement. Operational budget is prepared where instead of finance hourly units are used stating expected hours the employees will be working. Budgets are prepared by managers at every level and lower level managers generally prepare operational budgets.

The most common budget prepare by managers at different levels is cash budget. This budget estimates the expected cash inflow and cash outflow over a period of time. Cash inflow comes from sales and cash outflow is in the form of expenses. Business can find out net cash position by subtracting cash outflow from cash inflow.

Difference between Policies and Objectives

Basis	Policies	Objectives
1. Meaning	Policies are guidelines which facilitate the achievement of predetermined objectives.	Objectives are the ends towards which all activities of the enterprises are directed.
2. Purpose	Policies determine how the work is to be done.	Objectives determine what is to be done.
3. Nature	Policies prescribe the mode and the	Objectives are the ends points of planning.

	manner in which objectives can be achieved.	
4. Level	Policies are formulated at the top level, middle level and lower level management.	Objectives are determined by the owners or top management of the business.
5. Source	Derived from the objectives of the organisation.	Derived from the mission and philosophy of the organisation.

Difference between Policies and Strategies

Basis	Policies	Strategies
1. Meaning	Policies are guidelines which facilitate the achievement of predetermined objectives,	A strategy is a plan prepared for meeting the challenge posed by the activities of competitors or some other external environment forces.
2. Purpose/Aim	Formulated to deal with repetitive problems.	Formulated to counter environmental threats and capitalise on opportunities.
3. Concern/Coverage	Concerned with the company as a whole or particular departments.	Concerned with the company as a whole.
4. Nature of Plan	It is a type of standing plan to be used repetitively again and again,	It is a single use plan for meeting challenges. After its implementation, it is not used again.
5. Situation	The situations to be faced by a policy are comparatively known.	A strategy is formulated to deal with unknown environment in future.

Difference between Policy and Procedure

Basis	Policy	Procedure
1. Meaning	A policy is a guide for thinking and taking decision.	A procedure is a guide for action and contains steps to be taken in a chronological order.
2 Origin	It is derived from objectives of the enterprise,	It is derived from policies of the enterprise.
3. Flexibility	It is flexible.	It is more or less rigid.
4. Expression	Expresses in the form of general statement.	Expresses in more specific terms.
5. Scope for Discretion	It leaves some scope for managers discretion.	It gives no discretion to person concerned with its implementation.

Difference between Policies and Rules

Basis	Policies	Rules
1. Meaning	A Policy is a guide for thinking and taking decision.	Rules are specific statements to guide the behaviour.
2. Nature	A general statement.	The most specific statement.
3. Purpose	Guide to decision making.	Guide to behaviour.
4. Flexibility	Flexible: may have some exceptions.	Rigid: no exceptions or deviations.
5. Penalty	Penalty for violation not specified.	Penalty for violation.

Difference between Rules and Methods

Basis	Rules	Methods
1. Meaning	Guidelines to behaviour,	Standardised ways of performing routine and repetitive jobs.
2. Purpose	Ensures discipline.	Increases efficiency of operations.
3. Effect of violation	Penalty attached to violation.	No Penalty for violation.
4. Flexibility	Generally rigid statements.	Flexible statements for guiding and controlling operations.
5. Association	Associated with control.	Not associated directly with control.

EXERCISE – 1

1. What is meant by 'Planning'?
Ans.   It refers to thinking before hand.

2. Why planning is known as 'Futuristic'?
Ans.   Because it is related with future.

3. The planning function of management is conducted at which level of management?
Ans.   At all the three levels of management.

4. Which level of management more time is consumed on planning as compared to other levels?
Ans.   At top level of management.

5. One of the functions of Management is considered a base for all other functions. Name that function.
Ans.   It is planning.

6. 'Planning is done for achieving the organisational goals.' Do you agree? Give one reason in support of your answer.
Ans.   Yes, I do agree with this statement as planning determines the way to achieve organisationals.

7. How is planning a pervasive function? State.
Ans.   Planning is a pervasive function as it is required in all organisations and at all levels of management.

8. 'Planning strangulates the initiative of the employees and compels them to work in an inflexible manner.' What does it mean?
Ans.   It refers to planning reduces creativity.

9. Does mere planning ensure success?
Ans.   No, efforts have to be made to get success.

10. 'Planning always leads to success.' Do you agree? Give reason in support of your answer.
Ans.   No planning does not always lead to success Because planning is time consuming and it delays action

11. State any two types of plans.
Ans.   (i) Objectives, (ii) Strategy.

12.   Name the type of plans in which the move of competitors-is considered.
Ans.   It is strategy.

13.   In which type of plans the sequence of activities to complete a job is determined'
Ans.   Under procedure.

14.   No Smoking in the factory. This statement is related to which type of plans"
Ans.   It is related with rule.

15.   Name the type of plan which provides the broad contours of an organisation's business.
Ans.   Strategy.

16.   Name the type of plan which is time bound and linked with measurable outcome.
Ans.   Budget.

17.   Name the type of plan which provides the prescribed ways in which a task has to be performed considering the objective.
Ans.   Method.

EXERCISE – 2

1.   How does planning provide direction?

2.   Explain how planning reduces the risk of uncertainty.

3.   Explain how planning facilitates decision making?

4.   Define planning. List any two reasons why planning is essential.

5,   Explain 'objective' and 'policy' as types of plans using suitable examples.

6.   Explain 'method' and 'rule' as types of plan.

7.   Clarify the difference between standing plans and single use plans.

8.   What is budget? Give an example of a sales budget.

9.   Explain "Policy" and "Procedure" as types of plans.

10.   Explain 'objective' and 'strategy' as types of plan.

EXERCISE – 3

1.   Which quality of employee is restricted by the act of planning?
Ans.   (i) Decrease in the efficiency of initiativeness.
        (ii) Restriction on creativity.

2. Removal of mobile towers from residential area is being planned by the government to promote which value?

Ans. (i) Environment protection
(ii) Safety of birds
(iii) Safety of Health of Society

3. Government is planning to construct a ware house in remote area to store necessary goods. So as to make them available even at the time of bad weather regularly. Which values are being considered here to be achieved by the government?

Ans. (i) Stability in prices   (ii) Regular supply of goods
(iii) Fulfilling social responsibility   (iv) Control on hoarding & Black-Marketing

4. In order to reduce the cost, an organisation is planning the following:
(a) o reduce the charities to the social and religious institution.
(b) To arrange skilled workers from outside inspite of semi-skilled local employees.
(c) Increase the working hours.
(d) Increase the rate of remuneration.
Which value will be affected by the decisions?

Ans. (i) Reduction in social responsibilities due to non-cooperation in social work.
(ii) Increase in production due to efficient employees.
(iii) Deterioration in Health of employees due to prolonged working hours.
(iv) Reduction in employment opportunities for local persons.
(v) Increase in salary will increase social respect/standard of living.

5. Tobacco manufacturer is planning to sell its products outside the School & colleges. Which values are violated here from your point of view?

Ans. (i) Bad effect on students health
(ii) Deprivation of Morality.
(iii) instigation of social evil.

6. In an organisation executive director takes all the decision himself. He does give order only to the subordinates. Which value is overlooked here?

Ans. (i) Lack of feeling of ownness in an organisation.
(ii) Lack of manager's faith in his employees.
(iii) Wastage of time.

ORGANISING

CONTENT

☞ **INTRODUCTION :**

A process of implementing the plans by clearly defining the jobs, working relationships and effectively deploying, physical, human and financial resources for achieving organisation goals.

☞ **PROCESS OF ORGANIZING**

1. Identification and Division of Work.
2. Grouping the Jobs and Departmentalization.
3. Assignment of Duties.
4. Establishing Reporting Relationship

☞ **IMPORTANCE OF ORGANIZING**

1. Benefits of specialization
2. Role Clarity
3. Clarity in working relationship
4. Optimum utilization of resources
5. Co-ordination and effective Administration
6. Adoption to Change
7. Expansion and Growth
8. Development of Personnel

☞ **Organizing Structure Need for Orgamsation Structure**

1. Growth in size of organisation.
2. Overcoming communication problems.
3. Overcoming Coordination.
4. Need for Control.

☞ **Types of Organizing Structure**

A. Functional Structure
B. Divisional Structure

☞ **Formal and Informal Organisatons**

A. Formal Organisation
B. Informal Organisation

☞ **Delegation**

Importance of Delegation

1. Effective management
2. Employees Development
3. Motivation of employees
4. Facilitates organisational growth
5. Basis of management hierarchy
6. Better coordination
7. Reduces the work load of managers
8. Basis of superior-subordinate relationship

WEIGHTAGE

Units	Very Short Answer	Short Answer I & II	Long Answer I & II	Total
Unit-5(08)		4(2)		8(2)

5. ORGANIZING

☞ **MEANING OF ORGANIZING**

Once a specific plan has been established for the accomplishment of an organisational goal, the organizing function determines what activities and resources are required. It decides who will do a particular task, where it will be done and when it will be done.

Thus, organizing is the management function of assigning duties, grouping tasks, establishing authority and allocating resources required to carry out a specific plan.

☞ **Organising Process**

1. **Identification and Division of work :**
   The organising function begins with the division of total work into smaller units. Each unit of total work is called a job. And an individual in the organisation is assigned one job only. The division of work into smaller jobs leads to specialisation because jobs are assigned to individuals according to their qualifications and capabilities. The division of work and assignment of jobs leads to systematic working.

2. **Grouping the jobs and Departmentalization :**
   After dividing the work in smaller jobs, related and similar jobs are grouped together and put under one department. The departmentation or grouping of jobs can be done by the organisation in different ways.
   Following are the various ways of departmentalization
   (i)   On the basis of functions —
           Numerous activities are grouped into different departments on the basis of various functions. For example, Purchase Department for purchase functions, Finance Department for financing activities etc.
   (ii)   On the basis of type of products manufactured—
           In this case, activities are grouped into different departments on the basis of products manufactured or produced by organisation. For example, textile division, food division etc.
   (iii)   On the basis of territory—
           Here, activities are grouped into offices/branches on the basis of four directions (or locations) North, East, West, South (News) e.g., Southern Zone, Eastern Branch etc.

3. **Assignment of Duties :**
   Assignment of duties involves giving responsibility to various organisational positions for performing the activities relevant to these positions. Along with this, resources for performing the activities are allocated and authority is delegated to each position. Based on the responsibility, competence (education, experience, skills, etc) required for each position is prescribed.

4. **Establishing Reporting Relationship :**
    So, in the third step of organizing process all the individuals are assigned some authority matching to the job they have to perform.

    The assignment of the authority results in creation of superior-subordinate relationship and the question of who reports to whom is clarified. The individual of higher authority becomes the superior and with less authority becomes the subordinate. With the establishment of authority managerial hierarchy gets created (chain of command) and principle of scalar chain follows this hierarchy. The establishment of authority also helps in creation of managerial level.

☞   **Importance/Significance of Organising**

1. **Benefits in specialization :**
    In organising every individual is assigned a part of total work and not the whole task. Due to this division of work into smaller units and assignment of units according to the qualification leads to specialisation. The specialisation automatically comes when an individual is performing one job repeatedly.

2. **Role Clarity :**
    In the organising function the employees are assigned different jobs and the managers clearly define the jobs. The jobs are defined on the written document called job description which clearly spells out what exactly has to be done in every job.
    This description of job brings clarity in the minds of employees.

3. **Clarity in working relationship :**
    In the organising function it is clearly defined that what all and how much power and authority is enjoyed by different individuals or managers. Each manager knows very clearly to whom he can give order and from whom he has to receive the order. The superior-subordinate relation is clearly defined in organising.

4. **Optimum utilization of resources :**
    In the organising function there are very few chances of duplication of work or over-lapping of work because the jobs are assigned to different individuals by clearly defining the job in job description document, So, there are no chances that the same work is performed by two or more individuals.

5. **Co-ordination and effective administration :**
    In the organising function, the similar and related jobs are grouped under one department which leads to unification of efforts and harmony in work. The organising function establishes relation between different departments keeping in mind the co-ordination among different departments. By bringing clarity in working relationship administrative efficiency improver.

6. **Adoption to change :**
    Whenever the changes take place in the business environment then with the help of organising function these changes can be adopted systematically because organising function creates different departments and group related activities under each department. With this, changes can be adopted only in that area which may be affected by these changes and changes can be easily communicated

to whole organisation through departments. Organisational structures can be suitably modified according to changes.

7. **Expansion and Growth :**
   Organising helps in the growth and diversification of an enterprise. It allows a business enterprise to add more job positions, departments and even diversify their product lines. New geographical territories can be added to current assets of operation and this will help to increase customer base, sales and profit.

8. **Development of personnel :**
   Organising stimulates creativity amongst the managers. Effective delegation allows the managers to reduce their workload by assigning routine jobs to their subordinates. Managers can now use their time to explore areas for growth and innovation. Delegation also provides opportunity to the subordinates to utilize their talent and develop skills to perform complex and higher responsibility tasks.

☞ **Organisational Structure**

Organisation structure is the outcome of the organizing process. Structure, in general, is the pattern in which various parts or components of an object are interconnected, for example, structure of a building. Thus, organisation structure is defined as follows:

"Organisation structure is the framework within which managerial and operating tasks are performed to achieve desired objectives. It establishes relationship between people, work and resources."

1. **Job design**

   In the organising process the total work is divided into various jobs and the manager has to get the jobs done from his employees. So, it must be specified very clearly what all activities have to be performed in a particular job. What each individual has to do while performing the job. So, designing of job means clearly defining the contents of job as far as possible, expected results of jobs must be defined along with the job.

2. **Departmentation :**
   After division of work into jobs, the jobs are grouped together to form departments. While grouping the activities the managers must keep in mind that only the related or similar jobs are grouped under one department so that there can be specialisation. The manager can have different ways of grouping the jobs which are related to each other.

3. **Span of Management**
   Span of management means how many employees or subordinates can be effectively managed by one manager or how many subordinates are under one superior. When the authority and responsibility relationships are established in organising process then the managers must keep in mind the span of control. The span of control depends upon:

   (a) **Capacity and intelligence of level of managers:**
       If managers are smart and intelligent then they can have a large span. Which means more number of subordinates can work under them.

   (b) **The trust of managers in their employees :**
       The managers who have more trust and faith in their employees they can have a large span.

(c) **The employees intelligence level:**
If the employees are trained and professional then there can be large span but if they are unskilled then small span because unskilled employees need more guidance of superior so small span is needed.

(d) **Nature of job:**
If the routine job has to be performed then there can be large span but for specialised and challenging job small span of control is preferred. After deciding the span a scalar chain is developed of all the superiors and subordinates because the span of control clearly specifies who has to report to whom.

4. **Delegation of Authority :**
Delegation of authority means sharing of authority between the managers and subordinates. Generally while getting the work done from subordinates managers pass some degree or part of their authority to their subordinates. So that they can work as a team and achieve the group goal. This sharing of authority helps in deciding the group leader among the subordinates also. For example, if there are 10 salesmen working under one sales manager, then manager can authorise the salesmen to decide about delivery date, discount limits etc. And out of these 10 salesmen, sales manager can give authority to one person to report about the sale of all the salesmen.

☞ **Need for Organisation Structure**

1. **Growth in Size of Organisation :**
When an organisation grows in size, its number of employees increases; more functions may be added in the organisation. In order to manage increased number of employees and functions, suitable organisation structure is needed.

2. **Overcoming Communication Problems:**
In a large organisation, distance between decision-making centres and decision-implementation centres increases. This results in communication problems which can be overcome by suitable organisation structure as it establishes communication links.

3. **Overcoming Coordination Problems:**
Organisation structure is required to ensure coordination between different organisational functions as well as between sub-functions of a function.

4. **Need for Control:**
Need for suitable organisation structure is felt to ensure that functioning each organisational position is controlled suitably. Organisation structure facilitates this by prescribing which position is subject to control by which position.

☞ **Types of Organisational Structure**

I. **Functional Structure :**
Functional Structure is created by grouping the activities on the basis of functions required for the achievement of organisational objectives. For example, in a manufacturing organisation these functions are production, marketing, finance and human resource. For each of these functions, a department is created at the first level. At the second level, each function is further

divided and sub functions are indentified. For example, in marketing function, the sub-functions are sales, product promotion, product distribution and marketing research. The organization chart of functional structure has been given in figure.

☞ **Functional Structure**

☞ **Advantages**

1. **Occupational Specialization :**
   Functional structure leads to occupational specialization, that is, specialization in a particular field to activity. This specialization enhances employee efficiency.

2. **Easy supervision :**
   The supervisor becomes familiar with the type of task to be performed because all tasks are related to one function only. As a result he can supervise and guide the employees who are performing those activities.

3. **Better Control & Coordination :**
   It promotes coordination and control in a department as similar activities are performed in the department.

4. **It helps in increasing managerial efficiency :**
   Managers of one department are performing same type of function again and again which makes them specialised and improves their efficiency.

5. **Effective Training :**
   It makes training of the employees more easy as they are trained in limited types of skill i.e., employees of production department are given training of production techniques only.

6. **Easier employee learning :**
   It makes employee learning easier because of his continuous engagement in a particular field.

7. **Importance to all functions :**
It gives importance to all business functions as all functions are organized separately.

☞ **Disadvantages**

1. **Less Emphasis on Organizational Objectives :**
Functional structure puts more emphasis on performance of various business functions and less emphasis on organizatioal objectives. Therefore, no one is responsible for end results.

2. **Problem in Coordination :**
When the departments become too large the co-ordination decreases and results in delay of decision.

3. **Creates Conflicts :**
The departmental heads start thinking their departments as their functional empire and this leads to conflicts among various departments.

4. **Difficult to make accountable :**
When the organisational goal is not achieved then it becomes very difficult to make any one department accountable for this because all the departments are interrelated and it is very difficult to find out that which department is going against the organisational goal.

5. **Inflexibility :**
Employees get training of one function only i.e., the department to which they belongs so they can be shifted to other departments.

Suitability : Functional structure is suitable for:
1. Large organisations producing one line of product.
2. Organisations which require high degree of functional specialisation with diversified activities.

II. **Divisional Structure :**
In divisions structure, activities are grouped on the basis of products or geographical territories. This type of structure is divised by the business firm when are dealing in different categories of product. It helps in coping with the emerging complexities due to diversification of products. Similarly when organisation provides services throughout the country, it opts for divisional structure based on geographical areas. For example most of the bank and insurance companies have this type of divisional structure.

For example, if an organisation is producing soap, textiles, medicine, cosmetics etc. then all the activities to medicine will be grouped under medicine department, all the activities of textiles in textiles   department and so on.
Divisional structure is suitable only to multiproduct manufacturing large organisation

☞ **Divisional Structure**

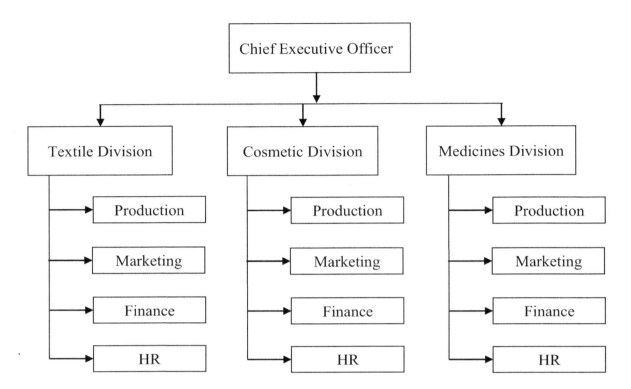

☞ **Advantages**

1. **Product specialisation :**
   All the activities related to one type of product are grouped under one department only which brings integration and co-ordination in the activities.

2. **Fast Decision making :**
   The decisions are taken much faster in divisional structure because there is no dependence on other departments for taking decisions.

3. **Accountability :**
   In this type of structure, the performance of individual departments can easily by assessed and you can hold the department accountable for non-accomplishment of objectives.

4. **Flexibility and more initiative :**
   It promotes flexibility and initiative because each divisional head gains experience in all functions related to a particular product.

5. **Expansion and growth :**
   New departments can be added without disturbing existing departments.

6. **Developing General Management Skills :**
   It helps in developing general management skills. As a result, succession to the post of CEO is not a problem.

☞ **Disadvantages**

1. **Less emphasis on organizational objective :**
   Each department focuses on their product only and they fail to keep themselves as a part of one common organisation.

2. **Interdivision Conflicts :** Divisional structure leads to conflicts among different divisions over the issue of allocation of organizational resources as each division tries to grab as much resource as possible.

3. **Conflict in Succession :**
   Conflict arises among divisional managers over the issue of succession to CEO.

4. **Costly :**
   It may lead to increase in costs since there may be a duplication of activities across products. Providing each division with separate set of similar functions increases expenditure.

☞ **Suitability and Divisional structure are suitable for**

1. Organisations producing multi-product or different line of products.
2. Organisations which require product specialisation.
3. Organisations which require each division to be self contained as under divisional structure each department has production, sale finance deptt.
4. Growing companies which plan to add more line of products in future.

☞ **Formal and Informal Organisation**

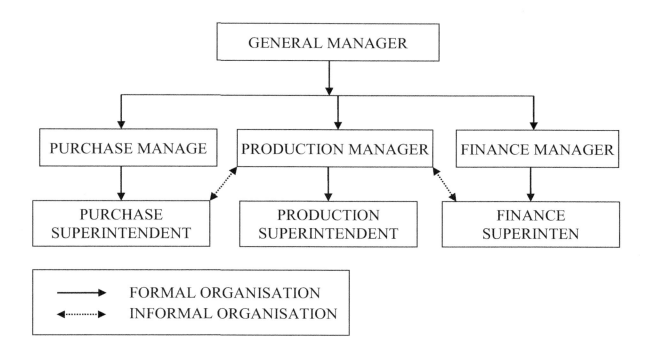

A. **Formal Organisation**

"It refers to the organisation structure which is designed by the
management to accomplish a particular task."

When the managers are carrying on organising process then as a result of organising process an organisational structure is created to achieve systematic working and efficient utilization of resources. This type of structure is known as formal organisational structure.

Formal organisational structure clearly spells out the jobs to be performed by each individual, the authority, responsibility assigned to every individual, the superior- subordinate relationship and the designation of every individual in the organisation. This structure is created intentionally by the managers for achievement of organisational goal.

☞ **Features of Formal Orgenisation**
1. The formal organisational structures created intentionally by the process of organising.
2. The purpose of formal organisation structure is achievement of organisational goal.
3. In formal organisational structure each individual is assigned a specific job.
4. In formal organisational every individual is assigned a fixed authority or decision making power.
5. Formal organisational structure results in creation of superior-subordinate relations.
6. Formal organisational structure creates a scalar chain of communication in the organisation.

☞ **Advantages of Formal Organisation**
1. **Systematic Working :**
    Formal organisation structure results in systematic and smooth functioning of an organisation.

2. **Achievement of Oranisational Objectives :**
    Formal organisatonal structure is established to achieve organisational objectives.

3. **No Overlapping of Work :**
    In Formal organisation structure work is systematically divided among various departments and employees. So there is no chance of duplication or overlapping of work.

4. **Clear Authority, Responsibility and Accountability :**
    Everyone knows precisely his authority, responsibility and accountability and works accordingly. Thus conflict is unlikely to emerge.

5. **Co-ordination :**
    Formal organisational structure results in coordinating the activities of various departments.

6. **Creation of Chain of Command :**
    Formal organisational structure clearly defines superior subordinate relationship i.e., who reports to whom.

7. **More Emphasis on Work :**
    Formal organisational structure lays more emphasis on work than interpersonal relations.

8.   **Clarity about Contributions of Employees :**
      Formal organization prescribes what each employee s expected to do. Therefore. everyone is very clear about his contributions to achieve group/organizational objectives.

☞   **Disadvantages of Formal Organisation**
1.   **Delay in Work Performance :**
      Forma organization puts emphasis on formal procedures, rules and methods in performing jobs. This delays the work performance unnecessarily.

2.   **Delay in Communication :**
      It puts emphasis on formal channel of communication which is mostly narrow. Thus, communication is delayed.

3.   **Job Dissatisfaction :**
      It puts emphasis on job performance based on formal interactions only whereas informal interactions among people are a natural phenomenon. Thus, employees feel job dissatisfaction.

4.   **Emphasis on Work Only :**
      Formal organisational structure gives importance to work only, it ignores human, creativity, talents etc.

B.   **Informal Organisation**
      "It refers to the natural grouping of people in the work situation to meet personal needs."
      In the formal organisational structure individuals are assigned various job positions. While working at those job positions, the individuals interact with each other and develop some social and friendly groups in the organisation. This network of social and friendly groups forms another structure in the organisation which is called informal organisational structure.

      The informal organisational structure gets created automatically and the main purpose of such structure is getting psychological satisfaction. The existence of informal structure depends upon the formal structure because people working at different job positions interact with each other to form informal structure and the job positions are created in formal structure. So, if there is no formal structure, there will be no ob position, there will be no people working at job positions and there will be no informal structure.

☞   **Features of Informal Organisation**
1.   Informal organisational structure gets created automatically without any intended efforts of managers.
2.   Informal organisational structure is formed by the employees to get psychological satisfaction.
3.   Informal organisational structure does not follow any fixed path of flow of authority or communication.
4.   Source of information cannot be known under informal structure as any person can communicate with anyone in the organisation.
5.   The existence of informal organisational structure depends on the formal organisation structure.

☞   **Advantages of Informal Organisation**
1.   **Fast Communication :**
      Informal structure does not follow scalar chain so there can be faster spread of communication.

2. **Fast Work Performance :**
Informal organization interacts continuously with formal organization in terms of work performance. This results in overcoming some constraints put by the formal organization in performing a job quickly, for example, following the short-cut procedure for doing a work instead of following the lengthy procedure prescribed for this purpose.

3. **Correct Feedback :**
Through Informal structure the top level managers can know the real feedback of employees on various policies and plans.

4. **Fulfillment of social needs :**
It helps to fulfill the social needs of the members. This enhances their job satisfaction since it gives them a sense of belongingness in the organization.

☞ **Disadvantages of Informal Organisation**
1. **Spread Rumors :** According to a survey 70% of information spread through informal organisational structure are rumors which may mislead the employees.

2. **No Systematic Working :** Informal structure does not form a structure for smooth working of an organisation.

3. **May Bring Negative Results :** If Informal structure organisation opposes the policies and changes of management, then it becomes very difficult to implement them in organisation.

4. **More Emphasis to Individual Interest :** Informal structure gives more importance to satisfaction of individual interest as compared to organisational interest.

☞ **Delegation of Authority**
"It refers to the process of entrusting responsibility and authority and creating account ability of the person to whom work or responsibility has been handed over."
In every organisation managers are assigned lot of work and manager alone cannot perform all the work. He divides the work among different individuals working under him according to their qualification and get the work done from them. The manager begins with sharing of his responsibilities with his subordinates. He deliberately passes some of his responsibilities to his subordinates. After passing the responsibilities the manager also shares some of his authority i.e., power to make decision with his subordinates so that the responsibilities can be carried on properly. To make sure that his subordinates perform all the work effectively and efficiently in the expected manner the manager creates accountability and this whole process is known as delegation.

☞ **Principle of Absoluteness of Accountability**
Delegation is a very important process to carry on the work systematically in the organisation. But delegation is not a process of abdication which means accountability is absolute. It can never be passed or delegated. After creating accountability on subordinates, the superiors also remain accountable. For example, if the sales manager is assigned a target of selling 1,000 units in one month, he divided this target among the five salesman working under him. One of the salesman fell sick. So, at the end of one month only 800 units could be sold. In such a situation the accountability lies with the manager although he has delegated or passed this target to his subordinates. But by passing or delegating the responsibilities he

cannot get rid of subordinates. He should have checked in between and supervised from time to time whether the work is going in right direction or not and taken timely action.

☞ **Elements/Process of Delegation :**
There are three elements of delegation
1. **Responsibility :**
   Responsibility means the work assigned to an individual. It includes all the physical and mental activities to be performed by the employees at a particular job position. The process of delegation begins when manager passes on some of his responsibilities to his subordinates which means responsibility can b delegated.

2. **Authority :**
   Authority means power to take decision. To carry on the responsibilities every employee need to have some authority. So, when managers are passing their responsibilities to the subordinates, they also pass some of the authority to the subordinates. The delegating authority is the second step of delegation process. While sharing the authority managers keep in mind that the authority matching to the responsibility should only be delegated. They shall not pass all their authority to their subordinates.

3. **Accountability :**
   To make sure that the employees or subordinates perform their responsibilities in their expected manner the accountability is created. Accountability means subordinates will be answerable for the non-completion of the task; creating accountability is the third and final step of delegation process. The accountability cannot be passed or delegated. It can only be shared with the subordinates which means even after delegating responsibility and authority the managers will be accountable for non-completion of task.

   If the production manager is given the target of producing 20 machines in one month's time and he divided this target between four foremen working under him i.e., 5 machines to be produced by each foreman but one foreman achieve the target and at the end of the month only 17 machines are manufactured, then production manager will be held accountable for non-completion of target as accountability cannot be transferred or shared: It is an absolute term.

   "Authority can be delegated but responsibility cannot." Explain?

   The word 'responsibility' can be used in two ways:
   (i) **'responsibility for'** and
   (ii) **'responsibility to'**
   'Responsibility for means obligation of a subordinate to complete the assigned job and it is called Operating Responsibility'.

   'Responsibility to' means accountability of a subordinate for his work performance in relation to the authority given to him and it is called 'Ultimate Responsibility'.
   Thus a superior can delegate only the operating responsibility to his subordinates but not the ultimate responsibility. The ultimate responsibility is always of the delegator, i.e. Superior. In the statement given in the question the meaning of responsibility is 'responsibility to' that cannot be delegated. It means the person who delegates authority remains accountable to his own boss for the work performance of his subordinate.

☞ **Importance of Delegation**

1. **Effective management :**
   In the delegation process managers pass routine work to the subordinate. So they are free to concentrate on other important matters. The main job of managers is to get the work done effectively and by delegating the authorities and responsibilities managers can get the work done effectively and efficiently from the subordinates.

2. **Employees Development :**
   As a result of delegation employees get more opportunities to utilise their talents. It allows them to develop those skills which help them to perform complex task. Delegation help in making better future managers by giving them chance to use their skills, gain experience of work related to higher job position.

3. **Motivation of employees :**
   In the delegation when the manager is sharing his responsibilities and authority with the subordinates it motivates the subordinates as they develop the feeling of belongingness and trust which is shown to them by their superiors. Some employees can be motivated by such kind of non-financial incentives.

4. **Facilitates organisational growth :**
   In the process of delegation when the managers are passing their responsibility and authority to the subordinates they keep in mind the qualification and capability of all the subordinates. This leads to division of work and specialisation which is very important for organisational growth.

5. **Basis of Management Hierarchy :**
   Delegation establishes superior-subordinate relationship which is the base for hierarchy of managers. The extent of power delegated to subordinates decides who will report to whom, and the power at each job position forms the Management Hierarchy.

6. **Better Coordination :**
   In delegation systematically responsibility and authority is divided and employees are made answerable for non-completion of task. This systematic division of work gives clear pictures of work to every one and there is no duplication of work clarity in duties assigned and reporting relationship brings effective coordination in the organisation.

7. **Reduces the work load of managers :**
   In the process of delegation, the managers are allowed to share their responsibilities and work with the subordinates which help the managers to reduce their work load. With the process of delegation the managers can pass all their routine work to the subordinates and concentrate on important work. Without delegation managers will be overburdened with the work.

8. **Basis of superior-subordinate relationship :**
   In the delegation process only two parties are involved that is superior and subordinate. If superiors share or pass their responsibilities and authorities to the subordinates it indicates good relationship between the superior and subordinate because superiors will transfer their responsibility and authority to their subordinates only when they have trust in them. So delegation improves the relations between superiors and subordinates.

☞ **Centralisation and Decentralisatoin**

Centralisation and Decentralisation are related terms as an organisation uses both the policies.

**Centralisation refers to concentration of power or authority
in few hands i.e., top level.**

An organisation is centralised when the decision-making authority is in the hands of top level management only.

**Decentralisation can be defined as even and systematic
distribution of authority at every level of management.**

Under decentralisation every employee working at different levels gets some share in the authority. Decentralisation is a policy matter and managers plan in advance whether to go for centralised or decentralised policy. Sometimes company follows a mixed policy of centralisation and decentralisation. They keep the important matters such as financial decisions, structural decisions with the top level management only and share the common decisions with the people working at different levels as generally an organisation can never be completely centralised or decentralised.

☞ **Relation between delegation and Decentralisation**

Decentralisation is extension of delegation. In delegation we multiply the authority with two whereas in decentralisation the authority is multiplied by many because systematic delegation taking place at every level will result in evenly distribution of authority and responsibility at every level and result in decentralisation. If delegation is restricted to certain levels only then there will be no complete decentralisation also.

For example, if the directors give the responsibility to production head to complete the target of 50,000 units per annum and authorise him to hire the required workers, decide their salaries and working conditions. The production head further shares his responsibility and authority with the production manager to achieve the target and select the workers. The production manager shares his authority and responsibility with the supervisors who directly deal with the workers and authorise them to select the workers. This sharing of authority and responsibilities between directors and production head, managers and subordinates will result in a systematic distribution of authority at every level automatically. That is why we say systematic delegation leads to decentralisation. In delegation the authority is shared between two persons only i.e., manager and subordinate whereas the decentralisation many people at every level are involved i.e., directors, production head, manager, subordinates etc.

☞ **Delegation is necessary in every organisation but decentralization is not necessary**

Delegation is an essential part of every organisation. No organisations can work without using the concept of delegation as there is no individual who can do all the work himself only. Delegation isa tool to get the work done effectively and efficiently through others whereas decentralisation is required when an organisation grows and expands and only top level cannot manage it. Specially in the present era due to liberalization and globalization fast decision is needed and quick decisions can be taken througr decentralisation only as it provides greater flexibility and freedom of action but still many organisation are working with little or no decentralisation. It is a matter of choice and preference of top level management and not compulsory.

☞ **Importance of Decentralisation**

1. **Develop initiative among subordinate :**

   Passing of authority at middle and lower level shows the trust and faith of top level in their subordinates and this trust and faith motivate the employees working at different levels as they are allowed to take decisions without seeking the approval of superiors.

2. **Develop managerial talent for future :**

   In the decentralisation managers working at lower and middle level also learn the art of making decisions. They get the experience of performing activities of top executives and learn to manage the authority given to them. So decentralisation process prepares the managers working at lower and middle level to perform the task of top level. So, whenever there is vacant job position at top level management, the managers working at lower or middle level can be promoted. This is how it level talent for future.

3. **Quick decision-making :**

   In the decentralisation process decision-making is not restricted in few hands only by decision-making power is entrusted to all the managers who are taking actions or performing the activities. This leads to faster decision because employees who have to perform the activities are allowed to take decision also.

4. **Relief to top level management :**

   In the process of decentralisation top level managers are not overburdened with the responsibilities and authority as they systematically pass the authority and responsibilities at different levels and they become free to concentrate on core and important issues.

5. **Facilitates growth :**

   Decentralisation grants more autonomy or freedom to lower level. This helps the subordinates to do the work in the manner best suited for their department. When each department is doing to their best then productivity increases and it will generate more revenue which can be used for expansion.

6. **Better control :**

   In decentralisation employees working at different levels take their own decisions and they are personally accountable for their decisions, they cannot pass the blame to their superiors. With decentralisation better control can be exercised through Score Card, Management Information System etc.

7. **Promotes initiative and creativity :**

   The initiative directly depends on the authority. When the employees at every level are given greater degree of autonomy and authority according to their responsibilities, this helps them to take initiative. On the other hand, when lower and middle level executives are performing the task of top level executives then it brings creativity.

8. **Improved team work :**

   In decentralisation all the managers and employees are sharing the decision-making powers, all are given some kind of autonomy and freedom of action. This sharing of decision and freedom of action integrate the employees as one team and develop team spirit among the employees.

Basis	Authority	Responsibility	Accountability
1. Meaning	It is right to command	It is duty for job performance.	It is answerability for results.
2. Origin	It emerges from formal position	It emerges from delegated authority	It emerges from responsibility.
3. Delegation	It can be delegated	It can be delegated partially	It cannot be delegated.
4. Flow	It flows downward from superior to subordinate,	It flows upward form subordinate to superior.	It flows upward from subordinate to superior.

Functional Structure Vs. Divisional Structure

Basis.	Functional Structure	Divisional Structure
1. Nature	Focus on functions such as production, marketing and finance.	Focus on products or product lines.
2. Formation	Based on functions. Simple Structure.	Based on products and supported by functions. Complicated structure.
3. Type of Specialisation	Specialized treatment to each functiàn.	specialized treatment to each product and to each function within the division.
4. Authority	Concentration-of authority at the top level of the enterprise,	Decentralisation of authority at the divisional level.
5. Autonomy	Various functions are interdependent and interrelated,	Each division is autonomous or independent.
6. Coordination	Very difficult for a multiproduct company.	Less difficult because all functions related to a particular product are integrated in the product divisions.
7. Control	Comparatively simple.	Comparatively complex.
8. Management Development	Difficult because of narrow functional specialisation.	Easier because autonomy to perform multiple functions is given to divisional heads.
9. Cost Factor	Economical as functional departments are not duplicated,	Costly as each division has to create its cross functional departments.
10. Responsibility for Profits	Cant be fixed on a single department.	Can be fixed on each division.
11. Suitability	Suitable for medium sized firms having a single product or a small number of related products.	Suitable for large firms having multiple products with distinct characteristics.

Formal Organisation Vs Informal Organisation

Basis	Formal Organisation	Information Organisation
1. Definition	It refers to the structure of well - defined authority and responsibility relationships.	It refers to the personal relationships which develop automatically when people work together.
2. Purpose	It is created to achieve predetermined objectives.	It has no predetermined objectives.
3. Formation /Origin	Formal relations are well planned and are created deliberately,	Informal relations are unplanned and they originate automatically.

4. Structure	The structure is well defined as it is on authority and tasks.	There is no clear cut structure as the emphasis is on people and relationships.
5. Flow of Authority	Authority flows from top to bottom, i.e., vertically downward.	Authority flows vertically as well as horizontally.
6. Communication	Formal organisation follows the official chain of command which can't be changed. Communication has to follow formal channels.	Informal organisation does not have a chain of command. There are no fixed patterns of communication.
7. Leadership	Managers provide leadership to the workers of their departments.	Informal leaders are chosen by the group members.
8. Flexibility	It follows a rigid structure.	It is loosely structured. It is highly flexible.
9. Behaviour of Members	Formal organisation reflects technical aspect of the organisation. It does not take care of human sentiments. The members are expected to behave as per rules and regulations of the organisation	Informal organisation reflects human aspects. It is based on the attitudes, likes and dislike, tastes, language, etc. of people. The members, are free to interact with any member freely.
10. Inter dependence	Formal organisation can exist independently of the informal organisation.	Informal organisation is dependent on the format organisation. It exists alongside the formal organisation.
11. Stability	Formal organisation is usually stable.	Informal organisation does not last so long.

Delegation Vs. Decentralisation

Basis	Delegation	Decentralisation
1. Nature	It refers to the entrustment of responsibility abd authority from a superior to his subordinate. Thus, it is individualistic.	It refers to the systematic delegation of authority to a lower level in the organisation. Thus, it is totalistic
2. Scope or Parties Involved	It has a narrow scope as it is restricted from one person to another.	It takes place when delegation is made to all the employees at a particular level.
3. Purpose	Its purpose is to lessen the burden of the superior,	Its purpose is to give greater autonomy (or freedom of action) to the lower levels.
4. Control vs. Freedom of action	The person who delegates authority keeps the power to control with himself. The subordinate does not have much freedom of action.	Control is exercised by the top management in a general manner. The divisional managers enjoy sufficient autonomy or freedom of action.
5. Need and Significance	Delegation is compulsory if an executive wants to get the help of others in getting things done.	Decentralisation is optional. Management may not think t necessary to decentralise authority.
6. Relationship	Delegation reinforces superior - subordinate relationship.	Decentralisation is a step towards creation of semi autonomous units.
7. Effectiveness	It can be effective in all organisations.	It can be effective in big organisations.

EXERCISE – 1

1. Which function of management is a means for translating plans into action and includes the designing of roles to be filled by suitably skilled people?
Ans. Organising.

2. Which function of management coordinates human efforts, assembles resources and integrates both into a unified whole to be utilised for achieving specified objectives?
Ans. Organising.

3. Which function of management is concerned with establishing relationships for the purpose of enabling people to work most effectively together in accomplishing objectives?
Ans. Organising.

4. Name the process of grouping the activities of similar nature.
Ans. Departmentalisation.

5. How does organising facilitate effective administration?
Ans. Organising provides a clear description of jobs and related duties. This helps to avoid confusion an duplication. Clarity in working relationships enables proper execution of work. This brings effectiveness in administration.

6. What is meant by organisational structure?
Ans. Organisational structure means the framework within which managerial and operating tasks are performed. It specifies the relationships between people, work and resources.

7. Define 'Span of management'.
Ans. Span of management refers to the number of subordinates that can be effectively managed by a superior.

8. How is 'Span of management related to organisation structure?
Ans. The span of management. to a large extent, gives shape to the organisation structure. This determines the levels of management in the organ isation structure.

9. Kshitij Medicines International Pvt. Ltd. is a diversified company and has seven branches all over the world. Each branch is concerned with the production and sales of only one type of medicine. What type of organisational structure would you suggest for the company and why?
Ans. Divisional structure.

10. Which type of organisational structure is suitable for high degree of specialisation?
Ans. Functional structure.

11. Name the type of organisation in which —
(a) Friendly relationship exists among the members
(b) Official relationship exists among the members.
Ans. (a) Informal organisation   (b) Formal organisation

12. Name the type of organisation which specifies clearly the boundaries of authority and responsibility and there is a systematic coordination among the various activities to achieve organisational goals.

Ans. Informal organisation.

13. "For effective delegation, the authority granted must be commensurate with the assigned responsibility." Why?

Ans. This is so because if authority granted is more than responsibility, it may lead to misuse of authority and if responsibility assigned is more than authority it may make a person ineffective.

14. How does the concept 'authority' arise?

Ans. Authority arises, from the established 'scalar chain' which links the various job positions and levels of an orgainsation.

15. The directors of Puneet Electronics, an organisation manufacturing T.V. components, have asked Shakti, their Marketing Manager to achieve a target sale of Rs. 5,00,000 per day. Shakti has delegated the task to Vaibhav, his Deputy Sales Manager working under him. Vaibhave couldnot achieve the targets. Is Shakti responsible for the failure of Vaibhav ? State the relevant principle in support of your answer.

Ans. Yes, Shakti is responsible. The relevant principle is 'Principle of absolute accountability'.

16. Name the type of organisation in which structure of jobs is created with clearly defined functions, authority and responsibility.

Ans. Formal organisation.

17. Which network of interaction facilitates emotional and mutual objectives to be fulfilled in an organisation?

Ans. Informal organisation.

EXERCISE – 2

---

1. A company has its registered office in Delhi, manufacturing unit at Gurgaon and marketing and sales department at Faridabed. The company manufactures the consumer products. Which type or organisational structure should it adopt to achieve its target? Give reasons.

Ans. The company should adopt **'Functional Structure'** to achieve its targets.

Reasons : The company has separate departments like manufacturing unit (Gurgaon), marketing and sales department (Faridabed), etc. That means, the size of the organisation is large, it has diversified activities and operations require a high degree of specialisation. So, it should about functional structure.

By adopting functional structure, the company gets the following advantages:

(i) Each functional area of business (production, marketing, finance and personnel) will be controlled by an expert/specialist. It will lead to specialisation.

(ii) It will lead to minimum duplication of efforts. This results in lower costs.

(iii) It helps in increasing managerial and operational efficiency and this results in increased profit.

(iv) It ensures that different functions (production, marketing, finance, etc.) get due attention.

2. Tanushree runs a factory wherein she manufactures shoes. The business has been doing well and she intends to expand by diversifying into leather bags as well as western formal wear, thereby making her complete provider of corporate wear. This will enable her to market her business unit as the one shop for working women. Which type of structure would you recommend for the expanded organisation and why?

Ans. I will recommend the **'Divisional structure'** for the expanded business.

Reasons : Tunushree wants to diversify products by manufacturing leather bags and western formal wear. That means, the organisation will grow; and will need to add more employees; create more divisions; and introduce new levels of management.

By adopting divisional structure, the company will get the following advantages:

(i)   It will facilitate growth and expansion. Not the business of Tansuhree will have multiple division shoes, bags and formal wear. Within each division, functions like production, marketing, finance, purchase, etc. will be performed to achieve the objectives of the business.

(ii)   Greater Accountability will be possible because the divisional manager can be held separately accountable for his division's profits, costs, etc.

(iii)   Product specialisation: A divisional head gains experience in all functions related to a particular product.

(iv)   Flexibility and initiative: It promotes flexibility and initiative because each division functions as an autonomous unit which leads to faster decision-making.

3.   The directors of Gunjan Ltd. an organisation manufacturing colour televisions, have asked their production manager to achieve a target production of 150 televisions per day. The production manager has asked his foreman to achieve this target, but he did not give him the authority for the requisition of tools and materials from the stores department. The foreman could not achieve the desired target. Can the directors blame the production manager, and can the production manager blame his foreman for not achieving the target? Explain in brief the relevant principles relating to this situation in support of your answer,

Ans.   Yes, the directors can blame the production manager, although he had delegated the task to his foreman because accountability cannot be delegated by a manager. The production manager shall still be accountable for the performance of the assigned tasks. (Principle of absoluteness of accountability)

However, the production manager cannot blame his foreman for not achieving the target because he did not give him the authority for the requisition of tools and materials from the stores department. Responsibility without authority will make the subordinate ineffective, i.e., he will not be able to perform his duties well. (Principle of authority and responsibility)

4.   Company manufacturing sewing machines set up in 1946 follows formal organisation structure. It is facing lot of problems such as delay in decision-making. As a result, it is not able to adapt to the changing business environment. The workforce is also not motivated, there is problem of red tapism and employees' turnover is very high.

(i)   Advise the company with regard to change it should bring about in its organisation structure to overcome the problems faced by it.

(ii)   Give reasons in terms of benefits it will derive from the changes suggested by you.

(iii)   In which sector can the company diversify keeping in mind the declining market for the product the company is manufacturing?

Ans.   (i)   The company should give due importance to informal organisational structure along with the formal structure. It enhances their job satisfaction. This will overcome the problem of   lack   of motivation. Informal groups can also provide useful communication channels, which   may   help   to transmit useful information quickly.

(ii)   Benefits of informal organisational structure:

(a)   Faster spread of information: Fixed lines of communication are not followed. Thus, the informal organisation leads to faster spread of information as well as quick feedback.

(b)   Fulfilment of social needs: It helps to fulfil the social needs of the members. This enhances their job satisfaction since it gives them a sense of belongingness in the organisation.

(c)   Fills inadequacies of formal structure: It contributes towards fulfilment of organisational objectives by compensating for inadequacies in the formal organisation. For example, employees' reactions towards plans and policies can be tested through the informal network.

(iii)   The company can diversify its activities by introducing embroidery machines. It can also design special machines keeping in mind the requirement of ready-made garment manufacturers, etc. By diversifying in the same field, it can get maximum utilisation of existing resources.

5.   A company manufacturing consumer goods has grown in size. It was a market leader but with changes in economic environment and with the entry of MN Cs its market share is declining. The company was following a centralised business model as even the minor decisions were in the hands of top level. Before 1991 this model was suitable for company but now the company is under pressure to reform.

What changes should the company bring about in order to retain its market share?

Ans.   The top management of the company must share decision-making authority with middle level and supervisory level also. It should introduce the concept of decentralisation instead of following complete centralisation. hi the current scenario of business environment, there is need for fast action and quick decision-making which is possible only with decentralisation.

Importance of decentralisation:

1.   **Relief to top management:** In a decentralised organisation, top level managers are not burdened by common day-to-day problems. Therefore, they have enough time to plan ahead, develop new strategies and concentrate on coordination and control.

2.   **Develops initiative amongst subordinates:** Decentralisation helps to promote self-reliance and confidence amongst the subordinates. This is because when lower managerial levels are given freedom to take their own decisions, they learn to depend on their own judgement.

3.   **Quick decision-making:** In a decentralised organisation, decision-making is not restricted in few hands only but decision-making power is entrusted to all the managers who perform the activities. This facilitates quick decision-making.

EXERCISE - 3

1.   "In big organisations delegation of authority is not required at all." Do you agree with this statement? Give reasons in support of your answer.

2.   Define the terms 'Responsibility', 'Authority' and 'Accountability' as elements of delegation.

3.   Distinguish between authority and responsibility on the basis of:
(A) Meaning   (B) Origin   (C) Flow   (D) Delegation

4.   Distinguish between authority and accountability on the basis of:
(A) Meaning   (B) Origin   (C) Flow   (D) Delegation.

5.   Distinguish between responsibility and accountability on the basis of:
(A) Meaning   (B) Origin   (C) Flow   (D) Delegation.

6.   "Authority can be delegated but accountability cannot" Explain the statement with an example.

7. The production manager asks the foreman to achieve a target production of 200 units per day, but he doesn't give him the authority to requisition tools and materials from the stores department. Can the production manager blame the foreman if he is not able to achieve the desired target? Give reasons.

8. In an electrical goods manufacturing company, there are four main activities: Marketing, Production, Finance and Personnel. The General Manager is planning to structure the organisation. Which type of organisational structure should he adopt and why? Give two reasons.

STAFFING

CONTENT

☞ **Introduction :**
A managerial function of placing the right man at the right jobs.

☞ **Importance of Staffing**
1. Filling the roles by obtaining competent personnel.
2. Placing Right person at the right job.
3. Growth of Enterprise.
4. Optimum utilization of human resources.
5. Helps in competing.
6. Improves job satisfaction and morale of the employees.
7. Key to effectiveness of other functions.

☞ **Staffing Process**
1. Estimating Manpower Requirements.
2. Recruitment.
3. Selection.
4. Placement and orientation.
5. Training and Development.
6. Performance Appraisal.
7. Promotion and Career Planning.
8. Compensations.
9. Separation

☞ **Components of Staffing**
1. Recruitment.
2. Selection.
3. Training

☞ **Source of Recruitment**
1. Internal Sources: 1. Transfer, 2. Promotion.
2. External Sources:
1. Direct Recruitment.
2. Casual callers.
3. Media advertising.
4. Employment exchanges.
5. Placement Agencies and Management Consultants.
6. Campus Recruitment.
7. Recommendations from present of employees.
8. Labour Contractors
9. Advertising on Television.
10. Web Publishing
11. Factory Gate

☞ **Selection Process**
1. Preliminary Screening.
2. Selection Test.

3. Employment interview.
4. Checking the reference and background.
5. Selection Decision.
6. Medical Examination.
7. Job offer.
8. Contract of Employment.

☞ **Training Methods**
1. On-the-Job Method.   2. Off-the-Job Method.

WEIGHTAGE

Units	Very Short Answer	Short Answer I & II	Long Answer I & II	Total
Unit - 6(6)	1(1)	---	5(1)	6(2)

6.   STAFFING

☞ **Meaning of Staffing**
   Staffing involves "finding the right person for the right job having the right qualification, doing the right job at the right time".
   OR
   "Staffing is the process of acquiring, employing, developing, remunerating, appraising and retaining people so that right type of people are available for right jobs"

☞ **Importance/Need/Benefits/Advantages of Staffing**
Efficient staff can help to attain number one position in market and inefficient staff can bring you down in market. The performance of an organisation depends upon the performance of its employees. Proper staffing ensures the following benefits to the organisation:

1.   **Filling the roles by obtaining competent personnel :** Staffing function is needed to fill the job position. There will be no use of job position unless and until these are occupied by employees and it is through staffing function only that employees are appointed to fill the vacant job.

2.   **Placing Right person at the right job :** Staffing ensures higher performance by placing right person on the right job by proper recruitment and selection. Employees are given a place according to their qualifications.

3.   **Growth of Enterprise :** By appointing efficient staff, staffing ensures continuous survival and growth of the enterprise. As organisation grow with the efforts of its employees only.

4.   **Optimum utilization of human resources :** Through manpower planning and job analysis we can find out the number of employees and type of employees required in the organisation. So there are no chances of overmanning and shortage of underutilization of personnel.

5.   **Helps in competing :** Two organisations can easily acquire same type of physical and financial resources but what helps organisation to win over the other is the efficient staff. The organisation with efficient staff can easily win over its competitors.

6. **Improves job satisfaction and morale of the employees :** Staffing function does not end only with appointment of employees. It includes training, promotion, compensation etc. All these activities help in motivating the employees and boost up the morale of the employees.

7. **Key to effectiveness of other functions :** No other function of management can be carried out without efficient staffing function because all the functions are performed by human beings and human beings join the organisation by staffing function only.

☞ **Staffing and Human Resource**
"It is a specialized functions which involves acquiring developing, appraising and maintaining human resources in the organisation. So as to achieve its objectives."

Managing the human resources is the most important function in an organisation because it is on their performance that the success of an organisation depends. **Human resource management is an important function of management which is concerned with managing and developing the human resources of an organisation in terms of their knowledge, skills, talents, attitudes and capabilities.** It involves determining the manpower requirements of an organisation, recruiting and selecting the best available employees, developing and motivating them. In other words, **Human Resource Management is that phase of management which deals with the effective procurement and utilization of manpower of human resources.**

☞ **The main functions performed by Human resource management**
(i)   Determining the number & types of employees required.
(ii)   Recruitment, selection & placement of employees.
(iii)   Providing training to the employees for improving their performance & career growth.
(iv)   Performance appraisals.
(v)   Motivating the employees by providing both financial & non financial incentives.
(vi)   Ensuring social security for employees & handling their grievances.
(vii)   Defending enterprises from legal complications.
(viii) Establishing amicable relations between union & management.
(ix)   Compensation or remuneration of employees keeping in mind their qualifications and other factors.

☞ **Staffing**
Staffing is referred as both line as well as a staff activity.
staffing is referred as line activity because like other functions such as planning, organising, directing, controlling, staffing is also performed by every manager.
staffing is a staff activity because it is an important area of management also like marketing management, financial management, we have human resource management department also in large organisations:
The steps involved in the staffing process are :
1. **Estimating man power requirement :** Staffing process begin with the estimation of manpower requirement which means finding out number and type (in the sense what should educational qualification) of the employees needed by the organisation. While estimating possibilities regarding internal promotions, retirements, resignation etc are also taken into consideration, estimation of manpower requirement should be based on the organisations strategic plan and not merely organisation structure.
Manpower planning involves two techniques in estimation

A. Workload Analysis — Specify no. & types of employees required.

B. Workforce Analysis— Specify there is understaffed, overstaffed or optimally staffed.

2.   **Recruitment :** It refers to the process of inducing the potential candidates to apply for the job. So that more option are available at selection step that is why it is also known as positive process, In other words, recruitment means making available the efficient employees in order to fill various post.

There are two sources for the recruitment of employees.

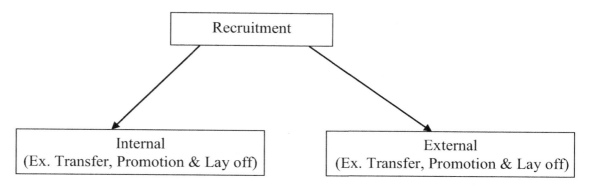

3.   **Selection :** It refers to choosing the most suitable and competent candidate to fill the vacant job in the organisational structure. It is important to keep in mind that the ability of the applicant and the nature of work must match. The selection is done through a process which involves test, interviews etc. Selection is considered a negative process because more candidates are rejected than selected through this process.

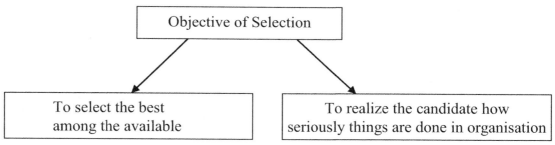

4.   **Placement and Orientation :** Placement refers to occupying of post by the candidate for which he is selected. After selection the employees is given appointment letter and is asked to occupy the vacant job position.

Before they start working in the organisation orientation programme is organised by the organisation. Orientation is the process of introducing a new employee to the organisation and organisation to the employee by providing relevant information such as working of organisation, it human resources policy, employment benefits, introduction of superior, co-workers and subordinate it is also known as induction.

5.   **Training and Development :** The last step in the process of staffing is imparting training and development facilities to the employees so that their efficiency and effectiveness is increased. Training refers to a process designed to maintain and improve current job performance. On the

other hand, development refers to a process designed to develop skills necessary for future activities.

☞ **Staffing Process**

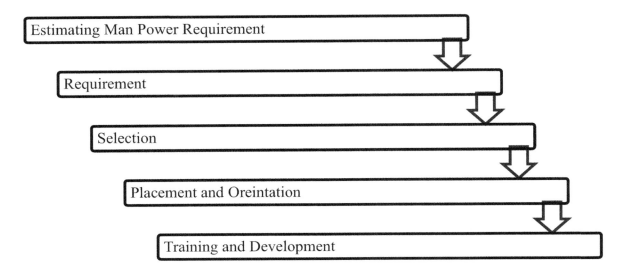

In most of the large scale organisations there is a separate human resource department which performs staffing function but in small organisations the line managers only perform all the functions. So small organisations in which there is no human resource department include following steps also in the staffing process.

1. **Performance Appraisal :** After taking training and performing the job for sometimes there is need that employees' performance must be evaluated. Performance appraisal refers to evaluating the performance of employees against some standards. The standards are made known to employees in advance. Superiors prepare a feedback report on the basis of performance appraisal.

2. **Promotion and Career Planning :** Promotion refers to being placed at a higher job position with more pay, job satisfaction and responsibility. Generally on the basis of feedback report of employee's performance they are given promotion and opportunities for higher job positions.

3. **Compensation :** It refers to price of the job. It includes pays, reward and other incentives given to employees. It includes direct as well as indirect payments. Direct payments such as wages, salary etc. Indirect payments such as medical facility, insurance etc. The managers must fix the right compensation on the basis of qualification, type of job etc.
   Direct financial payments are of two types:
   (i) **Time based :** This plan means salary/wages are paid on daily, weekly or monthly basis.
   (ii) **Performance based :** Under this method the payment is made to employees on the basis of number of pieces or units produced by the employees.

Some pay plans use time based payment in combination with some incentives such as bonus, commission etc.

Orgnisations must consider various factor before fixing the compensation such as Labour laws, Minimum Wage Payment Act, Union's Policy, Competitor's policy etc.

☞ **Components/Elements/Aspects**
Three important components of staffing are:

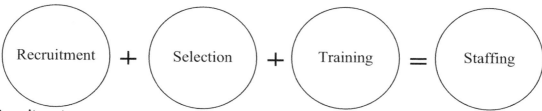

☞ **Recruitment**
Recruitment means inducing or attracting more and more candidates to apply for vacant job positions in the organisation. In general words recruitment means search for candidates who can perform the vacant roles and inducing them to apply and come forward to filling the vacant roles. The recruitment function is very important because the end result of recruitment function is receiving large number of applications to make selection from. **That is why it is also known as positive process as it provides wider choice.**

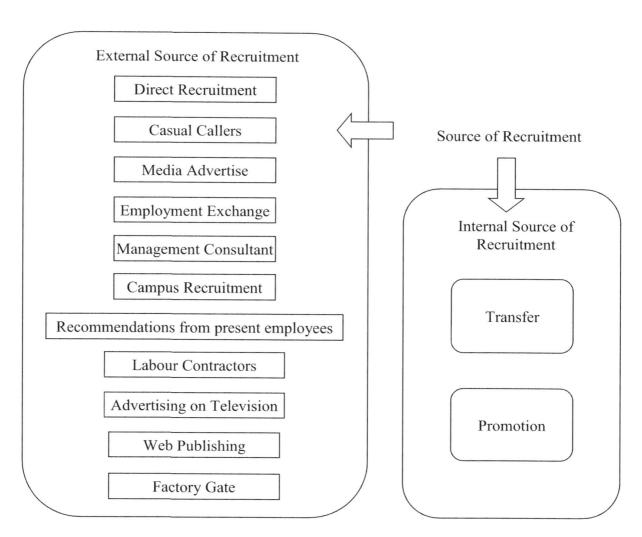

1. **Internal Source of Recruitment :** Under Internal source of recruitment the vacant job positions are filled by inducing the existing employees of the organisation. The vacant job positions are filled by using existing employees only and no outsiders are permitted in internal sources.

☞ **Under the internal recruitment following**

(a) **Transfer :** Transfer means shifting of employees from one job position to other at the same level of authority. Generally with the transfers there is no change in compensation level and authority level. There is no change even in his rank, responsibilities and prestige. Only the place of working is changed.
For example, transfer of clerk from accounts department to purchase department.

(b) **Promotion :** Promotion refers to shifting of employees from one job position to other with higher level of authority. In promotion the authority level, the rank, responsibilities of employees and prestige improve or increase. Generally with the promotions there is increase in compensation or salary also.
For example, promotion of clerk to accountant post.

☞ **Advantages of Internal Source of recruitment :**

(a) **Economical :** Filling the job internally is cheaper as compared to getting candidates from external sources as it does not involve any expense in the form of advertising for vacancies recruiting etc.

(b) **Source of Motivation :** The employees are motivated to do their jobs well so as to earn the desire promotion. Since the opportunity of promotion is implicit in internal recruitment, internal recruitment acts as a source of motivation for employees to improve their career and income levels.

(c) **Promotes loyalty :** it promotes loyalty among the existing employees since it gives them a sense of job security and opportunity for better prospects.

(d) **Minimizes Training Needs :** It minimizes training needs because they are aware of the major goals, policies, procedures and functions of the organisation.

(e) **Reduce Employees turnover :** The employees are already familiar with rules and regulations of organisation. So, less chances of turnovers.

(f) **Optimum utilization of human resource :** Transfer has the benefit of shifting workforce from the surplus departments to those where there is shortage of staff.

(g) **Benefit in training :** Transfer or job rotation is a tool of training the employees for hig her jobs. Or in other words through transfer employees get training also in the form of job rotation.

(h) **Employees satisfaction :** A promotion at a higher level may lead to a chain of promotions at lower levels in the organisation. Thus, many employees are satisfied.

☞ **Limitations of Internal Source of recruitment :**

(a) **Limited choices :** The management has a limited choice in choosing the most suitable candidates for the vacancies.

In case suitable candidates are not available internally, the organisation may have to compromise by taking less suitable persons from internal sources.

(b) **Absence of competition :** Internal employees may lose the drive for proving their worth since they may expect automatic promotion by seniority and sure prospect.

(c) **Reduces Productivity :** Frequent transfer of employees may reduce the overall productivity of the organisation.

(d) **No fresh talent :** When vacancies are filled through internal promotions, the scope for fresh talent is reduced.

(e) **Conflict among employees :** These may cause dissatisfaction and frustration among those employees who aspire for promotion but are not promoted.

(f) **Encourages Favourtism :** It may encourage favourtism i.e., appointment may be restricted to their kith or kin.

2. **External Source of Recruitment :** When the candidates from outside the organisation are invited to fill the vacant job position then it is known as external recruitment. In other words, when the organisation meets its manpower requirement from outside the organisation then it is external recruitment. Whenever large number of job positions are vacant then external recruitment is preferred.

☞ **The common methods of External sources recruitment are :**

1. **Direct Recruitment :** Sometimes the organisations paste notice at the gate of their office or factory or workshop stating the vacant job positions. The people who are interested in those jobs walk in for interview. This method of external recruitment is most suitable for unskilled job positions e.g., sweeper, peon etc.

2. **Casual callers :** Generally the large organisations maintain an application file in which they keep all the pending applications which the job seekers leave with the reception, sometimes the applications of suitable candidates who were not selected in previous year's selection process are also kept in application file. This application file is considered as waiting list. Whenever there is a job vacancy the suitable candidates from the waiting list are called.

3. **Media advertising :** The most common and popular method of external recruitment is advertising about the vacant job position. The organisations select the media of advertisement keeping in mind the requirement of job position. For example, for the job of an accountant the advertisement can be given in chartered accountant journal and for unskilled and lower rank job positions the advertisement can be given in local or regional newspaper. But for high rank and skilled job position the advertisement is given in national level reputed newspapers such as Times of India, Hindustan Times etc.

4. **Employment exchanges :** Employment exchanges act as middlemen between the job seekers and the organisations who have vacant job positions. The job seekers leave their bio-data and details of their qualifications with the employment exchanges and when the organisations approach employment exchanges the suitable candidates are sent. There are government as well as private employment exchanges. Government Employment Exchanges charge no fees or commission

whereas Private Employment Exchange charge commission or receive commission according to the salary of the employee.

5. **Placement agencies and Management consultant :** Placement agencies provide nation-wide service of matching demand and supply of work force. These agencies invite the bio data and record from various job seekers and send them to suitable clients. These agencies charge fees for providing such service.

6. **Campus Recruitment :** Sometimes the senior managers of the organisations visit various professional colleges, technical institutes to get fresh graduates or the people with the latest technological know-how. This type of recruitment is more common for engineers, computer programmers, MBAs etc. The organisations prefer fresh graduates because they can be moulded according to the recruitment of organisation.

7. **Recommendations from present employees :** Many firms encourage their employees to recommend the names of their relatives, friends and other known people to fill the vacant job position. The ogranisatation prefer recommendation by trusting the goodwill of the present employees and the organsations can catch hold of existing employees if there is any problem with the new employee recommended by him.

8. **Labour Contractors :** Jobbers and contractors are the people who Keep in touch with the labour in villages and rural areas and whenever there is vacancy or requirement for labour in factory or hi the construction site, they bring the labour from villages and supply to businessman. The jobbers and contractors charge commission for the same. This is suitable for labourers and unskilled workers. Labour contract is maintain close contact with labours and they can provide the required number of unskilled workers short notice.

9. **Advertising on Television :** A new trend of external recruitment is telecast on various channels regarding vacant job position. They telecast the requirement of the job along with the qualification necessary o apply.

10. **Web Publishing :** In internet there are certain websites specifically designed provide information regarding job seekers and companies which have vacant job position. These websites can be visited by job seekers as well as companies. The common websites are: Naukri.com, Monster.com etc.

11. **Factory Gate :** Sometimes a number of job seekers enquire at the factory gate about the vacant job positions in the workshop or in the factory. During the severe unemployment time many job seekers assemble at the factory gate to offer their services in the factory. This type of external recruitment is a!ss suitable for unskilled job positions e.g., sweeper, peon, machine operator etc.

    (a) **Fresh Talent :** The insiders may have limited talents. External sources facilitate infusion of fresh bioo with new ideas into the enterprise. This will improve the overall working of the enterprise.

    (b) **Wider Choice :** When vacancies are advertised widely, a large number of applicants from outside organisation apply. The management has a wider choice while selecting the people for employment.

(c) **Qualified Personnel :** By using external recruitment the management can make qualified and trained people to apply for vacant jobs in the organisation.

(d) **Latest Technological Knowledge :** Through campus placement organisation can get employees with latest technological knowledge.

(e) **Competitive Spirit :** Through external recruitment when out-siders join the organisation, this develops a competitive spirit in existing employees of organisation.

☞ **Limitations of External Recruitment :**

(a) **Dissatisfaction among Existing staff :** External recruitment may lead to dissatisfaction and frustration among existing employees. They may feel that their chances of promotion are reduced.

(b) **Lengthy Process :** Recruitment from outside takes a long time. The business has no notify the vacancies and wait for application to initiate the selection process.

(c) **Costly process :** It is very costly to recruit staff from external sources. A lot of money has to be spent on advertisement and processing of applications.

(d) **Chance of Employees turn-over :** The new employees may not adjust in the rules and regulations of the organisation which means more chances of turnovers.

(e) **Uncertain Response :** The candidates from outside may not be suitable for the enterprise. There is no guarantee that the enterprise will be able to attract right kind of people from external sources.

Comparison of Internal and External Recruitment

	Internal Recruitment	External Recruitment
1. Meaning	It involves search of candidates from within the organisation	It involves finding candidates from outside the organisation
2. Time Required	It a takes less time to recruit from internal sources	It takes very long time to recruit from external sources.
3. Economy	This process is cheaper. It does not involve any cost of contacting the external sources.	This process is costly as vacancies have to be notified in newspaper, etc.
4. Motivation	The existing staff is motivated to improve their performance.	The existing staff feels dissatisfied if external sources are used.
5. Talent or Quality	Choice of candidates is limited. The scope of fresh talent is diminished,	The business *can* hope for talented candidates from outside. This means infusion of new blood and new ideas into the enterprise.

☞ **Selection**

"Selection can be defined as discovering most promising and most suitable candidate to fill up the vacant job position in the organisation".

Selection Process : As end result of recruitment function organisations receive large number of applications and selection process begins at this stage by screening the applications. In selection the number of rejected applicants is generally more than the selected candidates that Is why selection is considered as a negatives process. In selection process various steps are performed which are give below:

1. **Preliminary Screening :** The candidates whose applications are selected are called for preliminary interview which is conducted by any of the personnel managers. No professional experts or specialised people are invited to take interview. Very general and basic questions related to job or status of person are questioned. The preliminary interview is conducted to check the confidence level of the candidate eliminate unqualified or unfit job seekers.

2. **Selection test :** The organisations prefer to conduct written test to find out the practical knowledge of the candidate. The type of test to be conducted depends on the requirement of the organisation. Known as own tailor-made test.
   The common types of tests conducted by the organisations are:

   (a) **Intelligence Test :** Is conducted to check the efficiency level and intelligence level of the candidates.

   (b) **Aptitude Test :** Is conducted to find out the potential of learning new skills, new methods and new job.

   (c) **Personality Test :** Is conducted to find out the human behaviour of candidate, approach, attitude, interest etc.

   (d) **Trade Test :** Is conducted to check the basic knowledge and skill of a candidate related to job.

   (e) **Interest Test :** Is conducted to find out the type of job in which candidate has more interest.

3. **Employment Interview :** The candidates who qualify the test are called for interviews. To conduct the final interview a panel of experts is called. The consultants who are specialised in their fields ask questions from the candidates to test his professional or specialised knowledge related to the job. The interview has many advantages over written test because in interviews you can find out the confidence level of the candidate along with his professional knowledge. Interview gives chance to candidate also to clarify thsqueries regarding salary, working conditions, posting etc.

4. **Checking the references and background :** After a candidate is declared successful in the interview then some information about him is gathered from those persons whose name figures in the column of References'. This information relates to the character, social relations, background, etc. of the candidate. To obtain this information the employer may also contact friends of the candidate, his past and present employers,

5. **Selection decision :** The candidates who pass the test, interview and references check are included in selection list and the managers select most suitable candidate from this list.

6. **Medical examination :** Before giving appointment letter the candidates selected are sent for medical fitness test. Some organisations appoint their own doctors to do the test and some sign contract with hospitals to do the test.

7. **Job offer :** The applicants who clear the medical test are given job offer through letter of appointment. In the letter the date of joining, terms and conditions of job etc. are mentioned. Generally a reasonable time is given to the candidate to join the organisation.

8. **Contract of employment :** When candidate accepts the job offer it refers to signing of contract of employment. While signing the contract of employment the employer and the candidate exchange certain documents. The common contents of contract of employment are job title duties, responsibilities, Pay, allowances, hours of work, leave rules, disciplinary rules, probation period etc.

    At this stage the candidate is asked to fill up a special application form, also called attestation form this candidate provides some important information about himself or herself which can be used for further references.

Training and Development
Meaning: -
        "Training means equipping the employees with the required skill to perform the job.
The candidates are sent for training so that they can perform the job in the expected manner."

Development refers to overall growth of the employee: It focuses on personal growth and successful employee's development. Development is much wider in concept as compared to training as training is only one part of development.

        Training is concerned with imparting technical knowledge in doing a particular job. But development is wider process concerned with growth of an individual in all respects. However, both training and development are related process. Training helps the employee in learning job skills whereas development shapes attitude of the employee. The term 'training' is used in relation to operative employee whereas 'development' in used in relation to executives and managers.

Difference between Training and Development

Basis	Training	Development
1. Meaning	It is a process of increasing knowledge and skills	It is a process of learning and growth.
2. Purpose	Its purpose is to enable an employee to do the present job better.	Its purpose is to enable the overall growth of an employee.
3. Orientation	It is job - oriented.	It is career-oriented.
4. Personnel trained/developed	Non-managerial personnel are trained.	Managerial personnel are developed.
5. Time perspective	Its time perspective is short-term.	Its time perspective is long-term.
6. Methods used	Methods used are vestibule training, apprenticeship training, etc.	Methods used are lectures, conferences, case studies, etc.

Importance of Training

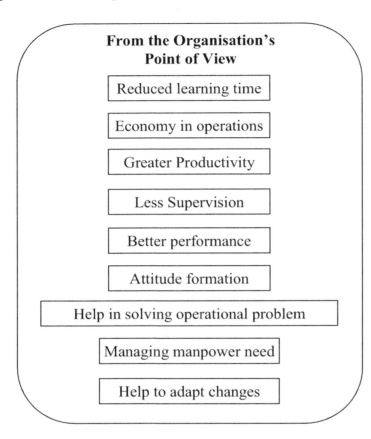
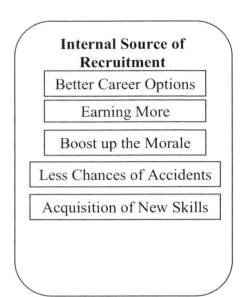

1.   **Reduced learning time :** A trained employee takes less time in learning the job as compared to untrained employee.

2.   **Economy in operations :** Trained personnel will be able to make better and economical use of materials and equipments. Wastage will also be low.

3.   **Greater Productivity :** A well trained employee usually shows greater productivity and higher quality of work output than an untrained employee.

4.   **Less Supervision :** If the employees are given proper training, the responsibility of supervision is lessened.

5.   **Better performance :** The performance of trained employees is always better than the performance of untrained employees as in the training programmes their qualities and capabilities are improved and employees get some experience of working on the job before they are actually assigned the job. This improves their performance and efficiency level.

6.   **Attitude formation :** The training and development aim at moulding the employees so that they develop positive attitude for the organisation, and to motivate them to ready to take the initiative and result in better support and cooperation among the employees.

7.   **Help in solving operational problems :** While performing various activities in the organisation, the organisation faces values problems such as problem of absenteeism, wastage of resources, dissatisfaction of

employees, lack of team work etc. Through the supervisory level training these operational problems can be avoided or removed in the organisation because supervisors are trained for improvement of superior subordinate relationship and for encouraging and motivating their subordinates.

8. **Managing manpower need :** Some organisations have specialised technique of production and the ready staff is not available. In that case the organisations hire untrained people and train them with the required skill according to their organisation's need. By training they solve long term problem of manpower requirement.

☞ **Benefits to the Employees**
1. **Better Career Options :** The efficient workers sharpen their skills during training. This helps them to prepare for promotion to higher jobs.

2. **Earning More :** The productivity of the workers is increased as a result of training. Because of this, they earn higher wages and bonus.

3. **Boost up the Morale :** Trained employees know their jobs well and have less number of accidents. They are satisfied with their jobs which increase their morale..

4. **Less Chances of Accidents :** Training makes employees more efficient so there are less chances accidents.

5. **Acquisition of New Skills :** Employees acquire new skills and knowledge which will help them improve their career prospects.

Methods of Training

Methods of Training :
There are mainly two methods of training:
1. On-the-job training   2. Off-the-job training

1. **On-the-job training :** When the employees are trained while they are performing the job then it is known as On-the-job training. Under this method the employees learn by doing. This method s sable only for technical jobs and the advantage of this method is employees can learn the practical problems while working on the job. The biggest disadvantage of on-the-job training is that it results in wastage of resources. Whenever employees are dealing with expensive and sophisticated machinery then on-the-job methods of training should be avoided.

2. **Off-the-job training :** Off-the-job training means training the employees by taking them away from their work position which means employees are given a break from the job and sent for training. This method of training is more suitable for managerial job positions as conferences, seminars are held to train the managers.

Difference between On the Job Training and Off the Job Training

Basis	On the Job Training	Off the Job Training
1. Meaning	Trainees learn while they are engaged in performing their jobs.	Trainees learn and develop skills without engaging in actual job performance.
2. Training place	Training is provided at the workplace itself.	Training is provided away from the workplace.
3. Training environment	Training environment consists of actual work situation, tools, etc.	Training environment is different from actual work situation.
4. Resource persons	Resource persons for providing training are concerned superiors,	Resource persons for providing training are experts in the field.
5. Training objective	Training objective is to provide vocational efficiency,	Training objective is to inculcate ideas are concepts.

Methods of Training

(a)   **Induction Training :** Induction Training, also known as orientation training, involves providing relevant information to new employees. Usually, induction training is provided by concerned superiors and persons from human resource department and other relevant departments. In many cases, even the chief executive also participates in induction training to make it more effective. Induction training covers various aspects introduction of organisation and its key personnel, terms and conditions of employment, human resource policies and practices and business rules and procedures.

(b)   **Vestibule School :** Vestibule school means duplicate model of organisation. Generally when the delicate machineries are involved then employers avoid using on-the-job methods of training. A dummy model of machinery is prepared and instead of using original machinery employees are trained on dummy model. Sometimes the accountants who have to make entries in inventory register or cash register they are first supplied the duplicate registers with the same columns as in original registers and when they become perfect in making entries in duplicate register then they are handed over original register. Vestibule school is an off-the-job method of training which makes use of benefit of on-the-job method.

(c)   **Apprenticeship programme/training :** The workers seeking to enter skilled jobs are sent for apprenticeship training programme which is an on-the-job method of training. In the Apprenticeship Programme, a master worker or a trainer is appointed who guides the worker or learner regarding the skill of job. The master worker performs the job and the trainee (learner) observes him performing. When the learner learns all the skills then slowly he starts taking up the job step by step and master worker becomes the observer. When the trainee becomes perfect in doing the job then master worker goes and trainee get full charge of job position. It is suitable for people seeking to enter skilled traits for example - plumbers - electricians, iron workers etc.

(d)   **Internship :** Internship is an agreement between the professional institutes and the corporate sector where professional institutes send their students to various companies so that they can practice the theoretical knowledge acquired by them through professional institutes. Under this training programme the organizations get people with fresh ideas and latest knowledge and the companies have to pay very less amount of salary which is called stipend. On the other hand, the students get chance to practice under the real situation. In short we can say under internship the class room sessions are backed with practical training.

EXERCISE – 1

Q.1   State the meaning of staffing.

Ans.   Staffing means' putting people to jobs'. It includes human resource planning, recruitment, selection training, development, promotion, compensation and performance appraisal of work force

Q.2   Name the first two steps in the process of staffing.

Ans.   (i) Manpower planning   (ii) Recruitment

Q.3   Mention two techniques of manpower planning.

Ans.   (i) Workload analysis   (ii) Workforce analysis

Q.4   What is workload analysis?

Ans.   It means assessment of the number and types of human resources necessary for the performance various jobs and accomplishment of organization objectives

Q.5   What is workforce analysis?

Ans.   It would reveal whether an organization in understaffed, overstaffed or optimally staffed.

Q.6   Name the concept related to searching for prospective candidate.

Ans.   Recruitment

Q.7   Why is recruitment called a positive process?

Ans.   Because candidates are invited to apply for the jobs.

Q.8   Why is selection considered to be a negative process?

Ans.   Because selection rejects more candidates than are employed.

Q.9   Name the process of discovering the most suitable candidate to fill the vacent job position.

Ans.   Selection.

Q.10   What is the objective of prelimainary screening?

Ans.   To eliminate unqualified and unfit job seekers.

Q.11   Name the concept which relates to forecasting and assessing manpower needs.

Ans.   Manpower Planning.

Q.12   Name the three important aspect of staffing.

Ans.   Recruitment, Selection and Training.

Q.13   What is the main purpose of recruitment?

Ans.   Recruitment seeks to attract suitable applicants to apply for available jobs.

Q.14   Identify the method of training under which training is conducted away from the actual work floor where actual work environments are created in a class room and the employees are trained on the dummy model.

Ans.   Vestibule Training.

Q.15   Name the method of training suitable for plumbers, electricians or iron - workers.

Ans.   Apprenticeship programma.

EXERCISE – 2

Q.1   Define " Placement" and "Orientation/Induction" in the context of staffing function of management

Q.2   Define" Recruitment" What is the purpose of recruitment?

Q.3   Explain 'transfers' and promotions' as internal sources of recruitment

Q.4   "Training is a process of increasing knowledge and skills, whereas development is a process of learning and growth." In the light of this statement, explain the difference between training and development.

Q.5   State any two merits and two demerits of internal sources of recruitment

Q.6   State any two merits and two demerits of external sources of recruitment.

Q.7   Explain 'Placement Agencies' and 'Campus Recruitment' as external sources of recruitment

Q8   Explain 'Telecasting' and 'Web Publishing' as external sources of recruitment

EXERCISE - 3

Q.1   Why is saffing an important function of management in all oragnisation ? Explain in brief any six reasons.

Q.2   Explain in brief the steps involved in staffing process.

Q.3   State any three merits and three demerits of internal sources of recruitment.

Q.4   State any three merits and three demerits of external sources of recruitment.

Q.5   Explain 'Management Consultants' Employment Exchange and 'Media Advertising' as external sources of recruitment

Q.6   Explain in brief any six external sources of recruitment of employees.

Q.7   State three advantage of training and development to the individual as well as to the organizations?

Q.8   Define 'Selection' What is the purpose of selection ? Explain in brief any six steps involved in the selection procedure of employees.

Q.9   Explain the term 'Development' Differentiate between "Training and Development on the basis of:
        (i) Focus   (ii) Result   (iii) Type of personnel   (iv) Time Period

DIRECTING

CONTENT

☞ **Introduction:**

A function of management that instructs, guides, counsels; motivates and leads the subordinates in such a manner that can help them to perform well in jobs for which they have been appointed.

☞ **Features/Characteristics of Direction**
1. Directing initiate action.
2. Continuing Function.
3. Directing takes place at every level.
4. Directing flow from top to bottom.
5. Performance Oriented.
6. Human Element

☞ **Elements of Directing**

I. Supervision

Role of Supervisor
1. Acting as a linking pin.
2. Scheduling the work.
3. Issuing orders and Instructions.
4. Guiding operatives.
5. Motivating operatives.
6. Monitoring performance..
7. Providing feedback.
8. Providing training.
9. Maintaining discipline.
10. Handling grievances.

II Motivation

Need Hierarchy Theory, Maslow's Need Hierarchy Theory
1. Basic Psychological Need.
2. Safety and Security Needs.
3. Social Needs Assiliation/Belonging need.
4. Esteem Needs.
5. Self-Actualization Needs.

☞ **Financial and Non-financial Incentives, Monetary or financial Incentives**
1. Pay and allowances.
2. Productivity-linked Incentives
3. Bonus.
4. Profit Sharing.
5. Co-Partnership/Stock Option.
6. Perquisites
7. Retirement Benefits.

☞ **Non Financial Incentives**
1. Status
2. Organisational Climate
3. Career Advancement.
4. Job Enrichment
5. Employee Recognition.
6. Job Security.
7. Employee Participation.
8. Autonomy Empowerment

III.   **Leadership**

☞   **Management Vs Leadership (Leadership styles)**

1.   **Authoritative**
           Advantages
           a. Satisfaction to Some subordinates.
           b. Motivating to some Superior.
           c. Fast Decision — Making
           d. No Exposure of Incompetence of subordinates.
           Disadvantages
           a. Disliked by subordinates.
           b. Lack of Motivation to Subordinates.
           c. Lack of Leadership Development

2.   **Democratic**
           Advantages
           a. Motivating to subordinates.
           b. High Productivity Safeguard to Leader.
           c. Leadership Development.
           d. Organisational Stability.
           Disadvantages
           a. Requirement of Highly Skilled Employees.
           b. Time Consuming.
           c. Sometime create frustration among employee.
           d. Disliked by employees

3.   **Laissez faire**
           Advantages
           a. Low Burden on Leader.
           b. Motivation to Subordinates.
           c. Higher Productivity.
           d. Development of Subordinates.
           Disadvantages
           a. Minimum Contribution of Leader.
           b. Requirement of Highly Competent Subordinates.
           c. Requirement of Highly Conductive Work Environment.

IV.   **Communication**
            Process of Communication
            1. Sender.
            2. Message.
            3. Encoding.
            4. Media.
            5. Decoding.
            6. Receiver.
            7. Feedback.
            8. Noise.

☞ **Channels of Communication**
A. **Formal Communication**
    1. **Vertical Communication**
        (i) Downward Communication
        (ii) Upward Communication

    2. **Horizontal Communication**
        (i) Diagonal Communication.

☞ **The common networks of formal communication**
(i) Single Chain Network.　(ii) Wheel Network　(iii) Circular Network.
(iv) Free flow Network　(v) Inverted V.

B. **Informal Communication**
Different networks of grapevine communication
(i) Single Strand　(ii) Gossip Chain.　(iii) Probability.　(iv) Cluster Chain.

☞ **Barriers to communication**
A. **Semantic Barriers**
    (i) Badly expressed message.
    (ii) Symbols with different meanings.
    (iii) Faulty Translations.
    (iv) Unqualified Assumptions.
    (v) Technical Jargon.
    (vi) Body language and gesture decoding.

B. **Psychological Barriers**
    (i) Premature Evaluation.
    (ii) Lack of Attention.
    (iii) Loss by transmission and poor retention
    (iv) Distrust.

C. **Organizational Barriers**
    (i) Organisational Policy.
    (ii) Rules and Regulations.
    (iii) Status Difference.
    (iv) Complex organisation.
    (v) Organisational Facilities.

D. **Personal Barriers**
    (i) Lack of confidence of superior in his subordinates.
    (ii) Lack of incentives.
    (iii) Fear of Authority.

☞ **Improving Communication Effective**
1. Clarify the idea before communication.
2. Communication according to the need of the receiver.
3. Consult others before communicating.

4. Use of Proper language, tone and contents of message.
5. Proper feedback.
6. Communication for the present as well as for future.
7. Follow up communication.
8. Good listener.
9. Open mind.
10. Completeness of message.

WEIGHTAGE

Units	Very Short Answer	Short Answer I & II	Long Answer I & II	Total
Unit-7(8)	1(2)	---	6(1)	8(3)

7.   DIRECTING

☞ **Meaning of Directing**
In the ordinary sense, directing means giving instructions and guiding people in doing work. But in the context of management of an organisation, directing refers to the process of instructing, guiding, motivating, leading, counseling and coaching people in the organisation to achieve its objectives. It is called Management in action.

"Directing is telling people what to do and seeing that they do it to the best of their ability."

☞ **Features/Characteristics of Directing Function**
1. **Directing Initiates Action :** Other functions prepare a base or setting of action i.e., how action has to be carried on the directing initiate or start action. By giving directions or instructions the managers get the work started in the organisation.

2. **Continuing Function :** Directing is a continuous process. A manager cannot just rest after issuing orders and instructions. He has to continuously guide, supervise and motivate his subordinates. He must continuously take steps to make sure that orders and instructions are carried out properly.

3. **Directing takes place at every level :** Directing is a pervasive function as it is performed by managers at all levels and in all locations. Every manager has to supervise, guide, motivate and communicate with his subordinate to get things done. However, the time spent in directing is comparatively more at operational level of management. Directing takes place wherever superior subordinate relation exists.

4. **Directing flow from top to bottom:** Direction are given by managers to their subordinates. Every manager can direct his immediate subordinate and take directions from immediate boss. Directing starts from top level and flows to lower level.

5. **Performance Oriented :** Directing is a performance oriented function. The main motive of directing is bringing efficiency in performance. Directing convert plans into performance. Performance is the essence of directing. Directing functions direct the performance of individuals towards achievement of organisational goal.

6. **Human Element :** Directing function involves study and moulding of human behaviour. It improves interpersonal and intergroup relationship. It motivate employees to work with their best ability.

☞ **Importance Directing Function**

"Directing is heart of Management"

1. **Initiation of Action:** Directing initiates action in the organisation. Through directing, a superior conveys to his subordinates what to do and how to do it. Which results in unity of direction without such an action, all organisational resources – both human and non human – remain unused.

2. **Integration of Employee Efforts :** In the organisation, every individual employee makes efforts to get his work done. But activities of all are co-related so performance of each individual affects the performance of others, their efforts contribute positively if these efforts are integrated. Directing integrates theses efforts.

3. **Means of Motivation :** Every individual has lot of potential to get things done but in the absence of proper motivation, this potential remains unused. So a manager with good leadership and motivational skill provides needed confidence, support, motivation and encouragement. Directing provides this motivation to the individuals to get maximum out of them.

4. **Facilitating Change in the Organisation :** An organiastion is required to make changes in its working because of changes in business environment. However, employees resist these changes as they become habitual to a particular way of working. Directing overcomes this resistance by convincing the employees how changes are beneficial to them. Not only that, even employees may be motivated to implement the changes effectively.

5. **Stability and Balance in the organisation :** Directing brings stability and balance in the organisation. An organisation has several groups of people – owners, managers, workers, etc. Each group may have its own goals which might be conflicting, for example, owners may want more profit workers may want more wages. Similarly, other goals may be incompatible. As a result, there is a possibit1 among various interest groups. Directing helps in integrating these conflicting interests, thereby bringing stability and balance in the organisation.

☞ **Element of Direction**

The directing function of management consists of four elements or sub-functions. These four elements are shown below:

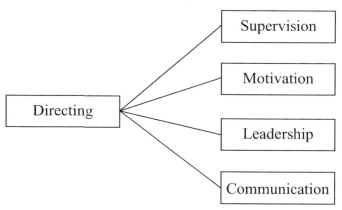

1. **Supervision :** The word supervision' consists of two parts:
    (i) Super (Means – Over and above)
    (ii) Vision (Means – Art of seeing objects)
    Supervision means overseeing the subordinate at work by their superiors and giving instruction to ensure optimum utilisation of resources and accomplish the desired objectives.

2. **Motivation:** Motivation means a process of stimulating people to action to accomplish desired goals.

3. **Leadership:** Leadership is the art or process of influencing the behaviour of people so that they will strive willingly and enthusiastically towards the achievement of organisational goal.

4. **Communication :** The word 'communication' has been derived from the Latin word 'communis' which means 'common', which consequently implies common understanding. Therefore communication is a process of exchange of ideas, views, facts, feelings etc. between people to have common understanding.

☞ **Supervision**

Meaning of Supervision:

Supervision : The word 'supervision' consists of two parts:
(i) Super (Means – Over and above)
(ii) Vision (Means – Art of seeing objects)
Supervision means overseeing the subordinate at work by their superiors and giving instruction to ensure optimum utilisation of resources and accomplish the desired objectives.

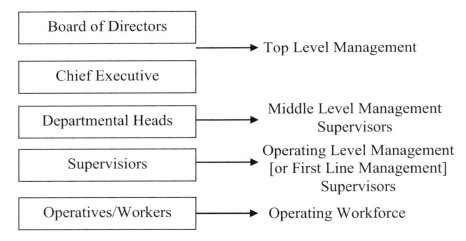

Meaning of Supervisor: The term 'Supeivisor' refers to a person who assigns work to subordinates and oversees their activities and performance. While executives at all levels carry out supervision work, the term supervisor' refers basically to an individual who supervises the operatives. The supervisor is in direct contact with the operatives/workers. In management, the first line managers at operating level management are called 'supervisors' because it is the primary or basic duty of first line managers to supervise the Operatives/Workers engaged in the basic operations (also called operating workforce). The first line manager may also be designated as 'Foreman', 'Chargeman', 'Overseer', 'Section incharge', 'Section Officer' and 'Superintendent'.

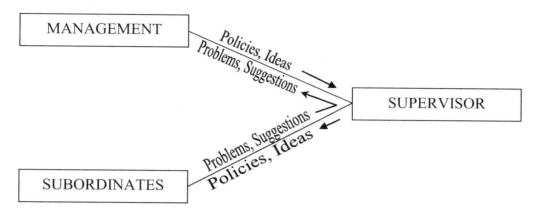

☞ **Function/Role of Supervisor**

1. **Acting as a Linking Pin.** A supervisor works as a linking pin between management and operatives (workers and other non — managerial employees). He conveys ideas of management to the operatives on the one hand and problems of operatives to the management to the other hand. This helps to avoid misunderstanding between management and operatives.

2. **Scheduling the Work.** The supervisor prepares work schedules for operatives to ensure steady and even flow of work. Work schedule involves laying down time of different activities as well as total time within which a work should be completed.

3. **Issuing Orders and Instructions.** The supervisor issues orders and instruction to operatives about how the work is to be done. Based on these orders and instructions, they perform various activities to complete the work according to work schedule.

4. **Guiding Operatives.** The supervisor guides operatives. In this function, he explains the plans and policies of management to operatives. He also solves their problems related to technical aspects of the work, working conditions etc.

5. **Motivating Operatives.** The supervisor motivates the operatives by creating enthusiasm among them, creating team spirit, creating friendly work environment and administering suitable financial incentives.

6. **Monitoring performance.** The supervisor continuously monitors performance of operatives. Continuous monitoring of performance aims at ensuring that the work is completed according to schedules and if there is any problem in work performance, it is overcome at the earlest.

7. **Providing Feedback.** The supervisor continuously provides feedback to management about the work done, cost involved, attendance of workers and problems being faced in completing the work. Based on this feedback, the management takes necessary actions.

8. **Providing Training.** The supervisor provides on — the — job training to operatives to develop relevant skills among them. This leads to building team of skilled and efficient workers.

9. **Maintaining Discipline.** The supervisor maintains disciplines among operatives both by enforcing organisational rules and regulations as well by inculcating sense of discipline among operatives.

10. **Handling Grievances.** The supervisor handles grievances of operatives which they have while working in the organisation. He makes efforts to overcome these grievances on his own level. If he is not in a position to handle any grievance, he refers it to the management.

☞ **Motivation**

The term motivation is derived from the word motive'. Motive may be defined needs, wants, implies within the individual.

Meaning of Motive, Motivation and Motivators:

1. **Motive :** A motive can be defined as an inner thought that directs or stimulates an individual to action. Needs of an individual give rise to such motives. For example, the need for water causes thirst on account of which a man searches for water. Some other motives are hunger, security, thirst, recognition etc.

2. **Motivation :** Motivation can be defined as stimulating, inspiring and inducing the employees to perform to their best capacity. Motivation is psychological term which means it cannot be forced on employees. It comes automatically from inside the employees as it is the willingness to do the work.

3. **Motivators:** Motivators are the incentives or techniques used to motivate the people in an organisation. Common motivators used by the managers are increment, bonus, promotion, recognition, respect etc.

☞ **Maslow's Need Hierarchy Theory**

The famous psychologist Abraham Maslow propounded 'Need Hierarchy Theory of Motivation'. His theory was based on human needs Maslow felt that within every human being, there exists a hierchy of five needs:

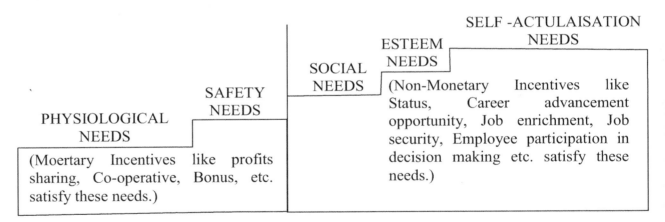

1. **Basic Physiological Needs:** Physiological needs are of primary nature. These needs are related to the survival and maintenance of human life.
    For ex. :- need for food, clothing shelter etc.
    These needs can be satisfied when the monetary incentives are offered by the employers.

2. **Safety and Security Needs :** Once the present day physiological needs are fulfilled then the people start thinking about their future as they want to secure their future by making sure that in future also they continue to satisfy their physiological needs.

Under safety and security there are two categories:

(a)   **Physical security.** Which means safety from illness, accident, fire etc.

(b)   **Economics security.** Which means having sufficient funds to meet the future physiological needs and to come out of physical security threat.

The people who have more of safety and security need active get motivated by monetary incentives.

3.   **Social Needs Assiliationl/Belonging need :** It means the need for love, affection, companionship, friendship etc. Once the people satisfy their physiological and safety needs then the social need becomes more active and to fulfill the social needs the managers prefer team-work, arrange formal and informal get- together so that employees can develop social relationships.

4.   **Esteem Needs :** These needs are related to the respect and recognition. When the above three needs are satisfied then people start demanding respect for themselves in a group. This need is more common in higher level employees. Esteem needs can be satisfied through non-monetary incentives.

5.   **Self-Actualisation Needs :** This need refers to realising or reaching to the aim of your life. Once the employee becomes what he wants to become it means satisfaction of his actualisation need. For example, when a solider faces bravely the bullet of enemy he seems to realise the self-actualisation need.

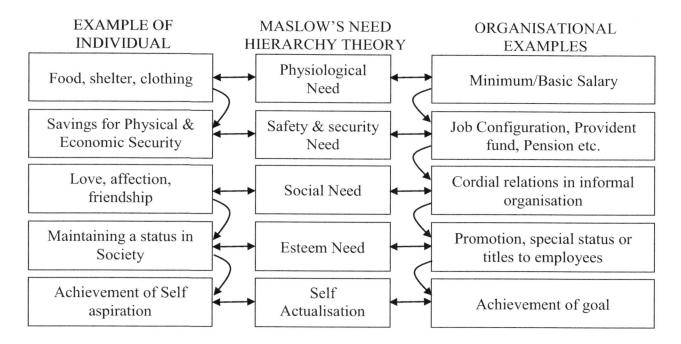

Maslow's theory is based on the following assumptions:

1.   People's behavior is based on their needs. Satisfaction of such needs influences their behavior.

2.   People's needs are in hierarchical order, starting from basic needs to other higher level needs.

3.   A satisfied need can no longer motivate a person; only next higher level need can motivate him.

4.   A person moves to the next higher level of the hierarchy only when the lower need is satisfied.

Thus, Maslow's Theory focuses on the needs as the basis for motivation.

Maslow felt that within every human being, there exists a hierarchy of five needs

☞ **Incentives**

Incentive is defined as follows:-

Incentive means all measures which are used to motivate people to improve performance.

OR

Incentive can be defined as monetary or non monetary reward offered to the employees for contributing more efficiency.

These incentives may be broadly classified in two categories — financial and non financial incentives.

☞ **Financial Incentives**

Financial incentives are in direct monetary form or measurable in monetary worth following are financial incentives.

1. **Pay and Allowances:** Pay and allowance constitute basic pay, increment and other allowances like dearness allowance, house rent allowance which improve performance level of employees.

2. **Productivity – linked Incentives :** These incentives are provided on the basis of productivity achieved by employees. Thus higher productivity attracts higher incentives.

3. **Bonus:** Bonus is a kind of yearly payment to employees either based on organisational performance or statutory requirements. For example, in India, employees are entitled to get 8.33 percent of their salary as bonus statutorily.

4. **Profit Sharing:** Profit sharing involves distributing a portion of organisation's profit among employees if the profit exceeds beyond certain level as jointly decided by management and employees.

5. **Co-partnership/Stock Option :** This involves issuing shares to employees below the market price of the shares. Employees become owners of the company to the extent of their shareholding. Stock option is very popular with IT companies.

6. **Perquisites :** Perquisites, simply called perks, are offered in various forms like car allowance, free housing, club membership, education allowance, leave travel allowance, etc. Generally, some perks are limited to higher-level managers.

7. **Retirement Benefits :** Retirement benefits are in the form of provident fund, pension, gratuity, etc. These benefits are available to employees after their retirement.

☞ **Non-Monetary/Non-Financial Incentives**

Incentives which put emphasis on non-financial aspects in motivating are known as non financial incentives. Objective of Non financial is to provide psychological and emotional satisfaction to the receiver.

1. **Status:** Status involves ranking of organisational positions. Status in an organisation is reflected in job title, size and furnishing of individual work cabin, company car, exclusive parking space, etc. Status motivates employees to a great extent.

2. **Organisational Climate :** Organisational climate indicate the characteristics which describe an organisation. Some of these characteristics are individual autonomy, consideration to employees, respect for each other etc.

3. **Career Advancement :** A person does not simply join an organisation for a job but for his career. An organisation may motivate its employees by providing them career advancement opportunity and developing them to progress on their career paths.

4. **Job Enrichment:** Job enrichment is a technique through which a job is made more motivating. In job enrichment, more responsibility is added in the job, need for using variety of skills is increased and more autonomy is provided for job performance.

5. **Employee Recognition :** Employee recognition involves appreciation for good performance done by employees through award, certificate for best performance, congratulating the employee for good performance etc.

6. **Job Security:** Employees need reasonable level of job security which ensures stability of income. Thus an organisation can motivate its employees by ensuring their job security.

7. **Employee Participation:** Employee participation means involving employees in decision making of the issues related to them. This creates feeling in the employees that they are important for the organisation which becomes motivating to them.

8. **Autonomy/Employee Empowerment:** It means giving more freedom to subordinates. This empowerment develops confidence in employees. They use positive skill to prove that they are performing to the best when freedom is given to them.

Difference between Monetary and Non-monetary Incentives

Basic of Difference	Monetary Incentives	Non- monetary Incentives
1. Measurement	These can be measured in terms of money.	These cannot be measured in terms of money.
2. Suitability	These are highly effective in case of workers.	These are effective in case of managers.
3. Levels of Satisfaction	These help in satisfying lower-level needs (foods, clothing and shelter)	These help in satisfying higher-level needs (esteem, status and self actualisation)
4. Visibility	These are visible as they are measurable in terms of money.	These may not be visible as they are measurable in terms of money.

☞ **Leadership**
Definition of Leadership:
"Leadership is the ability of influencing people to strive willingly for group objectives."
Management vs Leadership:

Leadership involves securing willing cooperation of subordinates by influencing their behaviour towards achievement of common goals of the organisation. It is a part of management.

Management is the creation and maintenance of an internal environment whereby individuals work together in groups efficiently and effectively towards the achievement of common objectives/goals. It includes leadership.

Sometimes, management and leadership are regarded as synonymous. But this is not true. A manager may not be a leader in the sense that he is not able to win trust and confidence of his subordinates. The subordinates do not look up to him for guidance and support. However, if a manager possesses leadership qualities, he is likely to be a more successful manager. He influence the behaviour of subordinates in such a manner that he is able to achieve willing cooperation and is able to make himself acceptable as their guide, counselor and source of support. He inspires the members of the group to make efforts for the accomplishment of organisational goals. Thus, a good manager should possess many of the qualities of an effective leader.

But a leader need not be a manager. It is not essential for a leader to be appointed formally or to have formal authority. That is, he need not necessarily hold a formal managerial position. There can be leaders of employee groups who are not managers. Employees look towards them for assistance, guidance and support.

Managership VS Leadership

Basis	Management	Leadership
1. Structure	Managers exist only as a part of formal organisation	Leaders can be found outside the formal organisation structure.
2. Focus	The focus of managers is on achieving the assigned organisational goals.	Leaders are concerned with the expectations and aspirations of their followers.
3. Authority	Managers possess formal authority,	Leaders have acceptance authority. Followers willingly grant them right to command and lead them.
4. Scope	Management is a wide term and includes leadership.	Leadership is a part of management. Thus, its scope is limited.
5. Appointment	Managers are formally appointed,	Leaders may not be formally appointed. They depend on their confidence and goodwill.
6. Approach	A manager (boss) fixes blames and finds faults. He believes in "I"	A leader solves problems and inspires enthusiasm. He believes in "We" and "You".

☞ **Leadership Styles**

Leadership style is defined as follows:
"Leadership style is the pattern of behaviour which a leader adopts in influencing behaviour of his subordinates."

(1) **Authoritative Leadership Style:**
An autocratic leader exercise complete control over the subordinates. He centralizes power in himself and takes all decisions without consulting the subordinates. He does not delegate authority. The leader gives order and expects the subordinates to follow them unquestioningly. He gives reward and puts penalty to direct the subordinate. **This style is also known as the Leader – Centred Style**

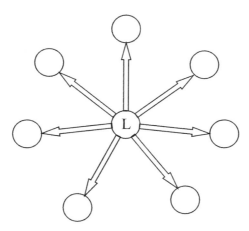

Advantages of Authoritative Leadership Style. Advantage or merits of authoritative leadership style are as follows:

1. **Satisfaction to Some Subordinates.** It provides satisfaction to those subordinates who prefer to work under centralized authority structure and strict control.

2. **Motivating to Some Superiors.** It is suitable to those superiors who derive satisfaction from having authority and exercising it to control their subordinates.

3. **Fast Decision — making.** It leads to fast decision — making as the leaders are not required to consult their subordinates in decision — making process.

4. **No Exposure of Incompetence of Subordinates.** In this style, incompetence of subordinates is not exposed because their role in planning, organizing, etc., which require thinking is very limited.

Disadvantages of Authoritative Leadership Style. Disadvantage or demerits of authoritative leadership style are as follows:

1. **Disliked by Subordinates.** Subordinates do not like this style, specially if emphasis is placed on negative motivation (demotion, penalty, etc.) for getting things done.

2. **Lack of Motivation to Subordinates.** There is lack of motivation for subordinates to work. They feel frustrated and their morale level remains low. As a result, organisational productivity is affected adversely.

3. **Lack of Leadership Development.** It results in lack of development of leadership in an organisation because subordinates rarely get opportunities to take initiative and to use their creativity.

Suitability. Autocratic style of leadership is suitable when:
(i)   subordinates are uneducated, unskilled, lack of knowledge and experience on part of subordinates.
(ii)   company follows fear and punishment disciplinary technique.
(iii) leader prefers to be dominant in decision making.

Now a days this style is less desirable as employees are becoming more educated and well-organised.

(2) **Democratic Leadership Style.**

Under this style leader takes decisions in consultation and participation with employees. He delegates and decentralizes the authority. Leader follows : the opinion of majority. He provides freedom of thinking and expression. He listens to the suggestions, grievances and opinion of the subordinates. **This style is also known as Group – Centred Leadership style.**

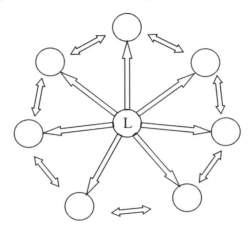

Advantages of Democratic Leadership Style. Advantages or merits of democratic leadership style are as follows:

1. **Motivating to Subordinates.** It is quite motivating to subordinates when their ideas and suggestions are given weight in decision making.

2. **High Productivity.** Subordinates feel that they are implementing their own decisions. As a result, they implement decisions whole-heartedly which leads high productivity.

3. **Safeguard to Leader.** Subordinates assume responsibility of performance results with their leader and support him. In this context, a famous saying is 'the fellow in the same boat with you will never bore a hole in it.

4. **Leadership Development.** It leads to leadership development because of active participation of subordinates in decision — making and decision implementation. Thus, a organisation rarely experience lack of suitable leaders.

5. **Organisational Stability.** It leads to organisational stability because of availability of trained employees with positive attitudes and high morale.

Disadvantages of Democratic Leadership Style. Disadvantages or demerits of democratic leadership style are as follows:

1. **Requirement of Highly Skilled Employees.** It requires highly skilled employees who may understand complexity of participative decision making. In absence of such employees, it becomes meaningless.

2. **Time Consuming.** Democratic leadership style require time in joint decision making between subordinate and leader which may result in delay in decision — making.

3. **Some time create frustration among employees.** Subordinates may develop the habit of expecting to be consulted on every issue and they may feel frustrated when they are not consulted.

4. **Disliked by Employees.** There are some employees who want minimum interaction with their superiors. As such, democratic leadership style is not suitable for such employees.

Suitability: Democratic style of leadership is suitable when:
(i)   when goal of company is to increase job satisfaction and independence of employees.
(ii)   when leader wants to share decision making with the subordinates.
(iii)   when subordinates have accepted the goal of organisation.

(3)   **Laissez faire Leadership Style:**
This style involves complete delegation of authority so that subordinates themselves take decision The managers explain the overall objectives, help the subordinates in this they provide resource for work performance and if need be they also advise the employees. This style is also known as individual centred style.

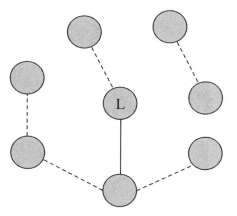

Advantages of Laissez Faire Leadership Style. Advantages or merits of laissez faire leadership style are as follows:
1. **Low Burden on Leader.** A leader prescribes policies and sets limits of actions for his subordinates. Therefore, his burden is lowered to a considerable extent.

2. **Motivation to Subordinates.** This leadership style is quite motivating to subordinates because they enjoy considerable autonomy in their functioning.

3. **Higher Productivity.** Since various groups are created on autonomous basis and their rewards are based on group performance, the members of the groups put on their best efforts to achieve group goals. This leads to higher productivity.

4. **Development of Subordinates.** This leadership style leads to development of subordinates because they work independently, use all their skills, and develop new skills to perform better.

Disadvantages of Laissez Faire Leadership Style. Disadvantages or demerits of laissez faire leadership style are as follows:

1. **Minimum Contribution of Leader.** In this leadership style, contribution of leader is minimum as he assigns all the activities to his subordinates. Unless he remains busy with other organisational matters, his relevance to the organisation is questionable.

2. **Suitable only for Highly Educated Employees.** This style is useful only when every employee is fully educated so that the work can be assigned to him with full confidence. This leadership style is not suitable for leading uneducated or semi-educated people.

3. **Requirement of Highly Conducive Work Environment.** Adoption of laissez faire leadership style requires highly conducive work environment in which various autonomous groups coordinate among them voluntarily. In the absence of such a work environment, there may be chaos in the organisation

Suitability: this style is suitable when
(i)   subordinates are well trained and highly knowledgeable.
(ii)   subordinates are self motivated and are ready to assume responsibility

Comparison between Leadership Styles

Basic	Authoritative Style	Democratic Style	Laissez-Faire Style
1. Decision Making	Leader takes all decisions alone with-out consulting subordinates; 'I' style.	Leader consults subordinates on proposed actions and decisions; 'We' style.	Subordinates themselves take decisions; 'You style.
2. Motivation technique	Threats and punishment.	Rewards and involvement,	Self-direction and self-control.
3. Focus	Boss-centred leadership.	Group-centred leadership.	Subordinates-centred leadership.
4. Delegation of authority	Complete control and supervision; no delegation of authority.	Delegation of authority,	Complete delegation of authority.
5. Opportunity to subordinates	No scope for initiative and self development.	Scope for initiative and self-development,	Full scope for initiative and self-development.
6. Role of leader	Strict manager, who commands and expects compliance,	Team manager, who operates according to majority opinion,	Contact person, who brings information and resources needed by subordinates to achieve group goals.
7. Communication	One-way (downward) communication.	Two-way (downward and upward) communication.	Free flow of communication.

☞ **Communication**
"Communication is the process of exchanging informance and understanding between two or more persons."

The common means and ways for transmission of ideas are:
(a) Spoken words;   (b) Written words
(c) Diagrams, Pictures, Graphs   (d) Gestures.

The communication is a two way process as it begins with sender and ends when the feedback comes from receiver to sender. Minimum two parties are involved in the process of communication i.e., the sender and the receiver.

Communication Process

The communication process begins when sender thinks of an idea or message to be conveyed to other person. Then the sender encodes the message i.e., plans out the words or the language in which the message must be sent to the other party. After encoding the message the sender transmits or transfers the message by using different ways and means. After transmission the message reaches to receiver. The receiver decodes the message to understand the message and give his response or feedback to the sender. When the feedback reaches back to sender then only the communication process ends which means the communication is a circular process which starts with sender and ends with sender.

Communication Process

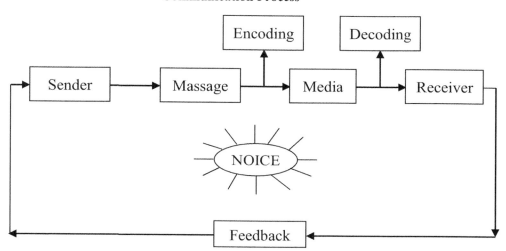

1. **Sender:** Sender is the person who conveys the message. The communication process begins immediately when the idea comes in the mind of sender.

2. **Message :** The contents of ideas or message or suggestions which sender wants to share with receiver is called message.

3. **Encoding :** Receiver cannot read the mind of sender. So sender converts the idea into a language or other communication symbols such as pictures, gestures etc. The is known as encoding.

4. **Media:** It is the way or means through which encoded message has to be transmitted to receiver. The common ways of transmission are phone, letter, Internet, message etc.

5. **Decoding :** Decoding refers to converting the encoded message into language and understanding the message.

6. **Receiver:** Receiver is the person who receives the communication and understands the message.

7. **Feedback:** After understanding the message the receives sends his response on that idea or message to sender. When response reaches the sender then only communication process ends.

8. **Noise :** Noise is any element which results in disturbance, distraction or interruption in the flow of information. The noise can be a loud sound made by any vehicle, disturbances in the telephone line, disconnection of line, losing of letter of documents on the way, poor connectively in the e-mail or Internet. Due to noise the message is not conveyed to receiver and receiver is not able to decode the message in the same manner as expected by the sender.

☞ **Forms of Organisational Communication**

(1)   **Formal Communication:**

Formal communication refers to interchange of information officially.

Formal communication refers to official communication taking place in the organisation. Whenever mere is exchange of views or message or information related to official matter such as assignment of task, fixing responsibilities, granting authority or setting up of targets, objectives etc. then it is known as formal communication.

Formal communication generally takes place in the written form such as issue of notice, letter, document etc. Verbal or oral channels are avoided in formal communication as there is no record or proof of such communication.

Classification of Formal Communication

A.   **Vertical Communication:** Vertical communication flows vertically, i.e., upwards or downwards through formal channels.

1.   **Downward Communication :** Downward communication refers to the flow of communication from a superior to subordinate. Examples: (i) Sending notice to employees to attend a meeting (ii) Ordering subordinates to complete an assigned work (iii) Passing on guidelines framed by top management to the subordinates.

2. **Upward Communication:** Upward communication refers to the flow of communication from a subordinate to superior, Examples: (i) Application for grant of leave (ii) Submission of progress report.

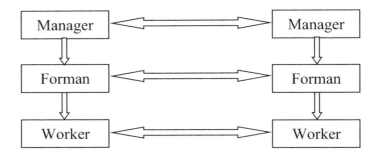

(Downward Communication) (Horizontal Communication) (Downward Communication)

B.   **Horizontal Communication :** It takes place between one department/division and another to coordinate different activities or to resolve inter-related problems. For example, a production manager may contact marketing manager to discus about product design, quality, etc.

Formal Communication Networks

Communication network indicates the pattern through which communication flows within the organisation.

1. **Single Chain Network :** The message flows in a direct vertical line along the scalar chain of command. It can flow from top to bottom or from bottom to top in a line. Thus, the flow of communication takes place through the formal channels, say from a superior to subordinate and vice versa. There is no horizontal communication in the chain network.

2. **Wheel Network:** It is the most centralized way of communication. Under wheel pattern all the information flows from one person only who is generally leader of the group. The other members have no communication link with each other. It is a common pattern of centralized organsiation.

3. **Circular Network :** In case of circular network, the message moves in a circle. Each person can communicate with his two neighbourhood collegus only as shown in Fig. The main disadvantage of circular network is that communication is very slow.

4. **Free flow Network:** Under such a network, there is no restriction on the flow of communication. Everyone is free to communicate with anyone and everyone in the organization. This network is informal and unstructured and so it allows free flow of communication as shown in Fig. Moreover, it is highly flexible. It is most decentralized organisation.

5. **Inverted V Network :** In this network a subordinate is allowed to communicate with his immediate superior and also with the superior of his superior. However in this pattern limited communication can take place.

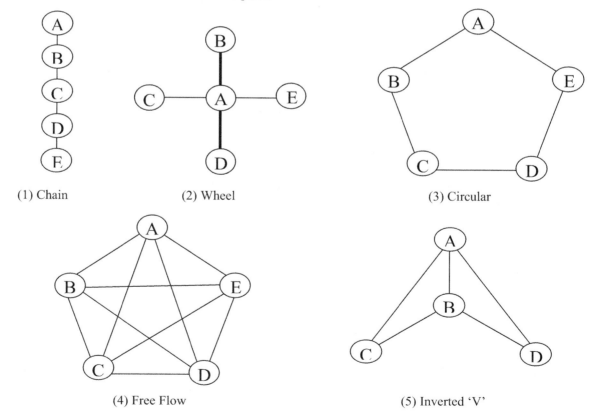

(1) Chain   (2) Wheel   (3) Circular

(4) Free Flow   (5) Inverted 'V'

Advantages of Formal Communication:

1. **Orderly Communication :** Flow of formal communication is orderly because everyone in sure about what to communicate with whom and from whom the required information may be obtained.

2. **Maintenance of Authority:** In formal communication, the authority of superior over subordinates is well maintained consequently it is convenient to control the subordinates and fix their responsibility.

3. **Easy fixation of Responsibility:** Formal communication leads to easy fixation of responsibility if there is any mis-communication or non communication of required subject matter. Based on this, appropriate penal action may be taken.

4. **Use for reference purpose:** Formal communication is used for reference purpose for example written policies procedures, rules, regulations etc are maintained as records which are used for reference in case of need.

5. **Authentic:** Formal communication is authentic because it is based on official prescription and uses official facts.

Disadvantages of Formal Communication:

1. **Slow communication :** Formal communication is usually slow. As a result in many cases information which passes through formal channel becomes delayed and loses its relevance.

2. **Costly miscommunication consequences :** Formal communication is treated as authentic and organisational members act upto that. Therefore, if anything is communicated wrongly, its consequences are very costly to the organisation.

3. **Distortion of Information :** Sometime the distance between the sender & the receiveris so big that the information passes through many hands & by the time it reaches the receiver it is distorted.

(2) **Informal Communication**

   In formal communication refers to interchange of information Unofficially.

Informal communication between different members of organisation who are not officially attached to each other is known as informal communication. Generally the social interactions, friendly talks and non official matters are discussed in the informal communication.

There is no fixed direction or path for the flow of information under informal communication. The information moves in a confusing and zig-zag manner. That is why the network of informal communication is known as Grap Vine

Informal Communication Networks

1. **Single Strand:** In single strand pattern each individual communicates to the other in sequence.

2. **Gossip:** Under gossip pattern one person tells many which means information is with one member of organisation and he shares the information with many other people in his social group.

3.   **Probability :** In probability network the individual communicates randomly with other individuals.

4.   **Clusters :** In the cluster grapevine, one person provides the information to a selected few to whom he trusts in the cluster.

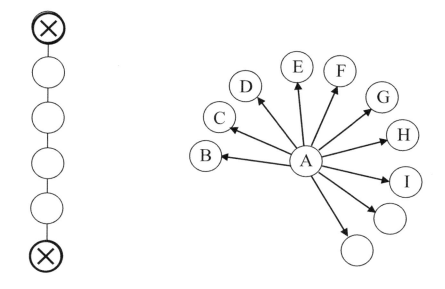

(1) Single Standard   (2) Gossip Chain

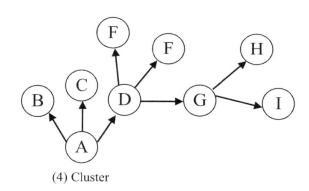

(3) Probility   (4) Cluster

Advantages of Informal Communication:

1.   **Fast Speed :** Informal communication travels at fast speed because of informal interactions among organisational members. Thus, information is available on timely basis.

2.   **Psychological Satisfaction :** Informal communication provides psychological satisfaction to organisational members. This helps them to overcome their work tension.

3.   **Easy solutions of the Difficult Problems :** There are many problems which cannot be solved with the help of formal communication. There is more freedom in informal communion which helps the solution of difficult problems.

4. **Communicating Reality of Situation :** In any cases, reality of organisational working is communicated only through informal communication as people do not prefer to communicate such a subject matter officially. Knowing reality of organisational functioning is quite important for top management.

5. **Knowledge of Attitudes of Organisational Members:** Informal communication helps top management to know the exact attitudes of organisational members. In the light of this knowledge, top management may take necessary actions to overcome the problems of negative attitudes, if any.

Disadvantages of Informal Communication:

1. **Unsystematic Communication :** This communication is absolutely unsystematic and it is not necessary that information reaches the person concerned.

2. **Unreliable Information :** Most of the information received through this communication is undependable and no important decision can be taken on its basis.

3. **Leakage of Confidential Information :** Sometimes, informal communication leads to leakage of confidential information of an organisation. This is harmful to the organisation.

4. **Difficult to Fix Responsibility:** In the case of informal communication, it is difficult to fix responsibility about who has spread a rumour because it is generated through interactions among organisational members which do not have fixed patterns.

Difference between Formal and Informal Communication

Basic	Formal Communication	Informal Communication
1. Status	It has official status	It has unofficial status
2. Sources of message	Sources of message are organisational policies, rules and other prescriptions.	Sources of message are informal relationship among persons.
3. Nature	It is well - planned, systematic and authorised.	It is spontaneous and unsystematic.
4. Objective	Its objective is to achieve organisational objectives,	Its objective is to meet social needs and personal interests of employees.
5. Contents	It contains work - related matters.	It contains personal views and feelings.
6. Flow	It flows through officially prescribed channels.	It flows through unofficially channels based on pattern of personal interactions.
7. Flexibility	It is quite rigid.	It is highly flexible.
8. Speed of Communication	Communication Speed of communication is slow.	Speed of communication is fast
9. Authenticity	It is highly authentic.	It is highly unauthentic.
10. Personal Touch	It lacks personal touch.	It has personal touch.
11. Fixation of Responsibility	Responsibility Fixation of Responsibility is easy.	Fixation of Responsibility is difficult.
12. Expression	It is mostly expressed in written form.	It mostly tends to be oral.

☞ **Barriers to Effective Communication**

Some times the message sent by sender does not reach the receiver in the same manner as expected by the sender. This filtration, misrepresentation of communication may cause misunderstanding. Therefore it is important for a manager to identify these barriers and take measures to overcome these. The barriers can be grouped in following categories:

Semantic Barriers, Psychological Barriers, Organisational Barriers, Personal Barriers.

A. **Semantic Barriers :** Sometimes the same words and sentences can be understood differently by different people in the organisation which means difference in the understanding levels of employees. For example, if the production manager announces in the meeting that there will be increase in budget of production department then employees may understand that their salary will increase but managers may understand it that expensive machinery will be purchased. Main causes for semantic problem can be

1. **Badly expressed message:** Sometimes due to lack of vocabulary manager may use wrong words, omission of needed words. Due to this the manager may fail to convey the same meaning to his subordinates.

2. **Symbols with different meanings :** Sometimes a word may have different meanings. Receiver may understand the other meaning. For example Price, Prize, Principle, Principal, Right, Write etc. or handle with care. Hold the handle of door carefully.

3. **Faulty Translation Barriers:** Sometimes the workers do not understand the language which is used by manager so workers get it translated. If translator is not efficient he may make mistake in translation. Due to wrong translation there may be transfer of wrong message.

4. **Unqualified Assumptions :** Sometimes the worker may misinter-pret the assumptions. For example boss may instruct the subordinate to "take care of goods". He may mean that take care of quality of goods whereas workers may understand that he is instructing to keep the goods safety.

5. **Technical Jargon :** While explaining to subordinates many specialized experts use technical words which may not be understood by the workers.

6. **Body language and gesture decoding :** Along with verbal communication another important mode of communication is body language and gestures shown by person who is talking. If the verbal communication is not matching with the body language, then workers may get confused and misunderstand the meaning Example - If manager is telling a joke but there are signs of anger on his face then worker will get confused.

B. **Psychological Barriers :** Emotional or psychological factors also act as barriers to effective communication. The state of mind has great influence over the information and its reflection. As a frightened person may not communicate properly similarly an angry person may not receive the communication effectively.

Some of the psychological barriers to effective communication are:

1. **Premature Evaluation :** It means deriving conclusions before completion of message. Sometimes people evaluate the meaning of message before the sender completes the message. In such case the receiver may not have an open mind. He may have some personal prejudice against the sender. He may resist change. He jumps to conclusions without logical deduction from the situation.

2. **Lack of Attention:** It means when receiver does not pay complete attention to the message as a result communication becomes ineffective. The reason can be preoccupied mind of receiver. For example, when worker is giving suggestion regarding method of production, the manager is preoccupied with an important file. Sometimes managers do not give attention due to extreme emotions for example, depression or jubilation. This lack of attention may disappoint the employees.

3. **Loss by Transmission and Poor Retention :** When communication passes through various levels, this results in filtering or loss of information. Specially when is oral information sometimes manager may not be able to retain all information for a longer time. They may ignore or misinterpret some of the information when they are not interested.

4. **Distrust:** Distrust between communicator and receiver also acts as a barrier to effective communication. They may not understand each other's message in the original sense, secondly they do not give much importance to the information exchanged between them.

C. **Organisational Barriers :** Factors related to organisational structure, authority relationship, rules, regulations may act as barriers to effective communication.
Some of the organisational barriers are:

1. **Organisational Policy:** If organisational policy does not support free flow of information it may result in barriers. For example in centralised organisation most of the information remains at toplevel only. People at lower level may not be able to communicate freely in centralised organisation.

2. **Rules and Regulations:** Rigid rules, regulations may also create barriers as following rules may lead to red tapism, delay of action and delay in movement of information.

3. **Status Difference:** Sometimes the people working at higher level do not believe in the information supplied by the lower level employees as they feel how would he know about my job and who is he to give me suggestions.

4. **Complex Organisation :** When the information passes through various levels then there can be screening or filtering of information at different levels. For example, while giving the feedback the subordinates filter all their negative points and highlight only their positive side.

5. **Organisational Facilities:** In large organisation free and effective flow of communication is possible only when facilities like social get together, complaint box, task force etc. exist. In absence of such facilities there can be delay and barrier to effective communication.

D. **Personal Barriers :** Certain personal factors of sender and receiver may influence the free flow of information. Some of the personal barriers are:

1. **Lack of confidence of superior in his subordinates :** If superiors have no confidence and trust in their subordinates then they pay no attention to their advice, opinion or suggestions.

2. **Lack of incentives:** if there is no incentive for communication then subordinates may not take initiative to give suggestions. For example if there is no reward given for giving some good suggestion then employees will take no initiative to give good suggestions.

3. **Fear of Authority:** Sometimes superiors conceal and hide information if they have fear of losing their authority over the subordinates.

Improving Communication Effectiveness

1. **Clarify the idea before communication:** In the first place we must be clear about what we want to communicate. The message can be conveyed properly only if it is clearly formulated in the mind of the communicator. The message should be encoded in direct and simple language so that the receiver is able to understand it without much difficulty.

2. **Communication according to the need of the receiver :** Whenever we communicate we must keep in mind the needs of the receiver of the message or it should be our effort to see that whatever message or information we send across must be of value to receiver. This will make receiver more respective. Sender must select the words according to the education level of receiver.

3. **Consult others before communicating:** Before communicating the message it is advisable to consult others. Effective communication is the responsibility of all persons in the organisation as all have to work towards a common goal. If plans are developed with consultation and involvement of subordinates, they will accept it with full cooperation.

4. **Use of proper language, tone and contents of message:** For an effective communication the words, tone and symbols used in message must be selected very carefully. The language used should not offend the sentiments of listener. The symbols used in message must be known to the listener.

5. **Proper feedback:** Feedback help to know the effect or success of communication given by sender. Communication is complete only when the message is understood by the receiver. We can never know whether receiver has understood the message or not unless we get the feedback. Feedback also provides opportunity for suggestions and criticism.

6. **Communication for the present as well as for future:** Communication must meet the need of present organisation as well as for future organsiation. There must be consistency in the past, present and future communication.

7. **Follow up communication :** There should be proper follow up of the information given by manager to subordinate. This follow up helps to remove hurdles, misunderstanding of instructions given by manager to subordinates.

8. **Good listener :** The sender must listen to receiver's words alternatively; on the other hand receiver must also listen with due attention. Patient and attentive listening solve many problems.

9. **Open mind :** The parties to communication must have open mind. They should not try to withhold information for their personal interest. They should not react before receiving and listening the full message.

10. **Completeness of message :** A message is effective only when it is given completely. The receiver should not be left guessing. It may lead to misunderstanding. A complete message carries all necessary facts and figures.

EXERCISE – 1

Q.1   Define directing.
Ans.   It is the process of instructing, guiding, counselling, motivating and leading.

Q.2   Name the elements of directing.
Ans.   Supervision, motivation, leadership and communication.

Q.3   Name the element of directing function under which the superiors share information with the subordinates in order to reach common understanding.
Ans.   Communication.

Q.4   What is positive motivation ?
Ans.   Positive motivation means motivation on the basis of positive rewards such as increase in pay, recognition, etc.

Q.5   What is negative motivation?
Ans.   Negative motivation means motivation on the basis of negative means like punishment threatening etc

Q.6   Give two examples of esteem needs.
Ans.   (i) Self-respect   (ii) Recognition.

Q.7   Give two examples of self-actualisation needs.
Ans.   (i) Growth   (ii) Self-fulfillment

Q.8   What is the aim of productivity-linked wage incentive?
Ans.   It is aimed at increasing the productivity at individual or group level.

Q.9   Name any monetary incentive offered over and above the wages/salary to the employees.
Ans.   Bonus.

Q.10   How does profit sharing help in motivating the employees of an organisation?
Ans.   It provides a share to employees in the profit, thus motivating them to improve their performance.

Q.11   Name the incentive scheme offering company shares at a set price to employees.
Ans.   Co-partnership.

Q.12   Give an example of retirement benefit.
Ans.   Provident fund.

Q.13   How can retirement benefit be a source of motivation?
Ans.   By imparting an advance feeling of financial security even in the post-retirement phase

Q.14   Name the incentive scheme used to enrich and make jobs interesting.
Ans.   Job enrichment.

Q.15   Give two examples of upward communication.
Ans.   (i) Application for grant of leave   (ii) Progress report.

Q.16   Give two examples of downward communication.
Ans.   (i) Instructions   (ii) Policies.

Q.17   Mention any two kinds of grapevine communication network.
Ans.   (i) Single strand network   (ii) Gossip network.

Q.18   Name the most popular grapevine network.
Ans.   Cluster.

Q.19   Name any two psychological barriers to effective communication.
Ans.   (i) Distrust   (ii) Lack of attention.

EXERCISE – 2

Q.1   State any three features of directing.

Q.2   Enumerate any three points of importance of directing as a function of management.

Q.3   Give the meaning of 'Monetary' and 'Non-monetary' incentives with two examples of each.

Q.4   What is 'Formal communication'? State the types formal communication.

Q.5   State any three 'semantic barriers' to communication.

Q.6   State any three 'organisational barriers' to communication.

Q.7   Explain any four types of 'Monetary incentives'.

Q.8   Explain any four types of 'Non-monetary incentives'.

Q.9   What are the elements of directing? Explain briefly.

Q.10   Explain different networks of grapevine communications.

EXERCISE – 3

Q.1   Explain the role and functions of a supervisor in an organisation.

Q.2   What is meant by 'Monetary Incentives'? State any five types of monetary incentives which contribute to the performance of employees.

Q.3   What is meant by 'Non-monetary Incentives'? State any five types of Non-monetary incentives which contribute to the performance of employees.

Q.4   Explain 'Pay and Allowances','Productivity-linked wage incentives' and 'retirement benefits' as monetary incentives for employees in an orgainsation.

Q.5   Explain Moslow's need hierarchy theory of motivation.

Q.6   Explain briefly the common barriers of effective communication.

CONTROLLING

CONTENT

☞ **Introduction :**
Ensuring that organisational's resources such as 'man, material, machinery etc are being used effectivel and efficiently."

☞ **Characteristics of Control**
1.   Pervasive Function.
2.   Continuous Process.
3.   Backward and Forward Looking process.
4.   Action Oriented Process.

☞ **Importance of Control**
1.   Helps in achieving organisational goals.
2.   Judging accuracy of standards.
3.   Better use of Resources
4.   Improve employee's motivation.
5.   Ensuring order and discipline.
6.   Better Coordination
7.   Controlling helps in minimising the errors.

☞ **Limitation of Control**
1.   Difficulty in setting quantitative Standards.
2.   No control o external factors.
3.   Resistance from employees.
4.   Costly affair.

☞ **Relations between Planning and Controlling**
1.   Meaning.
2.   Planning and controlling are interdependent and interlinked.
3.   Planning and controlling are both backward looking as well as forward looking.

☞ **Controlling Process**
1.   Setting performance standards.
2.   Measurement of actual performance.
3.   Comparing actual performance with Standards.
4.   Analysing deviations.
5.   Taking corrective actions.

WEIGHTAGE

Units	Very Short Answer	Short Answer I & II	Long Answer I & II	Total
Unit – 8(6)	1(1)	---	5(1)	6(2)

8.   CONTROLLING

☞ **Meaning of Controlling**
"Controlling is the process of verifying wheater actual performance is in conformity with planned performance and taking corrective action where necessary."

These are two aspects of Controlling System.
(i) Strategic Control
(ii) Operational Control

Strategic Control : refers to check how effective the strategies and the plans are because sometimes there can be deviation in actual performance and planned performance due to plans and strategies.

Operational aspect : refers to focus on managerial and other activities of the organisation. That is to find out whether the mismatch is due to fault in the actions or activities.

In both the aspects the managers try to find out the reasons for mismatch and take corrective measures.

☞ **Characteristics of Controlling**

1. **Controlling is a goal-oriented function :** Controlling means ensuring that activities in an organisation are performed as per the plans. The essence of control lies in managerial action taken to correct the performance. Mere measurement of performance and finding deviations does not achieve control. An effective control system facilitates timely corrective action so that deviations do not occur again and standards are accomplished. Thus, controlling is a goal-oriented function.

2. **Pervasive Function :** Control is pervasive function in the sense that it is required at all levels of management in every type of organisation. It is applicable to production, finance, marketing and organsiational activities. Every manager performs the controlling function irrespective of his status and the nature of his job.

3. **Continuous Process :** Controlling is a continuous process in the sense that it involves review of performance and revision of standard operations on a continuous basis. As long as an organisation exists, control continues to exist. Controlling is not an activity to be pursued in the end only, it has to be on a continuous basis. Activities should be supervised on continuous basis.

4. **Backward and Forward Looking Process :** Control is backward looking process in the sense that it compares actual performance which has, been or is being carried out with the planned performance. Control is a forward looking process in the sense that it improves future planning by suggesting revision of existing plans and targets and adoption of new plans on the basis of information derived from past experience. It looks at future through the eyes of past. Therefore, control is both a backward and forward looking process.

5. **Controlling improves future planning :** The controlling function measures actual performance against the standards and corrects the deviations from the standards and plans. This process helps in formulation of future plans in the light of the problems that were identified. Thus, controlling improves future planning by providing information derived from past experience.

☞ **Importance of Controlling**

1. **Helps in achieving organisational goals :** When the plans are made in the organisation these are directed towards achievement of organisational goal and the controlling function ensures that all the activities in the organisation take place according to plan and if there is any deviation, timely action is taken to bring back the activities on the path of planning. When all the activities are going according to plan then automatically these will direct towards achievement of organsiational goal.

2. **Judging accuracy of standards :** In controlling, actual performance is compared with standards set in this respect. To what extent these standards are accurate or inaccurate is indicated by controlling. For example, if a standard is not achieved even by putting the best possible efforts, it indicates inaccuracy in standard. Reverse of this is also true.

3. **Better use of Resources :** Controlling leads to adjustment in operations as quickly as possible. This adjustment is required either because of internal inefficiency or because of change in business environment Thus, organisational resources may be used in a much better way.

4. **Improving employee motivation :** An effective control system communicates the goals and standards of appraisal for employees to subordinates well in advance.

   A good control system also guides employees to come out from their problems. This free communication and care motivate the employees to give better performance.

5. **Ensures order and discipline :** Control creates an atmosphere of order and discipline in the organisation. Effective controlling system keeps the subordinates under check and makes sure they perform their functions efficiently. Sharp control can have a check over dishonesty and fraud of employees. Strics control monitor, employees work on computer monitor which brings more order and discipline in work environment.

6. **Better Coordination :** Controlling provides information about factors which are responsible for non — achievement of desired results. If there is lack of coordination between different individuals in a department or between different departments, it is highlighted by controlling. Based on this, suitable coordination methods can be adopted.

7. **Controlling helps in minimising the errors :** Small errors or small mistakes may not seriously affect the organisation. But if these errors are repeated again and again it will become a serious matter and can bring disaster for the organisation. An effective controlling system helps in minimising the errors by continuous monitoring and check. The managers try to detect the error on time and take remedial steps to minimise the effect of error.

☞ **Limitations of Controlling**
1. **Difficulty in Setting Standards :** Controlling uses standards set as the basis for further steps but stetting of these standards is very difficult, particularly in those areas where quantitative measurement of performance is quite difficult, for example, research and development, training, etc. In such areas. controlling becomes almost redundant.

2. **Resistance by Employees :** Employees resist controlling because they treat controlling as a kind of restriction on their freedom. Further, they develop a feeling that higher level management does not have faith in them. Therefore, control is exercised.

3. **Difficulty in Fixing Responsibility :** Controlling indicates what has happened actually (standards achieved or not) but it does not indicate who are responsible for this, particularly for non-achievement of standards as many people are involved together.

4. **Lack of Control on External Factors :** Controlling is mostly relevant for internal factors, as external factors are beyond control. There are many situations in which unsatisfactory result is caused by external factors. Therefore, the indication of controlling that standards have not been achieved becomes meaningless.

5. **Costly Affair :** Controlling is a costly affair as it involves collection of lot of information and its processing to identify deviations between standards and actual performance. Therefore, designing and operating a control system is limited to large organisations only.

☞ **Relations between Planning and Controlling between**
The relationship between planning and control can be divided into the following two parts:
(1) **Interdependence between Planning and Controlling.**
(2) **Both are backward looking as well as forward looking**.

(1) **Interdependence between Planning and Controlling :** Planning and Controlling are inseparable twins of management.
  - ➢ **Controlling is blind with planning :** Controlling involves comparison of actual performance with certain standards which are provided by planning. So, when there is no plan (i.e., the standards are not set in advance), managers have no basis for controlling.

  - ➢ **Planning without controlling is meaningless :** As plans are not made only on papers but these have to be followed and implemented in the organisation. The controlling function makes sure that everyone follows the plan strictly. Continuous monitoring and check in controlling function make it possible that everyone follows the plan.

So both the functions are interlinked and interdependent as for successful execution of both the function planning and controlling must support each other. For example, if the workers have produced 800 units the manager can know whether it is adequate or not only when there is a standard production set up by planners. So base of comparison comes from planning only. On the other hand, if the standard target is 1,000 units then controlling managers make sure that there is improvement in the performance and the employees achieve the set target.

(2) **Both are backward looking as well as forward looking :**
  - ➢ **Backward looking**
    - ❖ **Controlling :** As like a postmortem of past activities the manager looks back to previous year's performance to find out its deviation from standard.
    - ❖ **Planning :** As planning is guided by past experience and feed-back report of controlling function.
  - ➢ **Forward looking :**
    - ❖ **Planning :** As plans are prepared for future. It involves looking in advance and making policy for maximum utilisation of resources in future.
    - ❖ **Controlling :** As it involves finding the reasons for deviations and suggests the measures so that these deviations do not occur in future.

So this statement that planning is forward looking and controlling is backward is only partially correct as planning and controlling are both forward looking as well as backward looking.

☞ **Controlling Process**
(i) **Standards Setting Performance :** Standards are the criteria, set in both quantitative and qualitative terms against which actual performance can be measured. Standard are the bench marks towards which efforts of entire organisation are directed. In order to determine whether the actual performance is proceeding in the right way standards are required. As far as possible, standards must be set up in numerical or measurable terms. For example
  - ○ **Quantitative Standards –** (i) Standard output 1000 unit per day
    (ii) Standard sales Rs. 50 lakh per annum.
  - ○ **Qualitative Standards –** (i) Improving Goodwill
    (ii) Improving Labour relations.

(ii) **Measurement of Actual Performance :** Once the standards have been determined the next step is to measure the actual performance The various techniques for measuring are sample checking performance reports, personal observation etc However, in order to facilitate easy comparison, the performance should be measured on same basis that the standards have.
For example various ratios like gross profit ratio debtor turnover ratio return on investment current ratio etc. are calculated at periodic intervals to measure company's performance.

(iii) **Comparing Actual Performance with Standards :** The standards should be in quantitative terms of facilitate such comparison. This steps involves comparing the actual performance with standards laid down in order to find the deviations. **Deviation means difference between actual performance and Planned performance.**

Deviation are of two types :
(i)   Positive deviation It implies that actual performance is better than the standard performance
(ii)   Negative deviation It means actual performance is less than the standard performance
For example performance of a salesman in terms of unit sold in a week can be easily measured against the standard output for the week.

(iv)   Analysing Deviations : After identifying the deviations, various causes for same are analysed and the most exact cause or causes are identified in order to take corrective measures While analyzing the deviations 'Critical Point Control' and 'Management by Exception' techniques are used to save time

(v)   Taking Corrective Actions : The final step in the process of controlling involves taking corrective action. If the deviations are within acceptable limits, no corrective measure is required. However, if the deva3rs exceed the acceptable limits, they should be immediately brought to the notice of the management fan taking corrective measures, especially in the important and critical areas.

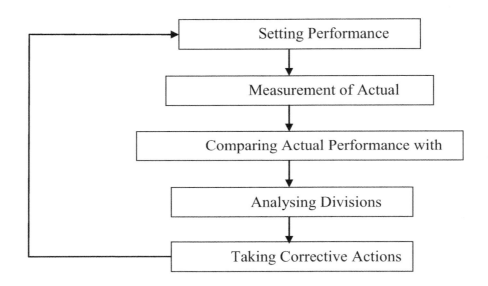

PROCESS OF CONTROLLING

Critical Point Control : - An ideal control technique should concentrate on key aspects of performance. There are several activities to be controlled. In practice, it is not possible or management to control each and every activity due to limited time.

Control should, therefore, focus on key result areas (KRA5) which are critical to the success of an organisation. The KRAs are set as the critical points. If anything goes wrong at the critical points, the entire organisation suffers.

For example, in a manufacturing organisation, an increase of 10 per cent in the labour cost may be more troublesome than a 20 per cent increase in postal charges.

Control by Exception/Management by Exception : - This principle of management control is based on the belief that – **"An attempt to control everything may end up by controlling nothing,"** Minor deviations from standards are insignificant for success. They should be ignored. Therefore, only significant deviations, which go beyond the permissible limit, should be reported to the management so that the management may take corrective action to deal with the situation.

Example 1: A manager establishes a quality control standard which says that 5 defects per 100 units produced are permissible. Under the "control by exception" principle, only significant deviations from this standard, i.e., 6 or more defects per 100 units should be reported to the manager.

Example 2: The management lays down a standard that the cost of production per unit should not exceed by 10% from the earlier period. If the actual cost exceeds by 10% (say by 15%), it should be reported to the management.

EXERCISE – 1

Q.1 State the meaning of controlling
Sol. Controlling implies the measurement of accomplishment against the standards and the correction of deviations to assure attainment of objectives according to plants.

Q.2 Which two aspects of performance are compared in controlling?
Sol. Actual with standards.

Q.3. What is the significance of standard?
Sol. Helpful in analysing deviation.

Q.4. What is deviation in controlling?
Sol. Difference between actual performance and standard performance.

Q.5. What is the term used to denote the situation under which standard performance and actual performance differ?
Sol. Deviation.

Q.6. Name the two techniques of analysing deviations.
Sol. Critical point control and management by exception.

Q.7. Which principle of management control is baded on the belief that an attempt to control everything results in controlling nothing?
Sol. Control by exception.

Q.8. How does controlling help in ensuring order and discipline?
Sol. Dishonest behaviour on the part of the employees is minimised by keeping a close check on their activities.

Q.9. What is critical point control?
Sol. Key areas that are critical for the success of an organisation should be the focus of control.

Q.10. What do you mean by 'Key result areas (KRAs)' in the context of controlling?
Sol. KRAs are the critical points which are critical to the success of an organisation.

EXERCISE – 2

Q.1. Define 'Controlling'. State the various steps involved in controlling-process.

Q.2. "Controlling function of management is a pervasive function." Explain.

Q.3. "Controlling is resisted by employees and it is a costly affair." Explain this statement.

Q.4.   How does controlling help in efficient use of resources?

Q.5.   "Planning and controlling are interrelated." Explain this statement giving two-points.

Q.6.   Define 'deviation' in controlling. Give examples.

EXERCISE – 3

Q.1.   Explain the various steps involved in the process of control.

Q.2.   Explain the importance of controlling in an organisation.

Q.3.   Discuss the relationship between planning and controlling.

Q.4.   "Planning and controlling are mutually inter-related and inter-dependent activities." How?

Part B:
Business Finance and Marketing

FINANCIAL MANAGEMENT

CONTENT

☞ **Introduction :**
Management of flow of funds
(A)   Business Finance
(B)   Financial Management

☞ **Objective of Financial Management**
1.   Ensuring availability of sufficient funds at a reasonable cost.
2.   Ensuring effective utilisation/deployment of such funds.
3.   Ensuring safety of funds.
4.   Avoiding idle finance.

A.   Investment Decision
Factor Affecting Investment Decision
1.   Cash flow of the project.
2.   Return on Investment.
3.   Risk Involved.
4.   Investment Criteria.

B.   Financial Decision
Factor Affecting Financing Decision
1.   Cost.
2.   Risk.
3.   Cash Flow Position.
4.   Control Consideration.
5.   Floatation Cost.
6.   Fixed Operating Cost.
7.   State of Capital Market.

C.   Dividend Decision
Factor Affecting Dividend Decision
1.   Earning.
2.   Stability of Dividends,
3.   Cash Flow Position.
4.   Growth Opportunities.
5.   Stability of Dividend.
6.   Preference of Shareholders.
7.   Taxation Policy
8.   Access to Capital Market Consideration.
9.   Legal Restrictions.
10.   Stock Market Reaction.
11.   Contractual Constraints

☞ **Financial Planning**

☞ **Objective of Financial Management**
1.　　To ensure availability of funds whenever these are required.
2.　　To see that firm does not raise resources unnecessarily.

☞ **Importance of Financial Planning**
1.　　It Facilitates Collection of Optimum Funds.
2.　　It Helps in Fixing the Most Appropriate Capital Structure.
3.　　Helps in Investing Finance in Right Projects.
4.　　Helps in Operational Activities.
5.　　Base for Financial Control.
6.　　Helps in Avoiding Business Shocks and Surprises.
7.　　Link between Investment and Financing Decisions.
8.　　It Links Present with Future.

☞ **Capital Structure**
Factor Affecting of Capital Structure
1.　　Cash Flow Statement.
2.　　ICR.
3.　　DSCR.
4.　　Return on Investment.
5.　　Cost of debt.
6.　　Tax Rate.
7.　　Cost of equity.
8.　　Floatation Costs.
9.　　Risk Consideration.
10.　　Flexibility.
11.　　Control.
12.　　Regulatory Framework.
13.　　Stock Market Condition.
14.　　Capital Structure of other Companies.

☞ **Fixed and working Capital**

☞ **Fixed Capital**
Factor affecting of Fixed capital
1.　　Nature of Business.
2.　　Scale of operation.
3.　　Technique of Production.
4.　　Technology Upgradation.
5.　　Growth Prospects.
6.　　Diversification.
7.　　Availability of Finance and Leasing Facility.
8.　　Level of Collaboration/Joint Venture.

☞ **Working Capital**
(i)   Gross Working Capital
(ii)   Net Working Capital

Factor affecting of Working capital

1.   Length of operating cycle.
2.   Nature of business.
3.   Scale of operation.
4.   Business cycle fluctuation.
5.   Seasonal factors.
6.   Technology and production cycle.
7.   Credit Allowed.
8.   Credit Avail.
9.   Operating Efficiency.
10.   Availability of Raw Materials.
11.   Level of Competition.
12.   Inflation
13.   Growth Prospects.

WEIGHTAGE

Units	Very Short Answer	Short Answer I & II	Long Answer I & II	Total
Unit – 9(12)	1(2)	4(1)	6(1)	12(4)

9.   FINANCIAL MANAGEMENT

☞   Meaning of Business Finance and Financial Management

(A)   Business Finance

"Money required for carrying out business activities is called Business Finance."

Finance is needed to:

(i)   Establish a business,
(ii)   To run a business.
(iii)   To modernize, expand and diversify the activities of business.
(iv)   For buying the assets; they may be tangible like machinery, factories, building etc. or intangible such as trademark, patent etc.
(v)   For running day to-day operations such as buying raw materials, paying wages, salaries etc.

Availability of efficient finance is very crucial for the survival and growth of a business. That is why finance is also called the life blood of the business.

(B)   Financial Management

"Financial management deals with planning, organizing, directing and controlling financial activities like procurement and utilisation of funds of an enterprise."

It is concerned with the following aspects:

(i)   Determining the long-term investments by the business and assessing the requirements of capital for the procurement of building, plant and machinery, etc.
(ii)   Raising of required capital by tapping sources of ownership and debt capital.

(iii)   Managing flow of funds/cash so as to pay for raw materials, wages and salaries, overheads, etc.

(iv)   Rewarding the equity shareholders, i.e., distribution of dividends.

(v)   Exercising financial controls through budgets, ratio analysis, etc.

☞ **Objective of Financial Management**
"The primary objectives of financial management is to maximize shareholders' Wealth, which means maximization of the market value or price of equity shares of the company."

Market price of equity shares increases if the benefits from a financial decision exceed the cost involved since there will be some value addition. Therefore, in order to maximise shareholders' wealth, financial management must aim at achieving the following specific objectives.

1.   **Ensuring availability of sufficient funds at a reasonable cost:** Whenever required, sufficient funds must be procured at a reasonable cost, keeping the risk under control so that some value addition takes place.

2.   **Ensuring effective utilisation/deployment of such funds :** When investment decision is taken, e.g. investment in land, building, plant and machinery, etc. the aim of financial management is to ensure that benefits or returns from the investment exceed the cost so that the value addition is even higher.

3.   **Ensuring safety of funds:** Financial management must aim at ensuring safety of funds procured by creating reserves, reinvesting profits, etc.

4.   **Avoiding idle finance:** Financial management must aim at avoiding idle finance because if excess funds are available, it will unnecessarily add to the cost and may encourage wasteful expenditure.

☞ **Finance Functions or Financial Decision**
The finance functions relate to three major decisions which every finance manager has to take
- **Investment Decision**
- **Financing Decision**
- **Dividend Decision**

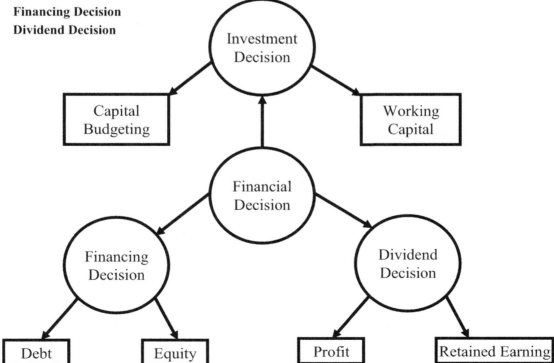

☞ **Investment Decision**

"**An Investment decision involves deciding how funds should be invested in
different assets of the business so that the funds give optimum returns.**"

Investment decision can be long term or short term.

Long term Investment Decision : "This is referred to as capital budgeting decision". It relates to the investment in long term assets/projects. For example (i) land, building, plant & machinery etc. (ii) opening new branch (iii) launching a new product line etc.

Since investment in long term assets is called fixed capital, therefore, this is also called Management of fixed capital.

Why the Management of fixed capital or investment or capital budgeting decisions are important?

OR

How Capital budgeting decisions can turn the fortune of a company?

The capital budgeting decisions are considered very important because of the following reasons:

1. **Long Term Growth :** The capital budgeting decisions affect the long term growth of the company. As funds invested in long term assets bring return in future and future prospectus and growth of the company depends upon these decisions only.

2. **Large Amount of Funds Involved :** Investment in long term projects or buying of fixed assets involves huge amount of funds and if wrong proposal is selected it may result in wastage of huge amount of funds that is why capital budgeting decisions are taken after considering various factors and planning.

3. **Risk Involved :** The fixed capital decisions involve huge funds and also big risk because the return comes in long run and company has to bear the risk for a long period of time till the returns start coming.

4. **Irreversible Decision :** Capital budgeting decisions cannot be reversed or changed overnight. As these decisions involve huge funds and heavy cost and going back or reversing the decision may result in heavy loss and wastage of funds. So these decisions must be taken after careful planning and evaluation of all the effects of that decision because adverse consequences may be very heavy.

☞ **Factor Affecting Investment Decision**

1. **Cash Flow of the Project :** Whenever a company is investing huge funds in an investment proposal it expect some regular amount of cash flow to meet day to day requirement. The amount of cash flow an investment proposal will able to generate must be assessed properly before investing in the proposal.

2. **Return on Investment:** The most important criteria to decide the investment proposal is rate of return it will able to bring back for the company in the form of income for e.g., If project A is bringing 10% return and project B is bringing 15% return then we should prefer project B.

3.   **Risk Involved :** With every investment proposal there is some degree of risk is also involved. The company must try to calculate the risk involved in every proposal and should prefer the investment proposal with moderate degree of risk only.

4.   **Investment Criteria :** Along with return, risk, cash flow there are various other criteria which help in selecting an investment proposal such as availability of labour, technologies, input, machinery etc.

The finance manager must compare all the available alternatives very carefully and then only decide where to invest the most scarce resources of the firm i.e., finance.

Short term Investment Decision : "This is referred to as working capital decision." It is concerned with the decisions about the level of cash, inventories and debtors.

Keeping adequate amount of the working capital at all the time in the business is called Management of the working capital.

How working capital decisions affect the liquidity as well as profitability of a business?

OR

How short term assets are more liquid but less profitable.

Keeping adequate amount of the working capital at all the times in the business is called management of the working capital. Adequate amount means that amount of working capital should neither be more nor less than required. Both these situations are harmful. If the amount of the working capital is more than required, it will no doubt increase liquidity but decrease profitability. For example, if large amount of cash is kept as the working capital then this excessive cash will remain idle and cause the profitability to fall. If the amount of cash and other current assets is very little, then a lot of difficulties will have to be faced in meeting daily expenses and making payment to the creditors. thus the objective of the management of working capital is to be determine optimum amount of both the current assets and current liabilities so that profitability of the business remains intact and there is no fall in liquidity. In short, liquidity and profitability are the main factors which affect the short4erm investment decision.

☞   **Financing Decision :**

"**Financing decision is concerned with the decisions about how much funds are to be raised from which long term source, i.e., owner's fund or borrowed funds".**

•   **Owners funds – Constitute equity share capital & retained earnings.**

•   **Borrowed/Debts funds – Constitute debentures loans, bonds etc.**

While taking this decision the finance manager compares the advantages and disadvantages of different sources of finance. The borrowed funds have to be paid back and involve some degree of risk whereas in owner's funds there is no fix commitment of repayment and there is no risk involved. But finance manager prefers a mix of both types. Under financing decision finance manager fixes a ratio of owner fund and borrowed fund in the capital structure of the company.

☞   **Factors Affecting Financing Decisions**

1.   **Cost:** The cost of raising finance from various sources is different and finance managers always prefer the source with minimum cost.

2.   **Risk:** More risk is associated with borrowed fund as compared to owner's fund securities. Finance manager compares the risk with the cost involved and prefers securities with moderate risk factor.

3. **Cash Flow Statement :** The cash flow position of the company also helps in selecting the securities. With smooth and steady cash flow companies can easily afford borrowed fund securities but when companies have storage of cash flow, then they must go for owner's fund securities only.

4. **Control Considerations :** If existing shareholders want to retain the complete control of business then they prefer borrowed fund securities to raise further fund. On the other hand if they do not mind to lose the control then they may go for owner's fund securities.

5. **Floatation Cost:** It refers to cost involved in issue of securities such as broker's commission, underwriters fees, expenses on prospectus etc. Firm prefer securities which involve least floatation cost.

6. **Fixed Operating Cost:** If a company is having high fixed operating cost then they must prefer owner's fund because due to high fixed operational cost, the company may not be able to pay interest on debt securities which can cause serious troubles for company.

7. **State Capital Market:** The conditions in capital market also help in deciding the type of securities to be raised. During boom period it is easy to sell equity shares as people are ready to take risk whereas during depression period there is more demand for debt securities in capital market.

☞ **Dividend Decision**
"Dividend decision relates to how much of the company's after-tax pro fit is to be distributed to the shareholders and how much of it should be retained in the business for meeting the investment requirements"
Dividend decision should be taken keeping in view the objective of maximizing shareholders wealth.

☞ **Factors Affecting Dividend decision**
The finance manager analyses following factors before dividing the net earnings between dividend and retained earnings:
1. **Earning :** Dividends are paid out of current and previous year's earnings. If there are more earnings then company declares high rate of dividend whereas during low earning period the rate of dividend is also low.

2. **Stability of Earnings :** Companies having stable or smooth earnings prefer to give high rate of dividend whereas companies with unstable earnings prefer to give low rate of dividend.

3. **Cash Flow Position :** Dividends involve outflow of cash. So, sometime it is possible that P & L a/c show high profit but the company falls short of cash. Company declare high rate only when they have surplus cash and vice-versa.

4. **Growth Opportunities :** Retained earnings are cheaper source as they do not involve floatation cost and any legal formalities. So, companies that have high growth opportunities retain more earnings to capitalize these opportunities. In case of lack of growth opportunities, companies prefer to pay a much higher proportion of their earnings as dividend.

5. **Stability of Dividend :** The stable dividend policy satisfies the investor. Usually the companies have a policy of stabilizing dividend per share. However, when a company is confident that its earnings potential has increased it may also increase the dividend per share. All other things being same, stable dividend may have a positive impact on market price of the share.

6. **Preference of Shareholders :** Shareholders are owners of company. The preferences of the shareholders is given due consideration while declaring dividends. There may be some shareholders who want atleast a certain amount to be paid as dividend (eg. Institutional investors) while some demand a regular income from their investments. (eg. Retired and old persons)

7. **Taxation Policy :** The rate of dividend also depends upon the taxation policy of government. Under present taxation system dividend income is tax free income for shareholders whereas company has to pay tax on dividend given to shareholders. If tax rate is higher, then company prefers to pay less in the form of dividend whereas if tax rate is low then company may declare higher dividend.

8. **Access to Capital Market Consideration :** Whenever company requires more capital it can either arrange it by issue of shares or debentures in the stock market or by using its retained earnings. Raising of funds from the capital market depends upon the reputation of the company. If capital market can easily be accessed or approached and there is enough demand for securities of the company then company can give more dividend and raise capital by approaching capital market, but if it is difficult for company to approach and access capital market then companies declare low rate of dividend and use reserves or retained earnings for reinvestment.

9. **Legal Restrictions :** The provisions of the companies act regarding payment of dividends must be considered while declaring dividends. Legal rules act as boundaries within which a company can operate in terms of paying dividends.

   Such as dividends can be paid only out of current year profit or past year profit after providing depreciation fund. In case company is not earning profit then it cannot declare dividend.

10. **Stock Market Reaction :** Dividend and the market value of the shares are directly related. It means that if the dividend is declared at a higher rate, it is considered to be good news. As a result, the price of the shares increases, Similarly, decrease in the dividend decreases the market price of the shares. Therefore, a finance manager should always keep in mind the effect on the market price of shares while determining the rate of dividend. (Note: Every company wishes that the market value of its shares should not fall.)

11. **Contractual Constraints :** Sometimes while providing loan to a company, the lender may place certain restrictions on the payment of dividends. Therefore, the company should ensure that the payment of dividend is according to the terms of the contract.

☞ **Financial Planning**

Financial planning essentially involves preparing a financial blue print of an oganisation's future business operations. Thus financial planning is defined as follows:

"Financial planning means estimating the funds requirement of a business and determining the sources of funds for current and fixed assets and future expansion prospects"

☞ **Process of Financial Planning**

1. **Determination of total capital requirement :** The financial planning begins with determination of total capital requirement. For this the finance managers do the sales forecast and if the future prospects appear to be bright and expect increase in sale, then firm needs to increase its production capacity which means more requirement of long term funds. Higher level of production and increase in sales will require higher fixed as well as working capital.

2. **Determination of sources of funds :** After estimating the requirement of funds the next step of financial planning is deciding how to raise this finance. Finance may be internally generated by the business or capital may have to be raised from external sources such as equity shares, preference shares, debentures, loans etc.

3. **Determination of suitable policies for proper utilisation :** Financial planning is broader in scope as it does not end by raising estimated finance. It includes long term investment decision. In financial planning finance manager analyze various investment plans and select the most appropriate. Finance manager make short term financial called budgets.

☞ **Objectives of Financial Planning**

Financial planning is done to achieve the following two objectives:

1. **To ensure Availability of Funds Whenever These are Required :** The main objective of financial planning is that sufficient fund should be available in the company for different purposes such as for purchase of long term assets, to meet day-to-day expenses etc. It ensures timely availability of finance. Along with availability financial planning also tries to specify the sources of finance.

2. **To See that Firm does not Raise Resources Unnecessarily :** Excess funding is as bad as inadequate or shortage of funds. If there is surplus money, financial planning must invest it in the best possible manner as keeping financial resources idle is a great loss for an organisation.

   Financial Planning includes both short term as well as the long term planning. Long term planning focuses on capital expenditure plan whereas short term financial plans are called budgets. Budgets include detailed plan of action for a period of one year or less.

☞ **Importance of Financial Planning**

Sound financial planning is essential for success of any business enterprise. Its need is felt because of the following reasons:

1. **It Facilitates Collection of Optimum Funds :** The financial planning estimates the precise requirement of funds which means to avoid wastage and over-capitalization situation.

2. **It Helps in Fixing the Most Appropriate Capital Structure:** Funds can be arranged from various sources and are used for long term, medium term and short term. Financial planning is necessary for tapping appropriate sources at appropriate time as long term funds are generally contributed by shareholders and debenture holders, medium term by financial institutions and short term by commercial banks.

3. **Helps in Investing Finance in Right Projects:** Financial plan suggests how the funds are to be allocated for various purposes by comparing various investment proposals.

4. **Helps in Operational Activities :** The success or failure of production and distribution function of business depends upon the financial decisions as right decision ensures smooth flow of finance and smooth operation of production and distribution.

5. **Base for Financial Control:** Financial planning acts as basis for checking the financial activities by comparing the actual revenue with estimated revenue and actual cost with estimated cost.

6. **Helps in Avoiding Business Shocks and Surprises :** By anticipating the financial requirements financial planning helps to avoid shock or surprises which otherwise firms have to face in uncertain situations.

7. **Link Between Investment and Financing Decisions :** Financial planning helps in deciding debt/equity ratio and by deciding where to invest this fund. It creates a link between both the decisions.

8. **It Links Present with Future :** Financial planning relates present financial requirement with future requirement by anticipating the sales and growth plans of the company.

☞ **Capital Structure**
Meaning :
    "Capital structure means the proportion of debt and equity used for financing the operations of business."

$$\text{Capital Structure} = \frac{\text{Debt}}{\text{Equity}}$$

In other words, capitals structure represents the proportion of debt capital and equity capital in the capital structure. What kind of capital structure is best for a firm is very difficult to define. The capital structure should be such which increases the value of equity share or maximises the wealth of equity shareholders. Debt and equity differ in cost and risk. As debt involve less cost but it is very risky securities whereas equity are expensive securities but these are safe securities from companies point of view.

Debt is risky because payment of regular interest on debt is a legal obligation of the business. In case they fail to pay debt security holders can claim over the assets of the company and if firm fails to meet return of principal amount it can even go to liquidation and stage of insolvency.

Equity securities are safe securities from company's point of view as company has no legal obligation to pay dividend to equity shareholders if it is running in loss but these are expensive securities.

Capital structure of the business affects the profitability and financial risk. A best capital structure is the one which results in maximising the value of equity shareholder or which brings rise in the price of equity shares.

    "Generally companies use the concept of financial leverage to set up capital structure."
Financial Leverage :
        "Financial leverage refers to proportion of debt in the overall capital."

$$\text{Financial Leverage} = \frac{D}{E} \qquad \text{Where, } D = \text{Debt} \qquad E = \text{Equity}$$

With debt fund companies funds and earnings increase because debt is cheaper source of finance but it is very risky to involve more debt in capital structure. More debt will result in increase in earning only when return on investment should be more than rate of interest on debt. In such cases company employ more of cheaper debt to enchance the EPS. Such practice is called Trading on equity.

"Trading on equity refers to the increase in profit earned by the equity shareholders due to the presence of fixed financial charges like interest."

Lets take following example.
Comparative statement of two companies showing EBIT EPS analysis is given as below :

Company P Ltd.

Total funds used Rs. 60 Lakh Interest Rate 10% p.a.
Tax Rate 30%
EBIT Rs. 8 Lakh

$$ROI = \frac{800000}{600000} \times 100 = 13.33\%$$

Debt:
Situation I – Nill
Situation II Rs. 20 Lakh
Situation III – Rs. 30 Lakh

13.3%   >   10%

EBIT – EPS Analysis (Return on Investment > Rate of Interest)			
Particular	Situation – I	Situation – II	Situation – III
Share Capital (Equity Share of Rs. 10 each)	60,00,000	40,00,000	30,00,000
Debentures	Nil	20,00,000	30,00,000
EBIT	8,00,000	8,00,000	8,00,000
Interest (-)	Nil	2,00,000	3,00,000
EBT	8,00,000	6,00,000	5,00,000
Tax (-)	2,40,000	1,80,000	1,50,000
EAT	5,60,000	4,20,000	3,50,000
No. of Shares of Rs. 10	6,00,000	4,00,000	3,00,000
EPS	**0.93**	**1.05**	**1.16**

For the Company Q Ltd., all the details are same except the EBIT - Rs. 4,00,000

$$ROI = \frac{400000}{600000} \times 100 = 6.67\%$$

6.67%   <   10%

EBIT – EPS Analysis (Return on Investment < Rate of Interest)			
Particular	Situation – I	Situation – II	Situation – III
Share Capital (Equity Share of Rs. 10 each)	60,00,000	40,00,000	30,00,000
Debentures	Nil	20,00,000	30,00,000
EBIT	4,00,000	4,00,000	4,00,000
Interest (-)	Nil	2,00,000	3,00,000
EBT	4,00,000	2,00,000	1,00,000
Tax (-)	1,20,000	60,000	30,000
EAT	2,80,000	1,40,000	70,000
No. of Shares of Rs. 10	6,00,000	4,00,000	3,00,000
EPS	0.47	0.35	0.23

Conclusion : Hence proved that in case Return on Investment is less than rate of interest the equity shareholder get less earning when debt is included in the capital structure.

Factor affecting the choice of capital structure.

1. **Cash flow Statement:** Before raising debt, a company is required to consider its cash flow position. A company must have enough cash at its disposal to carry out its daily operations, for investing in fixed assets and for the payment of interest and repayment of principle. Companies expecting a larger and stable cash inflow in future can employ a large amount of debt in their capital structure.

2. **Interest Coverage Ratio (ICR):** It refers to number of time companies earning before interest and taxes (EBIT) cover the interest payment obligation.

$$ICR = \frac{EBIT}{Interest}$$

High ICR means companies can have more of borrowed fund securities whereas lower ICR means less borrowed fund securities.

3. **Debt service coverage ratio (DSCR):** Debt service coverage ratio (DSCR) is one step further from ICR. While ICR deals only with interest payment obligation, DSCR deals with obligation of paying debt instalment too besides interest payment obligation. DSCR also takes into account payment obligation of dividend on preference shares if planned to be issued. Thus,

$$DSCR = \frac{Profit\ after\ tax + Depreciation + Interest + Non\ Cash\ Exp.\ written\ off}{Preference\ Dividend + Interest + Repayment\ obligation}$$

If DSCR is high then company can have more debt in capital structure as high DSCR indicates ability of company to repay its debt but if DSCR is less then company must avoid debt and depend upon equity capital only.

4. **Return on Investment:** Return on investment is another crucial factor which helps in deciding the capital structure. If return on investment is more than rate of interest then company must prefer debt in its capital structure whereas if return on investment is less than rate of interest to be paid

on debt, then company should avoid debt and rely on equity capital. This point is explained earlier also in financial gearing by giving examples.

5. **Cost of Debt:** If firm can arrange borrowed fund at low rate of interest then it will prefer more of debt as compared to equity.

6. **Tax Rate:** High tax rate makes debt cheaper. The rate of tax affects the cost of debt. If the rate of tax is high the cost of debt decrease. The reason is the deduction of interest on the debt capital from the profits considering it a part of expenses and a saving in taxes.

For example, suppose a company takes a ban of Rs. 100 and the rate of interest on this debt is 10% and the rate of tax is 30%. By deducting Rs. 10/- from the EBIT a saving of Rs. 3/- in tax will take place (if Rs. 10 on account of interest are not deducted, a tax of Rs. 3/- @ 30% shall have to be paid). On the one hand, an interest of Rs, 10/- has been paid and on the other hand Rs. 3/- have been saved. Thus, the real cost of the debt is not 10% but only 7%. Similarly, if the rate of tax is 40%, the real cost of debt would be 6%,

7. **Cost of Equity :** Another factor which helps in deciding capital structure is cost of equity. Owners or equity shareholders expect a return on their investment i.e., earning per share. As far as debt is increasing earning per share (EPS), then we can include it in capital structure but when EPS starts decreasing with inclusion of debt then we must depend upon equity share capital only.

8. **Flexibility :** Excess of debt may restrict the firm's capacity to borrow further To maintain flexibility it must maintain some borrowing power to take care of unforeseen circumstances.

9. **Floatation Costs :** Floatation costs are those expenses which are incurred while issuing securities (e.g., equity shares, preference shares, debentures, etc.). These include commission of underwriters, brokerage, stationery expenses, etc. Issue of shares, debentures requires more formalities as well as more flotation cost. Whereas there is less cost involved in raising capital by loans or advances.

10. **Risk Consideration :** Financial risk refers to a position which a company is unable to meet its fixed financial charges such as interest, preference dividend, payment to creditors etc. Apart from financial risk business has some operating risk also. It depends upon operating cost, higher operating cost means higher business risk. The total risk depends upon both financial as well as business risk. If firm's business risk is low then it can raise more capital by issue of debt securities whereas at the time of high business risk it should depend upon equity.

11. **Control:** Debt normally does not cause a dilution of control. A public issue of equity may reduce the management's holding in the company as there is threat of takeover also.

12. **Regulatory Framework :** A company has to operate in the framework provided by law. The Companies Act and the Securities and Exchange Board of India (SEBI) provide guidelines from time to time regarding raising of funds from the public.

13. **Stock Market Condition :** If the stock markets are bullish, equity shares can be easily issued even at higher price. However, during a bearish phase, a company may find it difficult to raise equity capital and hence it may opt for debt.

14. **Capital Structure of other Companies :** Some companies frame their capital structure according to Industrial norms But proper care must be taken as blindly following Industrial norms may lead to financial risk. If firm cannot afford high risk it should not raise more debt only because other firms are raising.

☞ **Meaning (Fixed Capital)**
   "Fixed capital refers to that capital which is used for the purchase of fixed assets, such as land, building, machinery, furniture etc."

Factors Affecting Requirement of Fixed Capital:

1. **Nature of Business :** The type of business Co. is involved in is the first factor which helps in deciding the requirement of fixed capital. A manufacturing company needs more fixed capital as compared to a trading, as trading company does not need plant, machinery etc.

2. **Scale of Operation :** The companies which are operating at large scale require more fixed capital as they need more machineries and other assets whereas small scale enterprises need less amount of fixed capital.

3. **Technique of Production :** Companies using capital-intensive techniques require more fixed capital whereas companies using labour-intensive require less capital because capital-intensive techniques make use of plant and machinery and company needs more fixed capital to buy plants and machinery.

4. **Technology Upgradation :** Industries in which technology up gradation is fast need more amount of fixed capital as when new technology is invented old machines become obsolete and they need to buy new plants and machinery whereas companies where technological upgradation is slow they require less fixed capital as they can manage with old machines.

5. **Growth Prospects :** Companies which are expanding and have higher growth plan require more fixed capital as to expand they need to expand their production capacity and to expand product on capacity companies need more plant and machinery so more fixed capital.

6. **Diversification :** Companies which have plan to diversify their activities by including more range of products require more fixed capital as to produce more products they require more plants and machineries which means fixed capital.

7. **Availability of Finance and Leasing Facility :** If companies can arrange financial and leasing facilities easily then they require less fixed capital as they can acquire assets on easy installments instead of paying huge amount at one time. On the other hand if easy loan and leasing facilities are not available then more fixed capital is needed as companies will have to buy plant and machinery by paying huge amount together.

8. **Level of Collaboration/Joint Ventures :** If companies are preferring collaborations, joint venture then companies will need less fixed capital as they can share plant and machinery with their collaborators but if company prefers to operate as independent unit then there is more requirement of fixed capital

☞ **Meaning of Working Capital**
"Working Capital means the portion of capital investment in short-term assets (or current assets) of a firm."

Types of Working Capital

(i) **Gross Working Capital : "This refers to the investment in all the current assets such as cash, bills receivables, prepaid expenses, inventories etc."** These current assets get converted into cash within an accounting year.

Examples of current assets in order of liquidity are:

Cash in Hand/cash at Bank	Debtors
Marketable securities	Finished goods inventory
Bills Receivable	Work in progress
Raw Materials	
Prepaid Expense	

(ii) **Net Working Capital/Working of Capital :** "This refers to excess of current assets over current liabilities "Current liabilities are to be paid within an accounting year e g bills payable creditors etc Current Liabilities are sources of funds acquiring current assets. Suppose company gets credit for maintaining stock then stock which is current asset gets created with the credit purchase which is current liability.

The net working capital can be negative also, when current liabilities exceed current assets. The net working capital indicates the liquidity position of the company. The positive net working capital implies positive liquidity position whereas negative networking capital indicates weak and poor liquidity position.

Factors Affecting the Working Capital

1. **Length of Operating Cycle :** The amount of working capital directly depends upon the length of operating cycle. Operating cycle refers to time period involved in production. It starts right from acquisition of raw material and ends till payment is received after sale. The working capital is very important for the smooth flow of operating cycle. If operating cycle is long then more working capital is required whereas for companies having short operating cycle, the working capital requirement is less.

2. **Nature of Business :** The type of business, firm is involved in, is the next consideration while deciding the working capital. In case of trading concern or retail shop the requirement of working capital is less because length of operating cycle is small. The wholesalers as compared to retail shop require more working capital as they have to maintain large stock and generally sell goods on credit which increases the length of operating cycle. The manufacturing company require huge amount of working capital because they have to convert raw material into finished goods, sell on credit, maintain the inventory of raw material as well as finished goods.

3. **Scale of Operation :** The firms operating at large scale need to maintain more inventory, debtors etc. So they generally require large working capital whereas firms operating at small scale require less working capital.

4. **Business Cycle Fluctuation :** During boom period the market is flourishing so more demand, more production, more stock, more debtor which means more amount of working capital is required. Whereas during depression period low demand less inventories to be maintained, less debtors, so less working capital will be required.

5. **Seasonal Factors :** The working capital requirement is constant for the companies which are selling goods throughout the season whereas the companies which are selling seasonal goods require huge amount during season as more demand, more stock has to be maintained and fast supply is needed whereas during off season or slack season demand is very low so less working capital is needed.

6. **Technique of Production :** If a company is using labour intensive technique of production then more working capital is required because company need to maintain enough cash flow for making payments to labour whereas if company is using machine-intensive technique of production then less working capital is required because investment in machinery is fixed capital requirement and there will be less operative expenses.

7. **Credit Allowed :** Credit policy refers to average period for collection of sale proceeds. It depends on number of factors such as creditworthiness, of clients, industry norms etc. If company is following liberal credit policy then it will require more working capital whereas if company is following strict or short term credit policy, then it can manage with less working capital also.

8. **Credit Avail :** Another factor related to credit policy is how much and for how long period company is getting credit from its suppliers. If suppliers of raw materials are giving long term credit then company can manage with less amount of working capital whereas if suppliers are giving only short period credit then company will require more working capital to make payments to creditors.

9. **Operating Efficiency :** The firm having high degree of operating efficiency requires less amount of working capital as compared to firm having low degree of efficiency which require more working capital Firms with high degree of efficiency have low wastage and can manage with low level of inventory also and during operating cycle also these firms bear less expenses so they can manage with less working capital also.

10. **Availability of Raw Materials :** If raw materials are easily available and there is ready supply of raw materials and inputs then firms can manage with less amount of working capital also as they reed not maintain any stock of raw materials or they can manage with very less stock. Whereas if the supply of raw materials is not smooth then firms need to maintain large inventory to carry on operating c ,e smoothly. So they require more working capital.

11. **Level of Competition :** If the market is competitive then company will have to adopt liberal credit policy and to supply goods on time. Higher inventories have to be maintained so more working capital is required. A business with less competition or with monopoly position will requires less working capital as i can dictate terms according to its own requirements

12. **Inflation :** If there is increase or rise in price then the price of raw materials and cost of labour will rise t will result in an increase in working capital requirement.

But if company is able to increase the price of its own goods as well, then there will be less problem of working capital. The effect of rise in price on working will be different for different businessman.

13. **Growth Prospectus :** Firms planning to expand their activities will require more amount of working capital as for expansion they need to increase scale of production which means more raw materials, more inputs etc. so more working capital also.

EXERCISE – 1

Q.1   What is the primary aim of financial management?

Or

Sate the objective of Financial Management.

Q.2   Define Financial Management.

Q.3   Name the financial decision which will help a businessman in opening a new branch of its business.

Q.4   Name the financial decision which affects the liquidity as well as profitability of a business.

Q.5   Why are capital budgeting decisions crucial for any business?

Q.6   It refers to investement in long-term assets. Mention this type of capital.

Q.7   How should fixed assets be financed?

Q.8   Fixed assets should never be financed though short-term sources. Do you agree?

Q.9   What does trading on equity refer to?

Q.10   "Cost of debt" is lower than the cost of "Equity share capital". Give reason why even then a company cannot work only with the debt.

EXERCISE - 2

Q.1   Explain the term 'Financial Management'. Briefly explain any three of its objectives.

Or

What is meant by 'Financial Management'? State the primary objective of Financial Management.

Or

What are the main objectives of financial management? Briefly explain.

Q.2   What is meant by 'financial management'? Explain any three decisions involved in financial management.

Or

There are three major decisions which an organisation has to take in respect of financial management. Enumerate and explain in brief, these decisions.

Or

Every manager has to take three major decisions while performing the finance function. Explain them.

Or

Enumerate any three important decisions taken in financial management.

Or

What is meant by financial management? State any two financial decisions taken by a financial manager.

Or

Financial management is based on three broad financial decisions. What are these?

Q.3   What is meant by 'Financing Decision' 9 State any four factors affecting the financing decision.

Or

Explain the following as factors affecting financing decision:
(i)   Cost
(ii)   Cash flow position of business
(iii)   Level of fixed operating cost
(iv)   Control considerations

Q.4   What is capital budgeting? Describe any two important features of capital budgeting.

Q.5   Explaing factors affecting capital budgeting decisions.

Q.6   Explain the meaning of Working Capital. Briefly explain any four factors that determine the working capital of a company.

Or

Explain briefly any five factors to be considered at the time of determining working capital requirement.

EXERCISE - 3

Q,1   What is capital budgeting ? Explain in brief, the various steps involved in the process of capital budgeting.

Q.2   Why is management of fixed capital (or capital budgeting decisions) important/necessary?

Q.3   Explain the meaning of Fixed Capital. Briefly explain any four factors that determine the fixed capital of a company.

Or

Explain the factors affecting requirements of fixed capital of a business

Q.4   What is meant by capital structure? What are the factors to be kept in mind while determining the capital structure of a company?

Q.5   What is meant by Dividend decision ? State any four factors affecting the dividend decision.

Or

Identify the financial decision which determines the amount of profit earned to be distributed ad to be retained in the business. Explain any four factors affecting this decision.

Q.6   What is financial planning? Explain in brief, the role of financial planning in the management of finance.

Or

Sound Financial planning is essential for the success of any business enterprise. Explain this statement by giving any six reasons.

FINANCIAL MARKET

CONTENT

☞ **Financial Market :**
Functions of Financial Market:
1. Mobilization of Savings and Chennellising them into Most Productive Use
2. Facilitate Price Discovery
3. Provide Liquidity to Financial Assets
4. Reduce the Cost of Transaction

☞ **Money Market :**
Instrument of Money Market:
1. Call Money
2. Treasury Bills (Ti - Bills)
3. Commercial Bills
4. Commercial Paper (C.P.)
5. Certificate of Deposits (C.D.)

☞ **Capital Market :**
Features of Capital Market:
1. Link between savers and investment opportunities.
2. Deals in long term investment.
3. Utilises intermediaries.
4. Determinant of capital formation.
5. Government rules and regulations

☞ **Types of Capital Market :**

Primary Market:
(a) Public issue through prospectus.
(b) Right issue.
(c) Preferential issue.
(d) Offer for sale.
(e) Private placement.
(f) e-IPOs.

Secondary Market:
(a) 22 regional stock exchanges.
(b) Two national level stock exchanges.

☞ **Functions of Stock Exchange :**
1. Economic Barometer
2. Pricing of Securities
3. Safety of Transactions
4. Contributes to Economic Growth
5. Mobilisation of Savings
6. Liquidity
7. Better Allocation of Capital
8. Promotes the Habits of Savings and Investment

☞ **Training Procedure**
1. Registration of Candidates
2. Selection of Candidates
3. Pursuing training programme
4. Evaluation of trainees
5. Issue of certificates

☞ **Depository Services**
Types of Depository Services
1. Dematerialisation
2. Rematerialisation
3. Transfer of securities
4. Settlement of trades

☞ **Benefits of Depository Services**
1. Elimination of bad delivery
2. Immediate transfer of securities
3. No need for duty stamps
4. Elimination of risks
5. Reduced transaction cost.
6. Transparency

☞ **Demat Account**
Procedure for Opening a Demat Account
1. Choosing a Depository Participant
2. Filling application form
3. Submitting application form and documents
4. Scrutiny by DP

☞ **SEBI :**
A regulatory body of stock exchange.

☞ **Functions of SEBI :**
1. Protective Functions
2. Development Functions
3. Regulatory Functions

WEIGHTAGE

Units	Very Short Answer	Short Answer I & II	Long Answer I & II	Total
Unit – 10(8)	1(2)	----	6(1)	8(3)

FINANCIAL MARKET

☞ **Meaning of Financial Market**

"Financial market is the market that directs the flow of funds into investment"
Money Market + Capital Market = Financial Market

☞ **Financial Market (Concept and Nature)**
Financial market refers to the whole network of all organisations and institutions that provide short term, medium term and long term funds. Financial markets enable the savers to invest their surplus fund and enable the borrowers to borrow funds to meet their requirements. Generally the investors are called surplus units and business enterprises are called deficit units. So financial Market transfers money supply from surplus units to deficit units. Financial market act as a link between surplus an deficit units and brings together the borrowers and lenders.

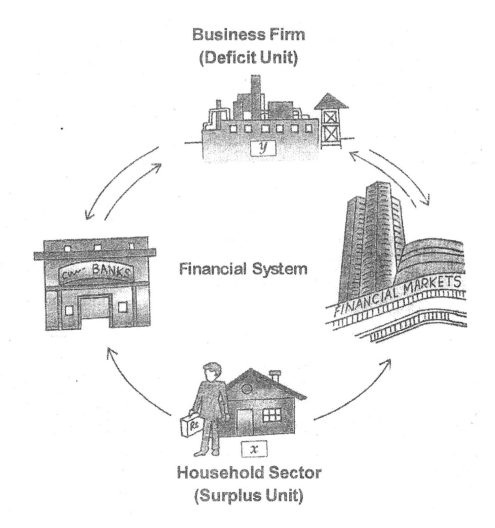

☞ **Functions of Financial Markets**

Financial markets perform following four important functions:

1. **Mobilization of Savings and Chennellising them into Most Productive Use:** Financial markets act as a link between savers and investors. Financial markets transfer savings of savers to most appropriate opportunities.

2. **Facilitate Price Discovery:** Price of anything depends upon the demand and supply factors. Demand and supply of financial assets and securities in financial markets help in deciding the prices of various financial securities.

. **Provide Liquidity to Financial Assets:** In financial markets financial securities can be bought and sold easily so financial market provide a platform to convert securities in cash.

4. **Reduce the Cost of Transaction:** Financial market provide complete information regarding price, availability and cost of various financial securities, So investors and companies do not have to spend much on getting this information as it is readily available in financial markets,

Classification of Financial Market

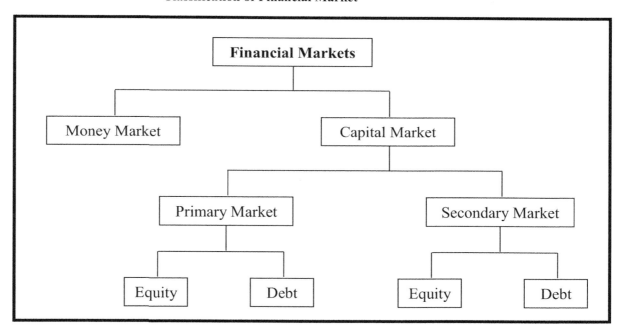

☞ **Money Market**

**"Money Market is the Market in which financial instruments
having short – term maturity period are dealt."**

Money Market is that market where transactions in Short – term securities are made. It means those securities where the payment period is upto one year. Since their Maturity period is very short, they are also called near money. These securities include chiefly Call Money, Treasury bills, commercial bills, certificates of deposits, commercial paper etc. Generally money market is the source of finance of for working capital.

✓ It has no physical location.
✓ Major participants of money market are RBI, LIC, GIG, UTI etc.
✓ Money of these institutions deals on telephone and fax only.

☞ **Instrument of Money Market**

1. **Call Money:** Call money is a method by which commercial ban borrow from each other to be able to maintain the minimum cash balance called cash reserve ratio (CRR), as required by the Reserve Bank of India.
   ✓ Call money is called interbank call money market.
   ✓ The maturity periods of call extremely short 1 to 15 days and its liquidity is just next to cash.
   ✓ The interest rate paid on call money is called call rate. It is very volatile rate. Which keeps on changing from day to day and sometimes from hour to hour.
   ✓ There is an inverse relationship between call rates and other Short – term instruments as when call rate increases the other securities become cheap such a certificate of deposit and commercial paper.

2. **Treasury Bills (T-Bills) :** Treasury Bills are issued by the Reserve Bank of India on behalf of the Central Government to meet its short term financial needs.
   ✓ The maturity period of Treasury Bills are 14 days, 91 days, 182 days or 364 days.
   ✓ These bills are generally purchased by the commercial banks, non-banking financial institutions, insurance companies, etc.
   ✓ They are negotiable instruments and so are freely transferable.

   ✓ They are issued at a price lower than its face value but it is redeemed at par. Thus the difference between issue price and face value represent interest.
   ✓ The minimum amount of T-Bills is Rs. 25,000.
   ✓ These are issued at discount that why it is also known as zero coupon bond & deep discount bond.

3. **Commercial Bills :** A commercial bill is a bill of exchange used to finance the working capital or used in credit purchase and sale.
   ✓ These are also known as Trade bills or accommodations bills drawn by one business firm on another.
   ✓ These have short term maturity period generally 90 days and can be discounted with bank even before the maturity period.
   ✓ When trade bill is accepted by a commercial bank it is known as a commercial bill.
   ✓ These are negotiable instruments and can be easily transferred.
   ✓ A trade bill is written acknowledgement of debt where drawer instruct or direct drawn to make payment within six time period.

4. **Commercial Paper (C.P.) :** Commercial paper is a short term unsecured promissory note which is issued by reputed public or public sector to raise the companies fund.
   ✓ It have maturity period ranging from 15 days to 1 year.
   ✓ It is issued at discount but redeemed at par
   ✓ Commercial bank and mutual funds are the main investor in cp.
   ✓ It is known as bridge financing because cp are used to meet the floatation cost which is used to raise long term funds.
   ✓ It was introduce in India for first time in 1990.

5. **Certificate of Deposits (C.D.) :** Certificates of Deposit (CD) are unsecured, negotiable, short term instruments in bearer from, issued by commercial banks and development financial institutions during tight liquidity. When the deposit growth of banks is slow but the demand for credit is high.
   ✓ They are issued to individual, corporation and companies.
   ✓ These help to mobilize a large amount of money for short periods.

☞ **Capital Market**

"Capital Market refers to that Market where transactions in long term securities are made".

Capital market means that market where transactions in long – term securities are made. This market offers help in meeting the long term financial needs of various sectors of economy. Transaction of securities in this market includes primarily the shares and debentures. This market encourage people to invest their small savings in productive activities. On the one hand, people earn appropriately and on the other hand, the economy develops.

☞ **Types of Capital Market**

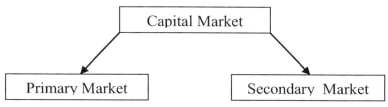

The main components of capital market are:
(A) **Primary Market.**
(B) **Secondary Market.**

(A) **Primary Market (New issue Market)**
"It refers to that Market in which securities are sold for the first time for collecting long term capital".

This market is concerned with new issues. Therefore, the primary market is also called New issue Market (NIM). Through the medium of this market both the newly established companies as well as the existing companies collect capital. In this market, the flow of funds is form savers to borrowers (industries), hence, it helps directly in the capital formation of the company. The money collected from this market is generally used by the companies to modernize the plant, machinery and building, for expanding business, and for setting up new business unit.

☞ **Methods of Floatation**
The securities may be issued in primary market by the following methods:
1. **Public Issue through Prospectus :** Under this method company issues a prospectus to inform and attract general public. In prospectus company provides details about the purpose for which funds are being raised, past financial performance of the company, background and future prospectus of company. The information in the prospectus helps the public to know about the risk and earning potential of the company and accordingly they decide whether to invest or not in that company. Through IPO company can approach large number of persons and can approach public at large. Sometimes companies involve intermediaries such as bankers, brokers and underwriters to raise capital from general public.

2. **Offer for Sale :** Under this method new securities are offered to general public but not directly by the company but by an intermediary who buys whole lot of securities from the company. Generally the intermediaries are the firms of brokers. So sale of securities takes place in two steps : first when the company issues securities to the intermediary at face value and second when

intermediaries issue securities to general public at higher price to earn profit. Under this method company is saved from formalities and complexities of issuing securities directly to public.

3. **Private Placement :** Under this method the securities are sold by the company to an intermediary at a fixed price and in second step intermediaries sell these securities not to general public but to selected clients at higher price. The issuing company issues prospectus to give details about is objectives, future prospectus so that reputed clients prefer to buy the security from intermediary. Under this method the intermediaries issue securities to selected clients such as UTI, LIC, General Insurance etc.

   The private placement method is a cost saving method as company is saved from the expenses of underwriter fees, manager fees, agent's commission, listing of company's name in stock exchange etc. Small and new companies prefer private placement as they cannot afford to raise from public issue.

4. **Right Issue (For Existing Companies) :** This is the issue of new shares to existing shareholders. It is called right issue because it is the pre-emptive right to shareholders that company must offer them the new issue before subscribing to outsiders. Each shareholder has the right to subscribe to the new shares in the proportion of shares he already holds. A right issue is mandatory for companies under Companies Act, 1956. The stock exchange does not allow the existing companies to go for new issue without giving pre-emptive rights to existing shareholders because if new issues to new subscribers then the existing equity shareholders may lose their share in capital and control of company i.e., it would water their equity. To stop this the pre-emptive or right issue is compulsory for existing company.

5. **e-IPOs :** It is the new method of issuing securities through on line system of stock exchange. In this company has to appoint registered brokers for the purpose of accepting applications and placing orders. The company issuing security has to apply for listing of its securities on any exchange other than the exchange it has offered its securities earlier. The manager coordinates the activities through various intermediaries connected with the issue.

(B) **Secondary Market**

**The secondary market is the market for the sale and purchase of
previously issued or second hand securities.**

In secondary market securities are not directly issued by the company to investors, the securities are sold by existing investors to other investors. Sometimes the investor is in need of cash and another investor wants to buy the shares of the company as he could not get directly from company. The both the investors can meet in secondary market and exchange securities for cash through intermediary called broker, In secondary market companies get no additional capital as securities are bought and sold between investors only so directly there is no capital formation but secondary market indirectly contributes in capital formation by providing liquidity to securities of the company. If there is no secondary market then investors could get back their investment only after redemption period is over or when company gets dissolved which means investment will be blocked for a long period of time but with the presence of secondary market, the investors can convert their securities into cash whenever they want and it also gives chance to investors to make profit as securities are bought and sold at market price which is generally more than the original price of the securities. This liquidity offered by secondary market encourages even those investors to invest in securities who want to invest for small period of time as there is option of selling securities at their convenience.

☞ **Stock Exchange**

Stock exchange is a platform where dealing take place in shares, debentures and bonds issued by the private sector companies, public enterprises, government, etc. Such shares, debentures and bonds are called securities. Only those securities could be traded that are included in the official list of stock exchange. The Securities Contracts (Regulations) Act, 1956 has defined stock exchange as an association, organisation or body of individuals, whether incorporated or not, established for the purpose of assisting, regulating and controlling business in buying, selling and dealing in securities.

Stock exchange is also called stock market or securities market.

Every stock exchange has a specific location. In India there are 24 recognized stock exchanges. These are in following locations:

S. No.		S. No.		S. No.	
1	Ahemdabad	9	Guwahati	17	Mumbai
2	Bangalore	10	Hyderabad	18	NSEI
3	Bhubaneshwar	11	Indore	19	OTCEI
4	Cheenai	12	Jaipur	20	Patna
5	Cochin	13	Kanpur	21	Pune
6	Coimbatore	4	Kolkata	22	Rajkot
7	Cuttack	15	Ludhiana	23	Sikkim
8	Delhi	16	Mangalore	24	Vadodara

Out of these stock exchanges NSEI and OTCEI are all India level stock exchanges and from business point of view Mumbai Stock Exchange is at No.1 followed by Kolkata and Delhi. The Mumbai Stock Exchange is popularly known as Dalal Street and Kolkata is popular as Lyons Range.

☞ **Functions of Stock Exchange/Secondary Market**

1. **Economic Barometer** : A stock exchange is a reliable barometer to measure the economic condition of a country. Every major change in country and economy is reflected in the prices of shares. The rise or fall in the share prices indicates the boom or recession cycle of the economy. Stock exchange is also known as a pulse of economy or economic mirror which reflects the economic conditions of a country.

2. **Pricing of Securities** : The stock market helps to value the securities on the basis of demand and supply factors. The securities of profitable and growth oriented companies are valued higher as there is more demand for such securities. The valuation of securities is useful for investors, government and creditors. The investors can know the value of their investment, the creditors can value the creditworthiness and government can improve taxes on value of securities.

3. **Safety of Transactions** : In stock market only the listed securities are traded and stock exchange authorities include the companies names in the trade list only after verifying the soundness of company. The companies which are listed they also have to operate within the strict rules and regulations. This ensures safety of dealing through stock exchange.

4. **Contributes to Economic Growth** : A stock exchange is a market in which existing securities are bought and sold. Through this process of reinvestment and disinvestment, saving get chennelized into their most productive investment use. This leads to capital formation and economic growth.

   If there would have been no stock exchanges, there would be low savings of the community, which means low investment and lower development of the country.

5. **Mobilisation of Savings** : Stock exchange helps in mobilisation of surplus funds of individuals, business firms and cooperatives for investment in popular securities, The procedure for purchasing securities through the stock exchange is simple. The stock brokers are always ready to help their clients with their specialised services.

6. **Liquidity :** The main function of stock market is to provide ready market for sale and purchase of securities. The presence of stock exchange market gives assurance to investors that their investment can be converted into cash whenever they want. The investors can invest in long term investment projects without any hesitation, as because of stock exchange they can convert long term investment into short term and medium term.

7. **Better Allocation of Capital :** The shares of profit making companies are quoted at higher prices and are actively traded so such companies can easily raise fresh capital from stock market. The general public hesitates to invest in securities of loss making companies. So stock exchange facilitates allocation of investor's fund to profitable channels.

6. **Promotes the Habits of Savings and Investment :** The stock market offers attractive opportunities of investment in various securities. These attractive opportunities encourage people to save more and invest in securities of corporate sector rather than investing in unproductive assets such as gold, silver etc.

Difference between Capital Market and Money Market

Basis	Capital Market	Money Market
1.Participants	The participants in capital market are financial institutions, bank, public and private companies, foreign investors and ordinary retail investor a from public.	The participants of money market are financial institutions, bank, public and private companies but foreign and ordinary retail investors do not participate in money market.
2. Duration	The capital market deals in medium and long term securities.	Money market deals with short term securities having maximum tenure of 1 year.
3. Instruments	The common instruments of capital market are equity shares, debentures, preference shares, bonds and other innovative securities.	The common instruments of money market are treasury bills, trade bills, CD, CP etc.
4. Investment outlay	The investment in capital market does not require huge financial investment as the value of securities is generally low i.e., Rs. 10 to Rs.100.	The instruments of money market are quite expensive so huge financial investment is required.
5. Liquidity	Capital market securities are considered liquid because of stock exchange but compared to money market instruments these are less liquid.	Money market securities enjoy higher degree of liquidity.
6. Safety	The instruments of capital market are riskier in respect to returns as well as in respect to principal repayment as issuing company may fail.	The instruments of money market are safe or less risky due to short duration and soundness of issues.
7. Expected Return	The expected return is higher in capital market as along with regular dividend or interest there are chances of gain.	The expected return of money market is less due to short duration.
8. Type of Capital	Companies approach capital market for fixed capital requirement	Companies approach money market for working capital requirement.

Difference between Primary Market and Secondary Market

S. No.	Primary Market	Secondary Market
1.	There is sale of new securities.	It is the market for existing or second hand securities.
2.	In primary market securities are directly issued by companies.	Securities are transferred between investors only.
3.	Primary market contributes directly for capital formation as funds are transferred from surplus units to deficit units.	Secondary market contributes indirectly for capital formation as funds are exchanged between surplus units only.
4.	All companies enter the primary market to raise capital for their operations.	Only listed companies' securities are bought and sold in secondary market.
5.	There is no fixed geographical area for primary market. All the institutions, banks, foreign investors etc. constitute primary market.	There is a fixed geographical area and working hours.
6.	Prices of securities are fixed by the management of the company.	Prices of securities are fixed by the demand and supply factors of stock exchange market.

☞ **Trading Procedure**

Trading procedure of stock exchanges is as follows:

1. **Selection of broker:** The first step is to select a broker who will buy/sell securities on behalf of the investor. This is necessary because trading of securities can only be done through SEBI registered brokers who are the members of a stock exchange. Brokers may be individual, partnership firms or corporate bodies.

   The broker charges brokerage/commission for his services.

2. **Opening demat account :** The next step is to open a Demat (Dematerialised) account with the depository participant. In the demat account securities are held electronically.

   These securities are hold in the electronic form by a depository. At present there are two depositaries in India NSDL (National Securities Depositing Ltd.) and CDSL (Central Depository Services Ltd.).

3. **Selection of securities and placing the order :** After opening demat account a person will engage him for buying or selling certain securities. Before placing an order, he can consult his friends and the broker. The order can be communicated to the broker either personally or through telephone, cell phone, e-mail or online link. The instructions should specify the name of securities to be bought or sold and price range with in which the order is to be executed.

4. **Executing the order :** According to the instructions of the investor, the broker buys or sells securities. The broker then issues a contract note. A copy of the contract note is sent to the client. The contract note contains the name and the price of the securities, names of the parties, brokerage charged. It is signed by the broker.

5. **Settlement :** This is the last stage in the trading of securities done by the brokers on behalf of their clients. The mode of settlement depends upon the nature of the contract.

   Equity spot market follow a T+2 rolling settlement. This means that any trade taking place on Monday, gets settled by Wednesday. All trading on stock exchanges takes place between 9:55 am and 3:30 pm. Indian Standard Time, Monday to Friday. Delivery of shares must be made in dematerialized form, and each exchange has its own clearing house, which assumes all settlement risk.

☞ **Depositary Services**

Emergence of electronic form of transactions in financial securities (shares, debentures, bonds, etc.) has led to conversion of securities in physical form (share/debenture certificates) into electronic form. Records of securities issued by various companies in electronic form are maintained by designated institutions. These institutions are known as depositories. At present, there are two depositories in India: National Securities Depository Limited (NSDL) and Central Depository Services (India) Limited (CDSL). These depositories provide various types of services related to securities to their clients through intermediaries, known as depository participants (DPs). These services are known as depository services. Thus, depository services are defined as follows:

Depository services are those services which are provided by a depository to its clients regarding maintaining their accounts of securities in electronic form

According to The Depository Act, 1996, "Depository service means any service connected with recording of allotment of securities or transfer of ownership of securities in the record of a depository.' A depository operates through depository participants (DPs). Therefore, there is no direct interaction between clients and the depository. A DP is an entity which is registered with the depository to work on behalf of the depository as well as clients. In India, there are two categories of DPs: those DPs who provide only depository services on behalf of the depositor like Stock Holding Corporation of India Limited and those DPs who provide both depository services as well as securities transaction services. In the second category, there are many DPs.

☞ **Types of Depository Services**

There are many types of depository services which are as follows:

1. **Dematerialisation.** Dematerialisation, usually known as demat, involves converting physical certificates into electronic form.

2. **Rematerialisation.** Rernaterialisation, known as remat, is reverse of demat, that is, converting electronic securities into physical certificates.

3. **Transfer of Securities.** Transfer of securities involves change of beneficial ownership of securities.

4. **Settlement of Trades.** Settlement of trades involves keeping records of settlement of trades done on stock exchange connected to the depository.

☞ **Benefits of Depository Services**

There are various benefits of depository services which are as follows:

1. **Elimination of Bad Delivery.** In the case of settlement of securities traded on a stock exchange, bad delivery means delivery of any security which is not in proper form like difference in signature of the security holder, expiry of validity period of transfer deed, inadequacy of stamp on the transfer deed, etc. In the case of bad delivery, the concerned company refuses transfer of the concerned securities. Since there is no need of transfer deed in the case of securities in electronic form, no question of bad delivery arises.

2. **Immediate Transfer of Securities.** In electronic form, there is immediate transfer of securities by debiting the account of security seller and crediting the account of security buyer. Both the steps take place simultaneously.

3. **No Need for Duty Stamps.** In case of transfer of securities in physical form, stamps meant for this purpose are used. Sometimes, availability of such stamps is a problem. In transfer of securities in electronic form, such stamps are not required as duty payable on the transfer is charged from the buyer at the time of settling his purchase account.

4. **Elimination of Risks.** In electronic form, many types of risks associated with dealing in physical securities like loss, theft, mutilation due to careless handling, forgery, etc., are eliminated.

5. **Reduced Transaction Cost.** Trading and giving/receiving of securities in electronic form require very little human interference. Therefore, brokers, through whom transactions are done, charge much lower brokerage resulting in low transaction cost.

6. **Transparency.** In trading of securities in electronic form, there is transparency as any person can verify his transaction records easily.

☞ **Demat Account**

Demat account is defined as follows:
"Demat account is an account which an investor is required to open with a depository through its any depository participant for availing depository services."

Procedure for Opening a Demat Account
"Procedure for opening a demat account involves the following steps:
1. **Choosing a Depository Participant.** The person who wants to open a demant account must select a depository participant (DP). There are two categories of DPs: institutions which provide only depository services and share brokers who provide security trading facilities along with depository services. A demat account may be either in single name or in joint names, subject to maximum three. Depending on his requirement, the person may choose a particular type of DR For example, if the person wants to transact in securities frequently, he should opt for a share broker as this will ease his operations.

2. **Filling Application Form.** For opening the demat account, the person is required to fill an application form which is available with the DR In this application, the various details of the person are filled along with details of his bank account (name of the bank, address of the branch, type of account and account number). The form must be duly signed by the person. In the case of joint account, details and signatures of all persons are required.

3. **Submitting Application Form and Documents.** The person is required to submit duly filled application form to the DP along with copies of required documents, photograph of the applicant and account opening charges. The required documents are PAN (Permanent Account Number) card and address proof.

4. **Scrutiny by Depository Participant.** On receiving the application form and documents, the DP securities these. If all these are in order, the DP opens the demat account and advises the person accordingly.

Benefits of opening Demat Account
Benefits for opening demat account are as follows:
1. It is safe and convenient to hold securities in demat form as compared to physical form as transfer of securities is Instant.
2. Any number of securities can be transferred In one delivery. This saves lot of time.
3. There is no risk of bad delivery in the case of purchase of securities,
4. It eliminates the risk of theft and damage of securities due to any reason.
5. The holder of securities is just required to inform only to the DP about change in his address, if any, instead of informing to all companies whose securities are held.
6. In the case of issue of bonus shares, rights shares and allotment of securities, these are credited in the account of the holder immediately.
7. Banks and other financiers prefer giving loans and advances against securities held in demat account, Therefore, raising such loans and advances becomes easier.

☞ **Securities Exchange Board of India (SEBI)**

Securities Exchange Board of India (SEBI) was set up on 12th April 1988 to regulate the functions of securities market. SEBI promotes orderly and healthy development in the stock market transactions. It was left as a watch dog to observe the activities but was found ineffective in regulating and controlling them. As a result on 30th Jan. 1992, SEBI was granted legal status with a view:

(i)   To protect the interests of the investors in securities,

(ii)   To promote the activities and development of the securities market, and

(iii)   To regulate the functioning of the securities market.

Reasons for Establishment

With the growth in the dealings of stock markets, lot of malpractices also started in stock markets such as price rigging, unofficial premium on new issue, delay in delivery of shares, violation of rules and regulations of stock exchange and listing requirements. Due to these malpractices the customers started losing confidence and faith in the stock exchange. So government of India decided to set up an agency or regulatory body known as Securities Exchange Board of India (SEBI).

Purpose and Role of SEBI

SEBI was set up with the main purpose of keeping a check on malpractices and protect the interest of investors. It was set up to meet the needs of three groups.

1.   **Issuers :** For issuers it provides a market place in which they can raise finance fairly and easily.

2.   **Investors :** For investors it provides protection and supply of accurate and correct information.

3.   **Intermediaries :** For intermediaries it provides a competitive professional market.

☞ **Objectives of SEBI**

The overall objectives of SEBI are to protect the interest of investors and to promote the development of, and regulate the securities market. This may be elaborated as follows:

1.   To protect the rights and interests of investors, particularly individual investors and to guide and educate them.

2.   To prevent trading malpractices like price rigging, insider trading, making misleading statements in prospectus, etc.

3.   To regulate stock exchanges and the securities market to promote their orderly functioning.

4.   To regulate and develop a code of conduct and fair practices by intermediaries like brokers, merchant bankers, etc., with a view to make them competitive and professional.

☞ **Functions of SEBI**

The SEBI performs functions to meet its objectives. To meet three objectives SEBI has been important functions. These are:

1.   Protective Functions

2.   Development Functions

3.   Regulatory Functions.

1.   **Protective Functions :** These functions are performed by SEBI to protect the interest of investor and provide safety of Investment. As protective functions SEBI performs following functions: Following are the protective functions of SEBI.

(i)   To check unfair trade practices (such as, to supply misleading statements to cheat the investors) in connection with security market.

(ii)   To check insiders trading in securities. [Insider trading means the buying and selling of securities by those persons (Directors, Promoters, etc.) who have some secret information about the company and who wish to take advantage of this secret information.]

(iii)   To provide education relating to dealing in securities to the investors.

(iv)   To promote code of conduct relating to security market.

2.   **Development Functions :** Thee functions are performed by the SEBI to promote and develop activities in stock exchange and increase the business in stock exchange. Under development categories following functions are performed by SEBI:

(i)   SEBI promotes training of intermediaries of the securities market.

(ii)   SEBI tries to promote activities of stock exchange by adopting flexible and adoptable approach in following way:

(a) SEBI has permitted internet trading through registered stock brokers.

(b) SEBI has made underwriting optional to reduce the cost of issue.

(c) Even initial public offer of primary market is permitted through stock exchange.

3.   **Regulatory Function :** These functions are performed by SEBI to regulate the business in stock exchange. To regulate the activities of stock exchange following functions are performed:

(i)   SEBI has framed rules and regulations and a code of conduct to regulate the intermediaries such as merchant bankers, brokers, underwriters etc.

(ii)   These intermediaries have been brought under the regulatory purview and private placement has been made more restrictive.

(iii)   SEBI registers and regulates the working of stock brokers, sub-brokers, share transfer agents, trustee, merchant bankers and all those who are associated with stock exchange in any manner.

(iv)   It undertakes inspection, conduct inquiries, and audit of the stock exchanges and intermediaries in the securities market.

(v)   It takes steps to check fraudulent and unfair trade practices in the securities market. It also checks insider trading in securities.

(vi)   SEBI registers and regulates the working of collective investment schemes including mutual funds etc.

(vii) SEBI regulates takeover of the companies.

EXERCISE – 1

Q 1.   What is a financial Market?

Q 2.   What is meant by Money Market ?

Q 3.   State any two features of Money Market.

Q 4.   What is meant by Capital Market?

Q 5.   Name the market for long-term funds.
[Hint: Capital market]

Q 6.   Name the borrowers of call money?
[Hint: Banks with temporary shortage of funds.]

Q 7.   Why are Treasury Bills considered negotiable instruments?
[Hint: Treasury bills are freely transferable by endorsement and delivery.]

Q 8.   Do treasury bills carry any rate of interest?
[Hint : Treasury bills do not carry any rate of interest. In fact, they are issued at a discount.]

Q 9.   Name two methods of IPO.

Q 10.   What is other name of Primary Market?
[Hint :New Issues market.]

Q 11.   Name the market which facilitates purchase and sale of old or existing securities. [Hint: Secondary Market]

Q 12.   Give any two methods of Floatation in the Primary Market.
[Hint: (i) Private placement. (ii) Public issue.]

Q 13. Give any two objectives of SEBI.

EXERCISE - 2

Q 1. State any four features of capital market.

Q 2. State the importance of money market.

Q 3. Differentiate between primary market and secondary market.

Q 4. Differentiate between capital market and money market.

Q 5. What is meant by "Money Market"? Briefly explain the concept of 'Cell Money'.

Q 6. What is meant by 'Primary Market'? Briefly explain the concept of 'Initial Public Offer'.

Q 7. What is meant by 'Money Market'? Briefly explain the concept of 'Certificate of Deposit.'

Q 8. What is meant by 'Money Market'? Briefly explain the concept of 'Commercial papers'.

Q 9. What is meant by 'SEBI'? Briefly explain its objectives.

Q 10. Briefly explain any four regulatory functions of the SEBI.

Q 11. State any four protective functions of the Securities and Exchange Board of India.

EXERCISE - 3

Q 1. Distinguish between 'Capital Market' and 'Money Market' on the following basis:
(i) Participants
(ii) Instruments traded
(iii) Duration of securities traded
(iv) Expected return
(v) Safety.

Q 2. Explain briefly any four protective functions of the Securities and Exchange Board of India.

Q 3. Why was Securities and Exchange Board of India (SEBI) set up? Explain any four objectives of SEBI.

Q 4. State any five functions of 'Stock Exchange'.

Q 5. State any five regulatory functions of Securities and Exchange Board of India.

Q 6. Explain the following money market instruments:
(a) Commercial
(b) Call money

Q 7. Briefly explain any five methods of floating new issues in the primary market.

Q 8. What is meant by Financial Market? Explain any two functions of Financial Market.

MARKETING MANAGEMENT

CONTENT

☞ **Introduction :**

A managing various functions of marketing

☞ **Features of Marketing :**
1. Need and Want.
2. Creating a Market offering
3. Customer Value.
4. Exchange mechanism.

☞ **Objective of Marketing Management :**
1. Creation of Demand
2. Market Share
3. Goodwill
4. Profitable Sales Volume through Customer Satisfaction

☞ **Functions of Marketing :**
1. Gathering and Analysing Market Information
2. Marketing Planning
3. Product Designing and Development
4. Standardization and Grading
5. Packaging and labeling
6. Branding
7. Customer Support Services
8. Pricing of Products
9. Promotion
10. Physical Distribution
11. Transportation
12. Storage or Warehousing

☞ **Marketing Management Philosophies :**
1. Production Concept.
2. Product Concept.
3. Selling Concept.
4. Marketing Concept.
5. Societal Concept.

☞ **Elements of Marketing Mix**
1. Product
2. Price
3. Promotion
4. Place

☞ **Product**
Product Mix

1. **Branding**
   Advantages of Brand Name
   1. Helps in Product differentiation
   2. Helps in Advertising
   3. Differentiate Pricing
   4. Easy Introduction of New Product.

☞ **Advantages to Customers**
   1. Helps in Identification of Product.
   2. Ensures Quality.
   3. Status Symbol.

2. **Packaging**
   Level of Packaging
   1. Primary Package
   2. Secondary Package.
   3. Transportation Packaging.

☞ **Importance of Packaging**
   1. Rising Standard of Health and Sanitation.
   2. Self Service Outlets.
   3. Product Differentiation
   4. Innovational Opportunities.

☞ **Functions of Packaging**
   1. Products Identification.
   2. Products Protection
   3. Facilitating Use of the Product.
   4. Product Promotion.

3. **Labelling**
   Functions of Labelling
   1. Complete Description of a Product.
   2. Identification of Product.
   3. Grading of Product.
   4. Promotion of product.
   5. Legal Information.

☞ **Price**
   Factors Determining Fixation of Price Determination
   1. Product Cost.
   2. The Utility and Demand.
   3. Extent of Competition in the Market.
   4. Government and Legal Regulations.

5. Pricing Objectives.
6. Marketing Methods Used.

☞ PLACE/PHYSICAL DISTIBUTION
Physical Distribution
Channels of Distribution
Types of Channel
1. Zero Level Channel/Direct Channel.
2. Indirect Channel.

☞ **Factors Determining Choice of Channels**
1. Product Related Factor.
2. Company Related Factor.
3. Competitive Factors.
4. Market Related Factor.
5. Environment Factors

☞ **Physical Distribution**
1. Order Processing
2. Transportation
3. Warehousing
4. Inventory Control

☞ **Promotion**
Elements of Promotion Mix
1. Advertising.
2. Personal Selling.
3. Sale Promotion.
4. Public Relation.

1. **Advertising**
Features of Advertising
1. Paid Form.
2. Impersonality.
3. Identified Sponsor.

☞ **Role of Accounting**
1. Creating Demand.
2. Creating Customer Loyalty.
3. Educating Consumers.
4. Enhancing customer confidence.
5. Supporting Dealers.
6. Facilitating New Product Introduction.
7. Creating Better Organisational

☞ **Objections to Advertising or Criticism of Advertising**
1. Effect of Advertising on Values, Materialism and Life Styles.
2. Advertising Encourages Sales of Inferior and Dubious Products.
3. Advertising Confuses Rather than Helps.
4. Some Advertisements are in Bad Taste.
5. Advertisement Costs are Passed on to the Customers in the Form of Higher Price

2. **Sale Promotion**
Sale Promotion Techniques for Customers
1. Rebate.
2. Discounts.
3. Refunds.
4. Premiums or gifts/or Product combination.
5. Quantity Deals.
6. Samples.
7. Contests.
8. Instant Draws and Assigned gifts,
9. Lucky Draw.
10. Usable Benefits.
11. Full Finance @ 0%.
12. Packaged Premium.
13. Exchange Offer.

3. **Personal Selling**
Features of Personal Selling
1. Personal form of communication.
2. Develop Personal relationship.
3. Flexible tool.

☞ **Qualities of a Good Salesman**
1. Physical Qualities
2. Mental Qualities
3. Social Qualities
4. Technical Qualities
   (i) Knowledge of Company
   (ii) Knowledge of Products.
   (iii) Knowledge of Competitors.
   (iv) Knowledge of Customers
   (v) Knowledge of Selling Techniques.

☞ **Public Relation**
Role of Public Relations
1. Creating better image.
2. Winning loyalty of public.
3. Understanding Public Opinions.
4. Overcoming Misundersanding.
5. Communicating New Developments.

WEIGHTAGE

Units	Very Short Answer	Short Answer I & II	Long Answer I & II	Total
Unit – 11(14)	1(2)	3(2)	6(1)	14(5)

11. MARKETING MANAGEMENT

☞ **Meaning of Market**
What is Market?
Traditionally the term 'Market is used to refer to a place where the buyer and seller meet and conduct buying and selling activities but now a days the focus of the term 'Market' is not on the place rather it is on the meeting of buyer and seller who can meet through telephone, mail or Internet. Thus, now-a-days, "Market refers to a group of actual and potential buyers of a product or service, where a seller can approach through various means of communication and transport" It may be noted that now a seller can reach any customer anywhere anytime and similarly a customer can reach seller anywhere anytime.

The term 'Market' is also used in:

Geographical Sense	:-	Local & District Market, National & International Market.
Product Sense	:-	Wheat Market, Cotton Market, Gold & Silver Market & Share Market.
Quantity Sense	:-	Wholesale Market and Retail Market.
Nature Sense	:-	Consumer Market and Industrial Market.

☞ **Meaning of Customer**
"Customer refers to the people or organisations that seek satisfaction of their needs and wants". They buy goods or services to get their needs and wants satisfied. They are also called seekers of satisfaction. Without customer there cannot be any marketing. The customer must have need, want and demand.

Need : It refers to basic necessities of life for example, food, cloth, shelter, water etc. These things are must for survival.

Want : Want refers to what customer desires to have after fulfilling his basic needs. Customer wants to have something more than the need and then want is created. For example, need is to drink water but we want to have cold drink, juice etc.

Demand : When want is bagged by purchasing power then it gets converted into demand. A customer may want to have a coke but he will demand it only when he has money to buy it so want with the purchasing power is called demand and it is demand which is more important for marketer or sellers.

☞ **Meaning of Marketer or Seller**
Who is a Marketer?
"Marketer is a person or organization who takes more active part in the process of exchange". The marketer arranges products or services and makes them available to the customers to satisfy their needs and wants. For example, Reliance satisfies the customers' need for petroleum, fruits etc. Some marketers offer only services to customers e.g. Punjab National Bank, Life Insurance Corporation etc.

Meaning of Selling & Marketing
Usually, people consider marketing and selling as similar terms but actually both are different concepts. The scope of marketing is much wider than that of selling which is just a part of marketing function.

☞ **Meaning of Selling**
"Selling is the process which is used to satisfy the needs of the seller who attempts to sell what he has without considering buyer's needs, by undertaking aggressive promotion efforts like persuasion and pressure, in order to earn profits through increased sales volume"
1. **Focus** - Selling focuses on the needs of the seller.
2. **Starting** - Selling starts with the product.
3. **Efforts** - The seller uses selling efforts like promotion, persuasion and pressure.
4. **Bending** - The seller attempts to bend the customer according to the product.
5. **Profits** - The seller seeks profits through sales volume.
6. **Orientation** - Selling is internal oriented,
7. **End** - Selling end when goods are converted into cash.

☞ **Meaning of Marketing**
"Marketing is the process which is used to satisfy the needs of the customers through the development of those products or services which can satisfy the needs of the customers better than the competitors."
1. **Focus** - Marketing focuses on the needs of the customer or target market.
2. **Starting** - Marketing starts with the customer need.
3. **Efforts** - Marketer uses integrated marketing efforts.
4. **Bending** - The marketer bends himself according to the customer needs.
5. **Profits** - Marketer seeks profit through customer satisfaction.
6. **Orientation** - Marketing is external oriented.
7. **End** - Marketing does not end as it provide after sale services.

☞ **Features of Marketing**
1. **Needs and Wants :** Marketing involves satisfying needs and wants of the target customers and developing goods and services that satisfy such needs and wants. Needs are the basic human requirements such as food, clothing, shelter to survive, while wants are demands for specific products. Needs give rise to wants. For example, we need entertainment but may want movie or disco. Similarly, a person needs food for survival but when he/she demands Pizza or Burger, his/her need becomes a want.

2. **Creating a market offering :** A good 'market offering' is the one which is developed after analysis needs and preferences of the potential buyers. For example, offering a cell phone, with good size of memory say, 2 GB), internet, camera, etc. at a reasonable price, say, Rs. 5,000.

3. **Customer Value :** The purpose of marketing is to generate customer value at a profit. The job of a marketer, therefore, IS to add to the value of the product so that the customers prefer it in relation to the competing products and decide to purchase it.

4. **Exchange Mechanism :** The process of marketing involves exchange of goods and services for money or for something of value to them.

What can be Marketed?

Generally it is a product or a service which is marketed.

In simple words, product is something what a seller sells and buyer buys. It can be defined as "Anything that can be offered to a market a satisfy a want or a need". Product does not always refers to physical product only form marketing point of view. It may include anything that can be offered to customer for satisfaction.

A product can be

(a)   A physical product like soaps, car, TV etc.

(b)   Services like banking, insurance, transport etc.

(c)   Experiences shows, theaters, movies etc.

(d)   Places - tourist places like Kerala, Malaysia, Singapore etc.

(e)   Ideas - like "say no to drugs", "no smoking" etc.

(f)   Information service like Export and Import Procedures etc.

Difference Between Selling and Marketing

Basis	Selling	Marketing
1. Focus/Emphasis	Selling focuses on the need of seller.	Marketing focuses on the need of customer.
2. Objective	Main objective of selling is to maximise the profit and sale.	Main objective of marketing is earning optimum profit with customer satisfaction.
3. Scope	Scope of selling is limited to exchange of goods or services for some considerations.	Scope of marketing is very wide. It includes activities like creation of demand, designing of product according to demand, using promotional technique and after sale survey to find out customer satisfaction
4. Start and end	Selling starts after production and ends with the sale of product.	Marketing starts much before production and continues even after sale.
5. Efforts	Seller uses promotional techniques and some manipulative tactics also to increase the sale.	Marketeer uses integrated market strategies to capture big share in the market.
6. Supremacy	Producer is considered king pin of market.	Consumer is considered king pin of market.
7. Approach	It involves fragmented approach to sell al that is produced by hook or by crook.	It involves integrated approach to identify and satisfy customer's approach.
8. Demand	It assumes demand for the products.	Demand is created by producing product according to need of customer.

☞ **Meaning of Marketing Management**

"Marketing management is a process of managing all the marketing activities". In other words marketing management can be defined

"As a process of planning, organizing, directing and controlling of the activities which help in exchanging goods and services between the manufacturer and the consumer"

☞ **Objectives of Marketing Management**

1. **Creation of Demand :** The marketing manager always tries to create the demand not by unfair means but by analysing the needs and wants of the customers and then producing the products which satisfy the customer's need. The usefulness of the product is made known to customers in advance. These efforts help the manufacturer to create the demand.

2. **Market Share :** Every business firm wants to capture a bigger share in the market so marketing techniques adopted by marketing manager help to get a big share in the market. Various promotional methods are used to make the goods popular. These selling efforts and promotional help the firm to capture a big share in the market.

3. **Goodwill :** Every business firm wants to create a better reputation and goodwill in the market. The goodwill can be created only by selling quality products at reasonable price. The image of the firms at built by using various image building techniques such as advertising, high quality, caring for customer satisfaction, after sale service, smooth supply etc.

4. **Profitable Sales Volume Through Customer Satisfaction :** Earning profit is the primary objective of every businessman but the marketing emphasis on profitable sale only with customer's satisfaction. The marketing manager does not want to increase sale and earn profit by supplying low standard products or by using unfair techniques. The marketing managers coordinate all the basic activities of the company and these activities are coordinated to meet the demands of the customers. The modern marketing techniques begin with customer and end with customer.

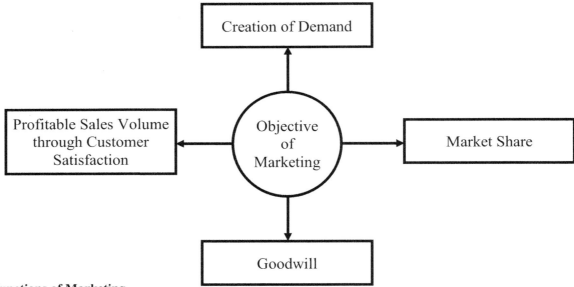

☞ **Functions of Marketing**

1. **Gathering and Analyzing Market Information :** The most important function of a marketer is to gather and analyze the market information. This is essential to find out the needs of the customers and to take various decisions regarding successful marketing of products. Marketer tries to understand what do customers want to buy and when, in what quantity and at what price? etc. He also tries to understand the motive behind this purchase i.e. whether the customer is buying the product as a necessity or for style. On the basis of all this information and analysis, the product is designed, labelled, branded, packed, promoted etc.

2. **Marketing Planning :** It involves making plans for increasing production and sales, promotion of product etc. and also laying down a course of action for achieving these objectives. For example, if a product has become popular in Punjab, the target of an organization should be to make it popular in rest of North India First, followed by remaining states. For this, proper plans are to be made.

3. **Product Designing and Development :** Another important function of marketing involves product designing and development. Product designing includes decision related to the quality standards to be used for shape or design of the product, packing, etc. in order to make the product attractive to the target customers and better than the competitor's product. For example, product designing for a color television includes shape, size, quality standard, technology etc.

4. **Standardization and Grading :** Standardization is a process of producing goods of predetermined standards so as to achieve the uniformity and consistency in products. This assures the buyers of the quality, price and packaging of the product.

   Grading refers to a process of classifying products into different groups on the basis of their features like size, shape quality etc. It is mainly done in case of agricultural products like wheat, rice, potatoes etc.

5. **Packaging and Labelling :** Packaging means designing the package for the product while labelling is concerned with putting label on the package. Packaging and labelling have been recognized as pillars of marketing. They not only provide protection to the product but also act as a promotional tool. Sometimes, the customers assess the quality of the product from its packaging. Packaging has played an important role in the success of many consumer brands like Colgate tooth paste, Taj Mahal tea, Lays potato wafers etc.

6. **Branding :** Branding is a process of giving a brand name to a product to differentiate it from competitors products, in building customer's loyalty and in promoting the product The most important decision under this strategy is whether to give a separate brand name or same brand to all products of a business firm. For example, (i) LG television, A.C. and washing machines (ii) Philips bulbs, tubes and television A.C. and washing machines.

7. **Customer Support Services :** The key to marketing success is the satisfaction of the customer. Therefore, an important function marketing i.e. to provide various customer support services like after sales service, procuring credit services, handling customer complaints, consumer information etc. These services helps in getting, keeping and growing the number of customers.

8. **Pricing of Products :** The amount of money which a customer is required to pay for purchasing the product is known as product price. Pricing has a great effect on the demand for a product. A little variation in price may increase the demand for competitor's product. Thus, while determining the price for a product, various factors like, types of customers, their income, firm's objective, product demand, competitor's policy etc should be considered.

9. **Promotion :** Promotion of product and services refers to providing information to the customers about the firm's products, their features, uses, prices etc. persuading them to buy these products. Advertising, Personal selling, Publicity and Sales Promotion are the main tools of promotion. A marketer has to decide about the promotion budget, promotion mix (i.e. combination of promotion tools) etc.

10. **Physical Distribution :** Another important function to be performed by marketer is the physical distribution of goods and services. The important decision areas under this involves selection of channel of distribution, transportation, inventory levels, storage and warehousing.

11. **Transportation :** Transportation means physical movement of goods from the place of production to the place of consumption. For example, Maruti cars are produced at Gurgaon but are available all over the country. Not only the finished goods are to be transported but also the raw material needs to be transported. A business firm analyses its transportation needs on the basis of factors like nature of the product, cost, location of the target market etc. and then take decisions regarding mode of transportation and other related aspects.

12. **Storage or Warehousing :** There is a time gap between production and consumption of goods. Thus it is an important function of marketing to provide for proper storage of such goods until they are demanded. For example, apples are produced in winter are stored in cold storages and sold even in summer. Moreover, there is a need for storage of adequate stock of goods to meet the demand in case of contingencies and to avoid unnecessary delays in delivery. Retailers, Wholesalers and Manufactures perform the function of storage. Also, Warehouse help in stabilizing prices by checking fluctuations. They also facilitate regular & even supply of products throughout the country & throughout the year.

☞ **Marketing Management Philosophies**

1. **Production Concept :** Some companies believe that it is easy to sell the product when products are inexpensive and are easily available. So the firms following production concept focus on lowering the cost of production by means of mass production and distribution but the drawback of this concept is that customers don't always buy products which are inexpensive and available.

2. **Product Concept :** Firms which follow the product concept propose that the way to realise business goal is by making products that are of high quality. These firms manufacture the products of superior quality but they must keep in mind that customers will buy the high quality only when they need or want t, only quality is not enough force. For example, the firm is dealing with a very high quality hair-dye but customer will demand it only when they have grey hair.

3. **Selling Concept :** This concept stresses on attracting and persuading customers to buy the product by making aggressive selling and promotional efforts. Thus, the focus of business firms is to ensure the sale of products through aggressive selling techniques such as advertising, personal selling and sales promotion without giving any consideration to customers' satisfaction. The main aim of selling is to convert the goods into cash by using fair or unfair means. But the buyers cannot be manipulated every time; hence selling can be successful only for short period but not during long period.

4. **Marketing Concept :** The marketing concept implies that a firm can achieve its goals by identifying the needs of the customers and satisfying them better than the competitors.

   This essentially involves that the firm must develop products and services that customers want, Customers satisfaction is the precondition for realizing the firms goats and objectives.

Pillars of the Marketing Concept:

(i)   Identification of market or customers.

(ii)   Understanding their needs and wants.

(iii)   Developing products or services accordingly.

(iv)   Satisfying their needs better than the competitors.

(v)   Doing all this at a profit.

5.   **Societal Concept :** Although marketing concept is satisfying the needs of customers in me best possible manner but then also is has attracted criticism from people who are concerned about society and environment. They argue that companies should not blindly follow the goal of customer satisfaction. This may lead to many social and environment ills for example, a customer may want to have drugs so just to satisfy customer the firms should not supply him drugs. Some products bring harmful effects on environment so these should not be supplied only to fulfill the goal of customer-satisfaction. The customer's satisfaction must be within the ethical ecological aspects of our society.

Comparative Study of Various Marketing Management Philosophies

Basis of Difference	Production Concept	Product Concept	Selling Concept	Marketing	Societal Marketing Concept
1. Starting Point	Factory	Factory	Factory	Market	Market and Society
2. Main Focus	Quantity of Production	Quality of Product	Attracting Consumers	Consumer satisfaction	Consumer welfare
3. Means	Balanced prices and easy availability	Product improvement	Advertising, personal selling and sales promotion	Various marketing activities	Various marketing activities including social welfare
4. Ends	Profit through maximum production	Profit through product quality	Profit through maximum sales	Profit through consumer satisfaction	Profit through consumer satisfaction and social welfare.

☞   **Marketing Mix**

"The set of all marketing tools or variables, that a firm uses to achieve its marketing objectives, in a target market is known as Marketing Mix"

OR

"Marketing mix are the set of marketing tools that firm uses to pursue its marketing objectives in the target market."   **- Philip Kotler**

In the concept of marketing on one side there is customer and on the other side there is producer or marketer. The firm looks for having transaction with the customer but to have a transaction the firm has to develop a product or service, design it, pack it, name it, price it, promote it and distribute it. All these decisions are the core of marketing mix. The elements of marketing mix can be classified into four categories and through fine mixing of these elements the superior value products or services are created for customers.

 **Elements of Marketing Mix**

The four main elements of marketing mix as classified are

I. Product II. Place   III. Price   IV. Promotion.

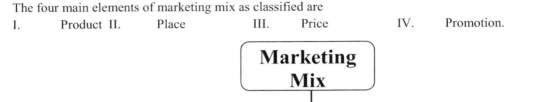

Product
- Quality
- Design
- Features
- Brand name
- Packaging
- Labelling
- Sizes
- Services
- Warranties

Price
List Price
Margins
Discounts
Credit terms
Pricing objectives
Pricing Strategies

Place
Channels of distribution
Order Processing
Storage or warehousing
Transportation
Inventory Control

Promotion
Advertising
Personal Selling
Sales promotion
Public Relations

1. **Product Mix :** Product mix refers to all decisions relating to the product. These decisions are mainly with regard to branding, packaging, labeling, colour, design, quality, size, after-sale service and weight of the product. These decisions play an important role in attracting the customers to the product.

2. **Price Mix :** Price mix refers to all those decisions which are concerned with the price fixation of any product or service. Under price mix, beside fixing the price of the product or service, decisions regarding credit sale, discount, etc., are also included.

3. **Place Mix :** Place mix refers to the combination of all the decisions relating to make products available to consumers. If the product is not available on the right time, in the right quantity and at the right place then the consumer will not be able to buy it.

4. **Promotion Mix :** Promotion Mix refers to the combination of various promotional tools to be used by an organization to provide information to the customer about a product and to persuade them to purchase it. These tools are advertising, personal selling, sales promotion and public Relation

I.   PRODUCT

Generally, the meaning of a product is considered as any physical thing like a mobile set, a book, a lipstick etc. But from marketing viewpoint, A product means everything which satisfies the need of Its buyer. In other words, services like Banking, Insurance, Education and Health, etc., are included with physical thing while defining a product. Not only this, but the opinions and information of other people also fall into the category of product.

In brief, anything that can be of value to the buyer can be termed as a product. The product can also be known as 'Bundle of Utilities'.

Types of Satisfaction Received from Product
A Product provides three types of satisfaction given as under:
1. **Functional Satisfaction :** To wear the shirt and cover the body with it is an example of functional satisfaction.

2. **Psychological Satisfaction :** To feel more confident and active after wearing the shirt provides psychological satisfaction.

3. **Social Satisfaction :** Getting recognition after wearing the shirt from the group of known people is a social satisfaction.

☞ **Product Mix**
"Product mix refers to all decisions relating to the product. These decisions are mainly with regard to branding, packaging, labeling, colour, design, quality, size, after-sale service and weight of the product. These decisions play an important role in attracting the customers to the product".
The detailed description of branding, packaging and labelling is given below:

(A) **Branding**
"Branding refers to that process through which a distinct identification of the product is established."

☞ **Various terms related to brand are :**
1. **Brand :** A brand is the identification of a product it can be in the form of name, symbol, or design etc. For Example, Surf, Dettol, Nike, etc. even various symbols such as etc. are also the brands.

2. **Brand Name :** The part of brand which can be spoken is called brand name. In other words we can say it is the verbal part of a brand, For example Detol, Surf.

3. **Brand Mark :** The part of brand which cannot be spoken but can be recognized is known as brand mark. For example, Maharaja sign of Air India, Red & Blue Ball of Pepsi, Right sign of Nike, star of Mercedes etc.

4. **Trade Mark :** A part of brand which is given legal protection is called trade mark. No the firm can use the name or sign for which a company get legal protection.

☞ **Qualities/Features of a Good Brand Name :**
While selecting a brand name attention must be paid to the following:
(i)   Brand name should be short and simple. For example, Lux, Dettol, Surf, etc. As long and complicated names are difficult to recognise and remember.
(ii) Brand names should be easy to pronounce as if it is difficult to pronounces the customer will hesitate to demand for it e.g., product names like Heinz etc. are difficult to pronounce.

(iii) Brand name should be suggsesive i.e., it must suggest the utility of the product for example, Hajmola suggest digestive properly. Ujjala suggests brightness, Hair and Care suggests care of hairs, etc.

(iv) The brand name should be unique and distinctive. The brand name should be very different and should not lose its identify for example, Ariel, Tide etc.

(v) Brand name should be selected after considering its meaning in other languages and cultures for example, the brand name Nova (given to Ambassador Car) means 'does not go' in Spanish. Such types of name should be avoided.

☞ **Advantages of Branding :**
To the Marketers :
1. **Helps in Product differentiation :** With branding marketer can differentiate his products from the competitors product.

2. **Helps in Advertising :** With the brand name advertising become more effective as it not only makes people aware about the features of product but also about brand which can provide these benefits.

3. **Differentiate Pricing :** With established brand name the firm can easily change high price for its product as compared to competitor's product.

4. **Easy Introduction of New Product :** The companies which use their company's name as brand name then it becomes very easy for such company to popularize the new product it is planning to introduce.

☞ **Advantages of Branding :**
To the Customers:
1. **Helps in Identification of Product :** Branding helps the customers to select the products easily as the brand which is giving them satisfaction can be selected easily over the competitor product.

2. **Ensures Quality :** Brand name gives quality assurance and customers can buy branded goods with no doubts about qualities of product.

3. **Status Symbol :** Use of branded goods adds to status symbol of customers and adds to their confidence level.

(B) **Packaging :**
"Packaging refers to the group of those activities which are related with the designing and production of the containers in which the products are packed."

☞ **Level of Packaging**
There are three levels of Packaging:
1. **Primary Package :** It refers to that container which is very close to the product. In some cases, it is kept throughout the entire life of the product, such as shaving cream tube, match box, etc. In other cases, it is kept till the consumer is ready to use the product, such as, plastic cover of Britannia Cake.

2.   **Secondary Package :** It refers to that container which is used for extra care of the product till the product comes into use, such as, card board box of shaving cream tube. When a consumer starts using the cream, he will dispose off the box but retains the primary packaging (e.g., plastic tube)

3.   **Transportation Packaging :** It refers to that packaging which a necessary to use for transportation, identification and storage. For example, a big card board box which is containing say 100 units of shaving cream tubes.

☞ **Importance of Packaging**

1.   **Rising Standard of Health and Sanitation :** Raising standards of living in the country have resulted in more use of packed goods and this also reduces the chances of adulteration.

2.   **Self Service Outlets :** The self services outlets are becoming very popular. In these stores generally products with attractive packing are picked by buyers more quickly.

3.   **Product Differentiation :** Packing help the customers to differentiate between goods on the basis of quality as with the type of packing customer can guess about the quality of goods.

4.   **Innovational Opportunities :** Recent developments in packaging have completely changed the marketing. For example new packing in soft drinks, chips, biscuits keep them fresh for a longer period. Even milk can be stored for 4-5 days without refrigeration. Scope of marketing is increasing with new innovations in packaging.

☞ **Functions of Packaging**

Following are the main functions performed by packaging:

1.   **Products identification :** Packaging ensures easy identification of a product. For example, Taj Mahal, Tea can be easily identified from a distance due to its blue color box.

2.   **Products Protection :** The most important function of packaging is to ensure protection of a product from spoilage, leakage, breakage etc. It also ensures effective protection during storage and transportation of a product.

3.   **Facilitating Use of the Product :** Packaging helps the customers to easily handle and use the product. For example, tubes of tooth pastes, bottles of cold drinks etc.

4.   **Product Promotion :** Packaging acts as an important promotional tool. The attractive color scheme or photograph used in packing helps in attracting the attention of the people and inducing them to purchase the product. Therefore, it plays the role of silent salesman.

(C)   **Labelling :**

"Labelling refers to the process of preparing a label".

Label is the carrier of information. it provides information like - name of the product, name of manufacturer, contents of products, expiry and manufacturing date, general instruction for use, weight, price etc.

Product labels can be

ut product to customer.

Apart from details of product some statutory warnings which are essential for some products must be printed on label. For example, on Tobacco, Liquor it is compulsory to mention that its consumption is injurious to health.

☞ **Functions of Labelling**

Following are the main functions of Labelling:

1. **Complete Description of a Product :** Labelling provides full details regarding the use, cautions in use, contents etc. of a product. For example, label of Maggi noodles describes the procedure of cooking noodles.

2. **Identification of Product :** it helps in identifying the product from among various products available in the market. For example, we can easily identify Head & Shoulders shampoo from among various shampoos sheerly by the colour of its label.

3. **Grading of Product :** Labelling helps in grading the product into different categories. For example, Sunsilk Shampoo comes in different categories such as for normal hair, oily hair, dry hair etc. All these categories have different labels.

4. **Promotion of Product :** A carefully designed label helps in attracting the customers and induces them to purchase the product. For example, the label on pack of Britannia Fifty mentions in different color 30% free.

5. **Legal information :** The last important function performed by labelling is to provide information required by law. For example, statutory warning that "smoking is injurious to health" on the package of cigarettes. Similarly appropriate safety warning needs to be put on the label of a product which is hazardous or poisonous.

II.   PRICE

"Price refers to the amount of money which the customer pays for the product or service he purchases". Pricing plays an important role in the marketing of a product or service. Price usually has an inverse relationship with the demand for product or service, An increase in the price of a product can decrease the demand and vice-versa, Therefore, a little variation hi the price of product can lead to increase in demand for competitor's product. Most of the firms competes with one another on the basis of this factor alone.

Pricing Mix : "Price mix refers to all those decisions which are concerned with the price fixation of any product or service. Under price mix, beside fixing the price of the product or service, decisions regarding credit sale, discount, etc., are also Included".

☞ **Factors Determining Fixation of Price Determination**

Following are the main factors affecting price determination:

1. **Product Cost :** The most important factor affecting the price of a product is its cost. Product cost refers to the total of fixed costs, variable costs and semi variable costs incurred during the production, distribution and selling of the product. Fixed costs are those costs which remain fixed at all the levels of production or sales. For examples, rent of building, salary etc. Variable costs refer to the costs which are directly related to the levels of production or sales. For example, costs of raw material, labour costs etc. Semi variable costs are those which change with the level of

activity but not in direct proportion. For example, fixed salary of Rs. 12,000 + upto 6% graded commission on increase in volume of sales.

The price for a commodity is determined on the basis of the total cost. So sometimes, while entering a new market or launching a new product, business firm has to keep its price below the cost level but in the long run, it is necessary for a firm to cover more than its total cost if it wants to survive admit cut-throat competition.

2. **The Utility and Demand :** Usually, consumers demand more units of a product when its price is low and vice versa. However, when the demand for a product is elastic, little variation in the price may result in large changes in quantity demanded. In case of inelastic demand, a change in the prices does not affect the demand significantly. Thus, a firm can charge higher profits in case of inelastic demand.

Moreover, the buyer is ready to pay up to that point where he perceives utility from product to be at least equal to price paid. Thus, both utility and demand for a product affect its price.

3. **Extent of Competition in the Market :** The next important factor affecting the price for a product is the nature and degree of competition in the market. A firm can fix any price for its product if the degree of competition is low. However, when the level of competition is very high, the price of a product is determined on the basis of price of competitor's products, their features and quality etc. For example, MRF tyres company cannot fix the prices of its tyres without considering the prices of Bridgestone Tyre Company, Goodyear tyre company etc.

4. **Government and Legal Regulations :** The firms which have monopoly in the market, usually charge high price for their products. In other to protect the interest of the public, the government intervenes and regulates the prices of the commodities for this purpose, it declares some products as essential products for example, Life saving drugs etc.

5. **Pricing Objectives :** Another important factor, affecting the price of a product or service objectives Following are the pricing objectives of any business:
   (a) **Profit Maximisation :** Usually the objective of any business is to maximise the profit During short run, a firm can earn maximum profit by charging high price. However, during long run, a firm reduces price per unit to capture bigger share of the market and hence earn high profits through increased sales.

   (b) **Obtaining Market Leadership :** It involves being a leader in terms of market share for a product. In such a situation, an organization which wants to play leader's role charges lower price than its competitors.

   (c) **Surviving in a Competitive Market :** If an orgamsation is struggling to survive in a competitive market, it charges lower price tp retain its market share.

   (d) **Attaining Product Quality Leadership :** When an organisation puts emphasis on attaining product quality leadership through research and development, it charges higher price in order to recover its research and development cost

6. **Marketing Methods Used :** The various marketing methods such as distribution system, quality of salesman, advertising, type of packaging, customer services, etc. also affect the price of a

product For example, a firm will charge high price if it is using expensive material for packing its product.

III. Place/Physical Distribution

"Place refers to the set of decisions that need to be taken in order to niche the product available." if the products are not made available to the customers the right time then customer would not be able to buy them, Place element is a process by which the goods are transferred from the place of production to the place of consumption.

Place Mix "Place mix refers to important decisions related to physical distribution of goods and services, These decisions are deciding the channel of distribution, physical distribution."

I. Channels of Distribution

"Channel of distribution refers to the people or middlemen who help in distributing the goods". Goods are produced at one place and customers are scattered all over the country so it is very difficult for the producer to distribute goods to the place of consumption for example, tea is produced in Darjeeling, Assam but it is consumed all over the country. It is very difficult for producer to distribute tea all over the country so he takes the help of some middlemen so that it can be supplied to all the consumers.

Channels of distributions are the firms and individuals who help in transferring the goods from place of manufacturing to place of consumption. The common type of channels of distributions are, Wholesaler and Retailer.

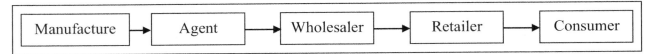

Channels of distributions make shopping easy for consumer and distribution simple of manufacturer for example, consumer can get variety of products by visiting one retail showroom whereas if there is no retailer then to buy various products he will have to visit various manufacturers which involves lot of efforts. Following diagram shows the situation of customer with and without channels of distribution.

For example, consumers need sugars, tea, rice, pulses.

Case when no Middlemen or Distribution Channel

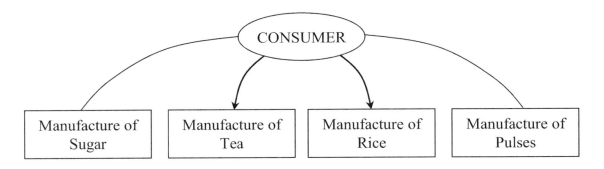

Case when Middlemen is Available

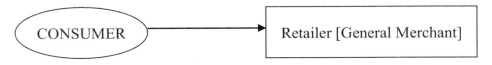

In above diagram we can see how customer's efforts are reduced with the presence of middlemen.

☞ **Channels Levels**

Types of Distribution Levels :

1. **Zero level channel/Direct Channel :** When the manufacturer instead of selling the goods to the intermediary sells it directly to the consumer then this is known as Zero Level Channel. Retail outlets, mail order selling, internet selling and selling through own sales force are the examples of this channel. Some companies which sell goods through this medium are as follows:

    - BATA SHOE CC, - EUREKA FORBES, - ASIAN SKY SHOP

    Zero level Channel can be explained with the help of the following diagrams:

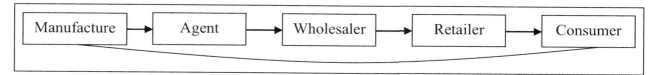

2. **Indirect Channel :** When a manufacturer gets the help of one or more middlemen to move goods from the production place to the place of consumption, the distribution channel Is called indirect channel. Following are the main types of it:

    (i)   **One Level Channel :** In this method an intermediary is used. Here a manufacturer sells the goods directly to the retailer instead of selling it to agents or wholesalers. This method is used for expensive watches and other like products. This method is also useful for selling FMCG (Fast Moving Consumer Goods). This channel is clarified in the following diagram:

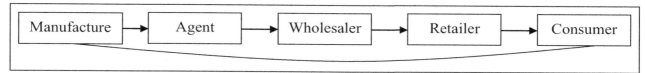

    (ii) **Two Level Channels:** In this method a manufacturer sells the material to a wholesaler, the wholesaler to the retailer and then the retailer to the consumer. Here, the wholesaler after purchasing the material in large quantity from the manufacturer sells it in small quantity to the retailer. Then the retailers male the products available to the consumers. This medium is mainly used to sell soap, tea, salt, cigarette, sugar, ghee etc. This channel is more clarified in the following diagrams:

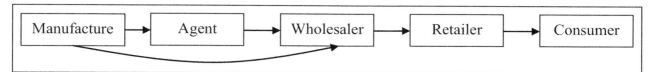

    (iii) **Three Level Channels :** Under this one more level is added to Two Level Channel in the form of agent. An agent facilities to reduce the distance between the manufacturer and the wholesaler. Some big companies who cannot directly contact the wholesaler, they take the help of agents. Such companies appoint their agents in every region and sell the material to them. Then the agents sell the material to the wholesaler, the wholesaler to the retailer and in the end the retailer sells the material to the consumers. This channel is more clarified in the following diagram:

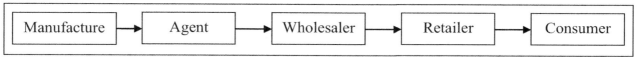

Factors affecting Choice a Channel/Physical Distribution of Commodity

Whether to have a small or long distribution path depends upon following factors:

1. **Product Related Factor :** Following are product related factors which help in deciding the channels of distribution:

    (a) **Value of product line.** If the unit value of product is high or for expensive product direct safe from company is preferred while for less costly products, longer channels are preferred.

    (b) **Product complexity.** Technically complex product requires expert advice and guidance so direct sale is preferred whereas for simple product longer channels can be used.

    (c) **Nature of product.** The customized product or product produced according to instruction of customers requires direct interaction of buyer and seller. So non intermediary whereas standardized product could be sold by using various intermediaries.

    (d) **Perishable or nonperishable product.** Direct selling is used for perishable product whereas nonperishable could be distributed with long channel.

2. **Company Related Factor :**

    (a) **Finance.** A company which has deep pocket or non financial problem should prefer direct sale while financially weak firms depend upon distribution channels or intermediary.

    (b) **Degree of control.** The firms wanting tight control over the distribution prefer short path or direct sale but firms which do not mind sharing the control appoint intermediaries for sale.

3. **Competitive Factors :** The type of channel selected by competitor also affects the selection of channel. As a company may select the same channel as selected by the competitor or sometimes the businessman prefers not to select the channel selected by competitor. For example, if competitor has chosen to sell the detergent powder through big retail house, the businessman may select the sale by appointing salesmen for door to door.

4. **Market Related Factor :** The channel path is greatly influenced by the market related factors. These factors are:

    (a) Nature of market. In industrial market direct selling is preferred. Whereas in consumer market distribution channels are appointed.

    (b) Size of the market If the number of customers are large then more intermediaries are used whereas when market consists of small number of consumers then short of direct channels are used.

    (c) Geographical concentration. When buyers are concentrated in a limited area the direct selling is preferred. Whereas if customers are scattered then more channels are used.

    (d) Quantity purchased. If order size is big then direct supply from firm is preferred whereas for small orders retailers are preferred.

5. **Environment Factors :** Other important factors which affect the choice of channels of distribution include environment factors such as trade policy, economic policy etc. For example, in a depressed economy shorter channels are preferred to distribute goods in economical way.

☞   Physical/Distribution

Physical distribution is an important element of marketing mix; it involves physical handling and movement of goods from the place of production to the place of consumption. It is concerned with the availability of the right quantity of goods to be customers at the right time and right place through the channels of distribution

"Physical distribution refers to all decisions relating to transportation, inventory, warehousing and order processing of goods"

1. **Order Processing :** It refers to placing order by the customer to the manufacturer via channel members. Accurate and speedy processing of order is essential to ensure timely delivery of goods to the customer in correct quantity/specifications.

2. **Transportation :** It refers to the mode of carrying goods and raw material from the place where they are produced to the place where they are to be sold. It is the most important element of physical distribution of goods. It also adds value to the good by ensuring their availability at the right place and right time.

3. **Warehousing :** There is a time gap between the production and the consumption of goods, thus it becomes essential to store them. For example, seasonal products like wheat, rice, coolers etc. In order to create time utility in them.

4. **Inventory Control :** inventory refers to the level of stock to be maintained. If a company maintains a high level of inventory, higher will be the level of service to customers but along with this the cost of maintaining the inventory will also be high because lot of capital would be tied up in the stock. Therefore, a firm is required to maintain a balance between customer satisfaction and level of inventory. Following are the factors which help in determining inventory level:

   (a) **Firm's Policy towards customer service :** If policy of a firm is to offer higher level of service to its customers, it needs to keep high level of inventory.

   (b) **Degree of accuracy of the sales forecasts :** The high level of inventory can be minimized if sales forecasts are accurate.

   (c) **Responsiveness of the distribution system :** If a firm is in a position to provide quick supply of goods in case of additional demand it will maintain low level of inventory. However, if it takes time to supply goods, it will maintain a high level of inventory.

   (d) **Cost of Inventory :** Cost of warehouse, tied up capital, manufacturing cost etc are included in cost of inventory. If this cost high, low level of inventory is maintained and vice

IV.   Promotion

"Promotion refers to the use of communication for providing information to the customer about a product and its uses persuading them to purchase it."

Promotion Mix : Promotion Mix refers to the combination of various promotional tools to be used by an organization to provide information to the customer about a product and to persuade them to purchase it. These tools are advertising, personal selling, sales promotion and public Relation

(I)   **Advertising :**
"Advertising means providing adequate knowledge about some special product service/idea to potential consumers so that they are stimulated to buy it."

☞   **Features of Advertising :**

1. **Paid Form :** Advertising is a paid form of communication. That is, the sponsor has to bear the cost of communicating with the prospects.

2. **Impersonality :** There is no direct face-to-face contact between the prospect and the advertiser. It is therefore, referred to as impersonal method of promotion.

3. **Identified Sponsor :** Advertising is undertaken by some identified individual or company, who makes the advertising efforts and also bears the cost of it.

☞ **Role of Advertising**

1. **Creating Demand.** Advertising plays significant role in creating demand for products by making people aware of new products and new uses of existing products. It attracts people's attention, creates interest in them and arouses desire in them for buying. All these lead to creation of demand.

2. **Creating Customer Loyalty.** Customer loyalty means repeated buying of products of the same brands. Advertising creates this loyalty through repeated communication of the product features.

3. **Educating Consumers.** Advertising educates consumers by providing useful information about how products value to them, how products can be used for better satisfaction, etc.

4. **Enhancing Customer Confidence.** Advertising leads to enhancing customer confidence in products advertised. Customers feel confident while buying adverted products as they are sure about product quality. Because of this confidence, they derive more satisfaction from the products.

5. **Supporting Dealers.** Advertising supports dealers by making people aware about positive features of products advertised. Thus, it creates ready market for the dealers and they do not have to make much effort for selling the products.

6. **Facilities New Product Introduction.** Advertising facilities introduction of new products. When a new product is introduced in the market, It is just like an alien (unknown) to people. Through advertising, positive features of newly introduced product are communicated making the product acceptable to people.

7. **Creating better Organisational Image.** Advertising helps in creating better organizational image. Through advertising, message may reach people how an organisation stands for serving the society. Creating better organisational image is a source of satisfaction for the organisation.

☞ **Objections to Advertising or Criticism of Advertising**

Advertising has been subject to lot of criticisms. The following are main objections raised on advertisements by a group of people. Along with objections the answers to these objections are also mentioned below:

1. **Effect of Advertising on Values, Materialism and Life Styles :** The major objection on advertisement is that it promotes materialism. The advertisements inform people about more and more products, the use of existing products and the new products are shown dramatically to attract the customers. This knowledge about more products induces the customers to buy more and more products. They start demanding the products which they don't even require. If there was no advertising we would be less aware of material things and we can be more contented.

    We do not agree with this objection as it is wrong to say that a person who is least informed is most contented or satisfied. The advertisement increases the knowledge of customers by informing them about various products along with their utilities. The advertisements only inform the customers, the final choice of buying or not, lies with the customers only.

2. **Advertising Encourages Sale of Inferior and Dubious Products :** The advertisements show all types of products irrespective of their quality. With the help of advertising anything can be sold in the market. The objection to sale of inferior goods is not correct because what is inferior and what is superior depends upon the economic status and preference. Every one cannot afford to buy superior quality expensive products but it does not mean they should not use the product. The lower income group people satisfy their needs with low cost inferior goods for example, those

who cannot afford to buy shoes of Nike or Reebok have to satisfy with local brand only. So it is not advertisements which encourage sale of inferior goods; it is ones pocket or financial capacity which decides this.

The real criticism of advertisement is that is encourages sale of duplicate products. Some producers exaggerate the use of products and innocent consumers get trapped in and buy duplicate products.

3. **Advertising Confuses Rather than Helps :** The number of advertisements shown in TV and Radio are increasing day by day for example, if we take T\ there are so many advertisements of different companies shown such as LG, Onida, Sony, BPL, Samsung, Videocon etc. each brand claiming they are the best. These claims by different companies confuse the customer and it becomes very difficult or him to make choice.

    We do not agree with this objection because advertisements give wide choice to customers and today's customer is smart enough to know and select the most suitable brand for him.

4. **Some Advertisements are in Bad Taste :** Another objection to advertisements is that advertisements use bad language, the way they are speaking may not appeal everyone, sometimes women are shown in the advertisements where they are not required for example, a woman in after shave lotion and in advertisements of suiting eta. Some advertisements distort relationship between employer-employee, mother-in-law and daughter-in-law etc. for example, in advertisement of Band Aid, detergent barm Fevistick etc.

    Although those types of advertisements should be avoided but it can't be an objection because good or bad taste differs from person to person. It is a matter of personal opinion as to what was not accepted by yesterday's generation is accepted by today's generation and they may not find it of bad taste.

5. **Advertisement Costs are Passed on to the Customers in the Form of Higher Price :** The most serious objection to advertisement is that it increases the price of product because the firms spend a huge amount on advertisement and these expenses are added to cost and consumer has to pay a higher price for the product or service.

    This objection is also not correct because with advertisements the demand for product increases which brings increase in sale and this leads to increase in production. With increase in production the companies can get the economies of scale which reduces the cost of production and thus the increase in cost due to expense on advertisements gets compensated. So if advertisement is used properly it brings reduction in cost the in long run.

(II)   Personal Selling :
"Personal selling refers to the oral presentation of the message in the form of conversion with prospective customers for the purpose of making sales".

Features of Personal Selling
*   Personal form of communication As it involves direct face to face interaction between the salesperson and the prospective buyer(s) for the purpose of making sales. Thus, there is a two – way communication.

- **Develop Personal relationship :** Personal selling allows a salesperson to develop personal relationship with the customers, which may help in repeat sales and direct feedback.
- **Flexible tool :** Personal selling is a flexible tool of promotion. The sales presentation can be adjusted to fit the specific needs of the individual customers.

☞ **Qualities of a Good Salesman**

A good salesman is one who presents an offering to a prospective customer in such a way that the latter appreciates it by his heart and tends to buy it. For being a good salesman, the person must possess the qualities of a good salesman which are as follows:

1. **Physical Qualities.** Physical qualities of a good salesman are sound health, good appearance, impressive voice, and impressive posture.

2. **Mental Qualities.** Mental qualities, also known as psychological qualities, of a good salesman are intelligence, sharp memory, self-confidence, hard working, determination, patience, enthusiasm, imagination, initiative, adaptability and sound judgment.

3. **Social Qualities.** Social qualities of a good salesman are maturity in behaviour, good manners, sincerity, courage, sound character, pleasing temperament, cooperative approach, tactfulness, effective communication and respect for others.

4. **Technical Qualities.** Technical qualities of a good salesman are as follows:

   (i) **Knowledge of Company.** Good salesman has relevant knowledge of the company for which he works. Knowledge of company includes knowing history of the company, management pattern, product lines, policies and any distinguished achievement Such knowledge is required to make sales presentation effective and to answer queries of customers.

   (ii) **Knowledge of Products.** Good salesman has complete knowledge of products which he offers to customers. Knowledge of products includes knowing all the relevant features of the products handled by the salesman. These features include technical dimensions of the products, their quality, price and any special features which make the products superior to comparable products.

   (iii) **Knowledge of Competitors.** Good salesman has relevant knowledge of competitors. Knowledge of competitors includes having knowledge about competitors, strength and weaknesses of their products and prices. Knowledge of competitors is relevant for answering queries of customers about competing products.

   (iv) **Knowledge of Customers.** Good salesman has relevant knowledge of customers: their buying motives, liking/disliking and attitudes about products offered.

   (v) **Knowledge of Selling Techniques.** A good salesman has knowledge of selling techniques so that he can adopt a technique which is the most relevant in the given situation.

Difference between Advertising and Personal Selling

Basis of difference	Advertising	Personal Selling
1. Forum	This is impersonal	This is personal.
2. Message	There is uniformity of message which means that the message is the same for all the customers.	The message has no uniformity which means it can be changed keeping in view the behaviour of the customers.
3. Flexibility	It lacks flexibility.	It is completely flexible.
4. Reach	Through its medium the message can be carried to numerous people at the same time.	Through this medium the message is conveyed to a single person or a group of persons at a time.
5. Cost	It is a relatively less costly method.	It is a more costly method.
6. Time	It takes a little time in conveying any information to the customers.	It takes more time in conveying information to the customers.
7. Media	TV., Radio, Newspapers and Magazines.	Through salesman.
8. Feedback	This gives no information about the reactions of the customers.	The reaction of the customers becomes immediately known or clear.
9. Role	To create and maintain interest in the product.	It immediately affects the decision to purchase.
10. Suitability	This method of promotion is useful for the ultimate consumers who are in large numbers.	This method is useful for industrial buyers and middlemen (e.g., dealers and retail sellers) who are less in numbers.

(III) **Sales Promotion :**

"**Sale Promotion refers to short term use of incentives or other promotional activities that stimulate the customer to buy the product**".

☞ **Sales Promotion Techniques for Customers**

Some of the sales promotion activities commonly used by the marketeer to increase the sale are:

1. **Rebate :** It refers to selling product at a special price which is less than the original price for a limited period of time. This offer is given to clear off the stock or excessive inventory for example, coke amounted 2 ltr bottle at Rs.35 only.

2. **Discounts :** This refers to reduction of certain percentage of price from list price for a limited period of time. The discounts induce the customers to buy and to buy more. Generally at the end of season big companies offer their products at discounted price to clear off the stock e.g. season's sale at Snow-white Jam Son's, Paul garments, Bhuvan garments etc.

3. **Refunds :** This refers to refund or part of price paid by customer on presenting the proof of purchase for example, Rs.2 off on presentation of empty pack of Ruffle lays.

4. **Premiums or gifts/or Product combination :** These are most popular and commonly used promotion tool. It refers to giving a free gift on purchase of the product. Generally the free gift is related to product but it is not necessary for example, Mug free with Bournvita, Shaker free with coffee, toothbrush free with toothpaste, etc.

5. **Quantity Deals :** It refers to offer of extra quantity in a special package at less price or on extra purchase some quantity free for example, buy three get one free e.g., this scheme of buy three get one free scheme is available on soaps.

6. **Samples :** It refers to distribution of free samples of product to the customers. These are distributed when the seller wants the customer must try the product. Generally when a new product is launched for example, when Hindustan Lever Limited surf excel it distributed the samples as it wanted the customers to try it.

7. **Contests :** It refers to participation of consumers in competitive events organised by the firm and winners are given some reward for example, Camlin Company organises painting competition, Bournvita quiz contest and some companies organise contest of writing slogans and best slogan is awarded prize.

8. **Instant Draws and Assigned gifts :** It includes the offers like 'scratch a card' and win instantly a refrigerator, car, T-shirt, computer etc.

9. **Lucky Draw :** In this draws are taken out by including the bill no. or name of customers who have purchased the goods and lucky winner gets free car, computer, A.C., T.V. etc. Draw can be taken out daily, weekly, monthly etc.

10. **Usable Benefits :** This include offers like 'Purchase goods worth Rs.5,000 and get a holiday package' or get a discount voucher etc.

11. **Full Finance @ 0% :** In this method, customers are given full financing facility interest free. They have to pay just installments on the product price without interest.

12. **Packaged Premium :** In this type of sales promotion the free gift is kept inside the pack. The gift is kept in limited products but the excitement of getting the gift induces the customer to buy the product for example, gold pendant in soap, gold coin in Tata tea etc.

13. **Container Premium :** This refers to use of special container or boxes to pack the products which could be reused by the customer for example, Pet bottles for cold drinks. This bottle can be used for steering water, plastic jars for Bournvita, Maltova etc. which can be reused by the housewife in kitchen.

14. **Exchange Offer :** It involves exchanging an old product with a new product by paying exchange price which is lower than the listed price of the new product, for example, 'exchange your old TV', 'exchange your old Refrigerator', etc.

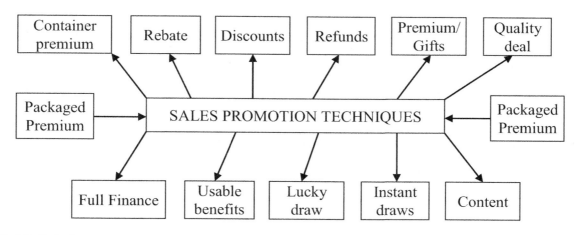

(IV)   Public Relations

In the present business environment, organisations, including business organisations, are putting high emphasis on public relations (PR). Public relations is defined as follows.

"Public relation is the action of an organisation for promoting goodwill between itself and the society."

☞   **Role of Public Relations**

Most of the large business organisations have separate public relations departments to undertake activities related to public relations. This is so because public relations plays the following roles:

1.   **Creating Better Image.** Public relations plays key role in creating better image of an organisation by maintaining good relations with public. This image is quite helpful for the organisation to promote its products.

2.   **Winning Loyalty of Public.** Public relations helps in creating public loyalty to the organisation. This loyalty is created by communicating relevant information to public, which is done by public relations.

3.   **Understanding Public Opinions.** Public relations helps in understanding public opinions about the organisation. Understanding public opinions helps an organisation to chalk out: its actions which are relevant to the public.

4.   **Overcoming Misunderstanding.** Sometimes, misunderstanding may be created in the public about the organisation or its any action. Such a misunderstanding may be overcome by communicating facts on the issues because of which misunderstanding has been created.

5.   **Communicating New Developments.** Public relations is a good mechanism to communicate new developments in the organisation. Communicating such developments is beneficial to both organisation and public.

EXERCISE – 1

Q.1   What is Marketing?

Q.2   Define marketing management.

Q.3   What is meant by 'Product Concept' of marketing?
Q.4   Give the consumer-oriented definition of marketing.

Q.5   What is meant by 'social concept' of marketing?
       [Hint: It means performance of marketing activities aimed at enhancing social well-being of the people.]

Q.6   What is Marketing Mix?

Q 7   What is the main pillar of marketing concept
       [Hint: Satisfying the needs of customers better than the competitors.]

Q.8   How does packaging act as a silent salesman 7

Q.9   What is meant by Trademark?
       [Hint: It refers to a brand name which is registered with the Government under the Trade Mark Act.]
Q.10   What is meant by direct channels of distribution?

EXERCISE – 2

Q.1   Differentiate between marketing and 'selling on the basis of :
       (a)   Meaning, and
       (b)   Process.

Q.2   Explain in brief the term 'Price Mix' as an element of 'Marketing Mix.'

Q.3   Explain 'Promotion Mix' as an element of 'Marketing Mix'.

Q.4   Explain any three qualities of a good brand name;

Q.5   Explain any three advantages of branding to the marketer.

Q.6   Explain any three factors affecting pricing of a product.

Q.7   Explain any three functions of packaging.

Q.8   Explain any three advantages of packaging.

Q.9   Explain any three advantages labelling.

Q.10   What is meant by 'direct channels of distribution'? List any four methods of direct distribution.

EXERCISE – 3

Q.1   Define marketing and state its basic objectives.

Q.2   What is meant by marketing management? Discuss the role of marketing.

Q.3   Explain the following functions of marketing:
       (i)   Gathering and analysing market information
       (ii)   Marketing planning
       (iii)   Product designing and development
       (iv)   Customer support services.

Q.4   What is meant by a product? Why is packaging of a product is necessary?

Q.5   Explain the concept of branding. What are the essentials of branding?

Q.6   Explain briefly the factors to which the marketers should pay attention while fixing the price of a product.

Q.7   Name the element of marketing mix which affects the revenue and profits of a firm. Explain any five factors which help in determining this element.
       [Hint: Pricing]

Q.8   Explain the factors determining the choice of channels of distribution depends.

Q.9   Describe briefly any five methods of sales promotion.

Q.10   'Bending the customer according to the Product' and 'Developing the product according to the customer needs' are the two important concepts of marketing. Identify the concepts and differentiate between the two.
       [Hint: Selling concept and Marketing concept.]

CONSUMER PROTECTION

CONTENT

☞ **Introduction :**
It refers to protecting the interest of consumer.

☞ **Importance of Consumer Protection :**

A.   From Customers point of view:
1.   Consumer ignorance.
2.   Unorganised Consumer.
3.   Widespread exploitation of Consumer.

B.   From Businessmen's point of view:
1.   Long term interest of business.
2.   Business uses society's resources.
3.   Social responsibilities
4.   Moral/Ethical justification.
5.   Government intervention.

☞ **Need of consumer Protection in India :**
1.   Poverty and unemployment.
2.   Illiterate consumer.
3.   Consumers are not organised.

☞ **Legal Protection for Consumers :**
1.   The protection Act 1986.
2.   The Contract Act 1982.
3.   The sale of goods Act 1930.
4.   The essential commodities Act 1955.
5.   The agricultural Produce Act 1937.
6.   The prevention of food adulteration Act 1954.
7.   The standard of weights and measures Act 1976.
8.   The trade mark Act 1999.
9.   The Competition Act 2002.
10.   The bureau of Indian Standard Act 1986.

☞ **Consumer Rights :**
1.   Right to safety.
2.   Right to information.
3.   Right to choice.
4.   Right to be heard.
5.   Right to seek redressal.
6.   Right to consumer education.
7.   Right to basic needs.
8.   Right to healthy environment.

☞ **Consumer Responsibilities :**
1. To provide adequate information to the seller
2. To exercise caution in purchasing
3. To insist on cash memo or receipt
4. To file complaint against genuine grievances.
5. To be u quality conscious.
6. To be cautions against false and misleading advertisements
7. To exercise his legal rights

☞ **Ways and Means of Consumer Protection :**
1. Self regulations by Business.
2. Business Association.
3. Consumer Association.
4. Consumer Organisation.
5. Government

☞ **Three Tier Consumer Grievances Machinery under the Consumer Protection Act :**
1. District Forum.
2. State Commission.
3. National Commission.
Role of Consumer Protection.
Role of The Press.
Role of Universities

WEIGHTAGE

Units	Very Short Answer	Short Answer I & II	Long Answer I & II	Total
Unit – 12(6)	1(2)	4(1)	---	6(3)

12. CONSUMER PROTECTION

Who is Consumer?
A consumer is defined as any person who buys any products or hires or avails of any service. The product or service must be paid for either wholly or partly, or any have to be paid at a later date. The services covered by the Consumer Protection Act include supply of electricity, banking, financing, transport, communication, construction, medical treatment, etc.

☞ Meaning of Consumer Protection
What is Consumer Protection?
Consumer Protection is a very wide term. It includes providing information to the consumers about their rights and responsibilities and also helps in getting their grievances redressed and protecting their interest The concept of consumer protection is beneficial not only for the consumer but also for the businessmen. To protect the consumers against unfair trade practices of the producers & sellers is called Consumer Protection.

☞ **It covers the following three aspects :**
(i) **Physical protection of consumers.** This aspect includes measures to protect the consumers against products that are unsafe or injurious to health and hygiene.
(ii) **Protection of economic interest.** This covers measures to protect the consumers against deceptive and other unfair trading practices and to provide him adequate means to get his grievances redressed.
(iii) **Protection of public interest.** This covers measures to prevent monopolistic and restrictive trade practices to safeguard the interests of general public.

☞ **Importance of Consumer Protection**
In the present business environment, scope of unethical practices has increased significantly because of increase in product demand and decrease in social moral values. In this situations, consumer protection has become important from the point of view of both consumers and business.

A. **From Consumers Point of View :**
1. **Consumer Ignorance :** Because of illiteracy or lower level of education, many consumers can't differentiate between good and bad products and can't even read the contents, date, price, quantity, etc. printed on the packets. Even the educated consumers are many a time not aware of the quality standards and can't differentiate between pure and adulterated goods. This ignorance may give opportunities to some suppliers to cheat the consumers by selling sub-standard goods and charging higher prices.

2. **Unorganised Consumers :** We have a very few organisation of consumers in India looking at the size of her population. Because of lack of powerful consumer movement, the consumers feel the need of adequate legal protection against the malpractice of producers and traders.

3. **Widespread Exploitation of Consumers :** The consumers are widely exploited by dishonest producers and traders. For example, they may sell sub-standard or duplicate goods which are not safe for human consumption, or they may charge higher prices of scarce goods. False advertising is another method to exploit the innocent consumers. Thus, there is a strong case for the protection of consumers against such malpractices.

☞ **From Businessmen's pint of View :**
Business needs consumers as much as consumers need business. Therefore, business should also join hands in protecting consumer's interest. It's importance is highlighted by the following facts.
1. **Long Term Interest of Business :** Long term interest of the business lies in the satisfaction of its consumer. It is a satisfied consumer who not only leads to repeat sale but also provides positive feedback to other consumer. In this way the number of customers for that firm goes up and the firm continues to live for a long time. Paying attention to the satisfaction of the consumers is nothing but consumer's protection.

2. **Businessman Uses Society's Resources :** Every business uses various resources, e.g., material, machinery, human, capita!, etc. All these resources supplied by society. From this point of view, it becomes the responsibility of business to provide better facilities to society. By doing this and through the medium of consumer protection business gets an opportunity to discharge its responsibility towards society.

3   **Social Responsibilities :** It is the social responsibility of business to protect the interests of its owner and all other related constituents like – employees, consumers, suppliers, competitors, government, etc. Consumers happen to be the most important of all the related constituents. Therefore, more attention should be paid to the protection of their interests. Doing this is nothing but consumers protection. Therefore, business through the medium of consumer protection can discharge its social responsibility to a large extent.

4.   **Moral/Ethical Justification :** It is the moral responsibility of business to take care of the consumer's interest. The business should keep away from the evils of adulteration, inferior quality, misleading advertisement, hoarding of goods, black – marketing, less weighing and measuring. By doing so they can discharge their moral responsibility and it can be said that business is helping the cause of consumer protection.

5.   **Government Intervention :** By ignoring consumers interest business is almost inviting government intervention. Government intervention may spoil the image of business. That is why every firm wants to avoid such as situation. Such a situation can be avoided only if the consumers' interest is taken care of. Doing so means taking care of consumers' protection. Therefore, by being a partner in protecting consumers' interests government intervention can be avoided and reputation of the firm can also be maintained.

☞ **Need for Consumer Protection in Developing Countries like India**

In the developing countries like India there is more requirement or need for consumer protection because of the following reasons:

1.   **Poverty and Unemployment :** In a developing country most of the customers are poor and unemployed and these customers are taken for granted as they cannot object to any product or service. They accept anything which is offered to them at low price as they have to buy it to live. The poor consumer is the most harassed and the most helpless creature in India and other developing countries.

2.   **Illiterate Consumer :** In developing countries like India most of the consumers are uneducated and illiterate and cannot differentiate between the pure and adulterated product. Consumer cannot read the contents, date, price, quantity etc. So they rely blindly on the information of the suppliers. This ignorance gives more chances of frauds and manipulation to the supplier who tries to cheat the illiterate consumer by supplying substandard and low quality products at higher prices.

3.   **Consumers are not Organised :** Another reason for more requirement of consumer protection in India is that in India consumers have not yet organised themselves to have powerful consumer movement. There is lack of effective and alert agencies to secure redressal of their grievances. Due to lack of consumer organsiations there is more need for consumer protection in countries like India.

☞ **Legal Protection to Consumer**

Government of India has provided various laws and legislations to protect the interest of consumer and some of these regulations are:

1.   **The Consumer Protection Act 1986 :** This Act has been presented as an important Act in the Indian History. It was passed by the parliament in 1986 and came into force with effect from 1 July, 1987. The main aim of enactment of this act is to protect and promote the interests of the consumers. The main features of this act are:

(i)   To safeguard the consumers from unfair trade practices, harmful and defective goods, deficient services and other forms of exploitations.

(ii)   It has laid down various rights and responsibilities for consumers.

(iii)   The act has established a three tier machinery, District Forums, State Commission and the National Commission, for redressal of consumers' grievances.

2. **The Contract Act 1982 :** This Act defines the conditions on the basis of which the promises made by parties to a contract will be binding on them and also the remedies available to the parties in case of breach of contract.

3. **The Sale of Goods Act 1930 :** The various safeguard and reliefs to the customers are provided under this act, when the goods are not according to the expressed conditions or warranties.

4. **The Essential Commodities Act 1955 :** This act aims to control production, supply and to provide fair distribution of goods. It also checks inflationary trend in the prices of the goods and take action against black marketers, hoarders.

5. **The Agricultural Produce (Grading and Marketing) Act 1937 :** This act is formed to assure quality of agricultural products. This Act provides grade standards for agricultural commodities. The quality mark which is supplied by this act is "AGMARK". This mark is given only when goods are produced by following minimum standards.

6. **The Prevention of Food Adulteration Act 1954 :** This Act is formed to check Adulteration of food articles and ensure their purity so that the health of general public can be maintained.

7. **The Standard of Weights and Measures Act 1976 :** This Act provides protection to consumers against malpractices of under-weight, under measure. The provision of this Act is applicable on those goods which are sold or distributed by weight and measure.

8. **The Trade Mark Act 1999 :** This act has replaced the Trade and Merchandise Marks Act, 1958. This Act provides protection to the consumers for wrong use of trade mark.

9. **The Competition Act 2002 :** This Act has replaced the monopolies and restrictive trade practices Act 1969. This Act is formed to encourage healthy competition and protect consumers from companies which hamper competition.

10. The Bureau of Indian Standard Act 1986 : This Act is formed to provide special marks to products which fulfill some minimum quality standards. The common mark issued under this Act is ISI mark. This act has set up a grievance cell where consumer can make a complaint about a product which is not up to a quality mark and are having 181 Mark.

☞ **Consumer Rights**

Although businessmen is aware of his social responsibilities even then we come across many cases of consumer exploitation. That is why government of India provided following rights to all the consumers under the Consumer Protection Act:

1. **Right to Safety :** It means a consumer has right to be protected against the marketing of such goods and services that are harmful to life and health. For example, electrical appliances can cause

serious injury if they are manufactured with substandard products or do not conform to the safety norms. Thus, the consumer should be educated to use ISI marked electrical appliances.

2.   **Right to Information :** A consumer has the right to get true and complete information about the quality, quantity, price, contents, date of manufacture and expiry etc of the goods and services which he intends to buy. It is for this reason that the Consumer Protection Act has made it compulsory for the business firms to provide such information on the package and label of the product.

3.   **Right to Choose :** Consumers have the freedom to choose products of their choice. It further implies that suppliers are bound to supply a variety of products to the customers and allow the consumers to choose a product from amongst those available. The supplier must offer a variety of products in terms of quality, size, prices etc. so that the consumers can purchase the products according to their preferences.

4.   **Right to be Heard or Right to Representation :** According to this right, consumer is allowed to file a complaint and to be heard if he finds himself exploited or is not satisfied with the goods and services. Many business organisations have set up their own consumer service and grievances cell on the basis of this right. Moreover, many other organisations are also working under this direction and aim at redressal of consumer's grievances.

5.   **Right to Seek Redressal :** The right to seek redressal is justified for dignified living because this right provides an opportunity to an exploited consumer to get relief in case a product or service falls short of his expectations. This right assures justice to consumers against exploitation and includes compensation for any loss or injury suffered by the consumers, replacement of goods or repair of defects in the goods to their full satisfaction.

6.   **Right to Consumer Education :** The consumer should have knowledge about the various right and relief provided by the legislations to product their interest. Many business firms, consumer organisations and even government is taking active part in educating people in this respect. The concept of consumer education has been introduced in school curriculum and various university courses too. Also, media is being used in this respect.

Apart from the above six rights two additional rights are recommended by the UNO (United Nations Organisation)
These are:

7.   **Right to Basic Needs :** Every human being has the right to fulfill his basic needs and to lead a dignified life. The goods and services included in the basic needs are food, clothing, health care, drinking water, sanitation, shelter etc. Likewise, education, energy and transportation etc. are essential for a dignified living.

8.   **Right to Healthy Environment :** Healthy environment enhances the quality of life. According to this, a consumer has the right healthy and peaceful environment. This right insists on providing a pollution free, tension free and healthy environment for us all at all times.

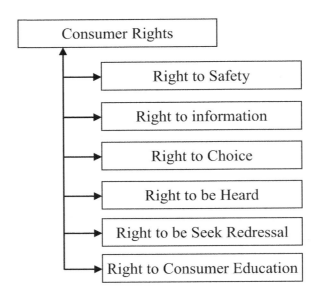

☞ **Consumer Responsibilities**

Various efforts have been made by government and nongovernment organisations to protect the interest of consumer but exploitation of consumer will stop only when consumer himself will come forward to safeguard his own interest. Consumers have to bear some responsibilities which are given below:

(i)   **To provide adequate information to the seller :** The consumer has the responsibility to provide adequate information about his needs and expectations to the seller. This would enable the seller to provide right kind of products and services to the consumers.

(ii) **To exercise caution in purchasing :** The consumer must try to get full information on the quality, design, utility, quantity, price, etc. of the product before purchasing it. Thus, he should not buy blindly.

(iii) **To insist on cash memo or receipt :** The consumer must get a cash memo or receipt as a proof of purchase of goods from the seller. This would help him in making a complain to the seller in case of any defect in the goods. Further, if the goods (e.g. pressure cooker, T.V., Fridge, etc.) carry any warranty, the buyer must obtain the warranty card mentioning the cate of purchase, and period of warranty. It must also bear the signature and stamp of the sever.

(iv) **To file complaint against genuine grievances :** The consumer must file a complaint with the seller or manufacturer about any defect or shortcoming in the products and services, He should neither consider it a waste of time nor overlook the defect considering it a small loss.

(v)   **To be quality conscious :** The consumer should never compromise on the quality of goods. While making a purchase, the consumer must look for standard quality certification marks such as ISI, Agmark, Wool mark, FPO (Fruit Product Order) Hall Mark, eco mark etc. For example, electric, electric iron must carry ISI mark.

ECOMARK

(vi) **To be cautions against false and misleading advertisements :** The manufacturers/sellers often exaggerate the quality of their goods through advertisement. It is the responsibility of the consumer not to be carried away by such advertisements. If he finds any discrepancy in the features advertised and the actual features of the product, he must bring it to the notice of the seller or advertiser.

(vii) **To exercise his legal rights :** The consumer has right to safety, right to be informed, right to choose, right to representation, right to seek redressal and right to seek information. If any of these rights in violated by the manufacturer or seller, the consumer must file a complaint with the legal machinery constituted under the Consumer Protection Act, 1986.

☞ **Ways and Means of Consumer Protections**

In India large number of consumers are living below poverty line and large number are illiterate and unaware of their right so consumer protection movement cannot be the same as followed by developed countries. In India it has to be a social movement wherein people of all walks of life have to play their role. Following are some ways and means of consumer protection followed in India:

1. **Self Regulations by Business :** Large Business houses have realized that they can prosper and grow for a long period of time only by giving due importance to consumers. Socially responsible firms follow quality standards and have started customer grievances cell to attend the complaints of consumers.

2. **Business Associations :** Various business associations such as Federation of Indian Chamber of Commerce and Industry (FICCI) and Confederation of Indian Industry (CV) have framed a set of code of conducts which lay down guidelines for dealing with customers.

3. **Consumer Awareness :** It is not easy to exploit an educated and well aware consumers. Consumer must be well aware about his rights, responsibilities and relief available to him under consumer protection act.

4. **Consumer Organisations :** Consumer organisations play an important role in educating consumers regarding their rights, duties. These organsiations also help consumer to get relief in case of exploitation.

5. **Government :** Government of India has framed a set of laws and legislations to protect the interests of consumers and the most important act framed by Govt. is Consumer Protection Act 1986. This act has provided three tier redressal agencies i.e., District Forum, National Commission and State Commission. Some Important Terms Defines in Consumer Protection Act and Some Important Questions answered in Consumer Protection Act

Q.1   Who is a Consumer?
Ans.   According to consumer protection act a consumer is
        (a)   One who buys goods or hires services for some value.

(b)   Any user of such goods or beneficiary of services with approval of the buyer.

(c)   Any one who uses the goods bought or services hired for earning livelihood by self-employment.

Q.2   When or under what circumstances the complaints can be filed?

Ans.   Complaints can be filed and compensation can be claimed by the consumer with respect to

(i)   an unfair trade practice has been adopted by a trader or manufacturer, e.g., offered goods hazardous to life and health.

(ii)   the goods bought suffer from any defect.

(iii)   the services hired suffer from any deficiency.

(iv)   a trader has charged for goods a price in excess of the price displayed on the label/package.

Q.3   Where the complaints can be filed or which judicial machineries are available to deal with consumer grievances?

Ans.   There are three important judicial machineries or three important redressal forums available to deal with consumer grievances. These are:

(i)   District Forum to deal with complaints where the value of goods and compensation claim does not exceed Rs.20 Lakh. (In 1987 it was only 1 lakh)

(ii)   State Commission to deal with cases where the value of goods or compensation is more than 20 Lakh but does not exceed 1 crore. (In 1987 it was Rs.10 Lakh)

(iii)   National Commission to take up all cases exceeding the value of Rs. 1 crore. (Earlier it was Rs. 10 Lakh)

Appeals against district forum can be filed in State Commission within 30 days and the person who is declared guilty has to deposit Rs.25,000 or 50% of fine amount whichever is less.

The appeal against the State Commission can be filed with National Commission within 30 days and the person who is declared guilty by State Commission has to deposit Rs.35,000 or 50% of amount of compensation whichever is less.

Q.4   Within what period the complaint can be filed?

Ans.   The complaint must be filed within 2 years from the day of course of action.

Q.5   What reliefs or remedies are available to consumer on complaints filed by him? Ms. Following reliefs are available to consumer:

(a)   Removal of defects from the goods.

(b)   Replacement of the goods.

(c)   Refund of the price paid.

(d)   Compensation of loss or injury suffered.

(e)   Removal of deficiency in service.

(f)   Discontinuance of unfair trade practices.

(g)   Stopping the sale of hazardous market.

(h)   Withdrawal of hazardous goods from market.

(i)   Payment of adequate cost to grieved party.

(j)   To issue corrective advertisement to neutralize the effect of a misleading advertisement.

Q.6   Who are not considered as consumer under Consumer Protection Act 1986?

Ans.   Following persons are not considered as Consumer under Consumer Protection Act:

(i)   The person who obtains goods for re-sale.

(ii)   The person who uses the goods without the approval of the buyer.

(iii)   The person who avails of the services without the approval of the hirer.

(iv)   The person who obtains goods without any consideration.

(v)   The person who hires or avails of any services without consideration.

Q.7   Who can file a complaint?

Ans.   A complaint can be filed by:

(i)   Any consumer.

(ii)   Any registered Consumer Association.

(iii)   The central or state government.

(iv)   One or more consumers on behalf of numerous consumers.

(v)   A legal heir or representative of a deceased consumer.

☞ **Three Tier Consumer Grievances Machinery Under the Consumer Protection Act**

1.   **District Forum :** District Forum consists of a president and two other members. One of whom should be woman. The president can be retired or working judge of District Court. They are appointed by state government. The complaints for goods or services worth Rs.20 lakhs or less can be filled in this agency. The agency sends the goods for testing in laboratory if required and gives decisions on the basis of facts and laboratory report. If the aggrieved party is not satisfied by the jurisdiction of the district forum then they can file an appeal against the judgment in State Commission within 30 days by depositing 25,000 or 50% of the penalty amount whichever is less.

2.   **State Commission :** It consisted of a president and two other members. One of whom should be woman. The president must be a retired or working of high court. They all are appointed by state government. The complaints for the goods worth more than 20 lakhs and less than Rs.1 crore can be filed in State Commission on receiving complaint the State Commission contacts the party against whom the complaint is filed and sends the goods for testing in laboratory if required. in case aggrieved party is not satisfied with the judgement then they can file an appeal in National Commission within 30 days by depositing Rs.35,000 or 50% of penalty amount whichever is less.

3.   **National Commission :** The national commission consists of a president and four members one of whom shall be a woman. They are appointed by Central Government. The complaint can be flied in National Commission if the value of goods exceed Rs.1 crore. On receiving the complaint the National Commission informs the party against whom complaint is filed and sends the goods for testing if required and gives judgment. If aggrieved party is not satisfied with the judgment then they can file a complaint in Supreme Court within 30 days.

Redressal Agencies Under the Consumer Protection Act, 1986 and their Jurisdiction

Basis	District	State Commission	National Commission
Composition	It consists of a president and two other members.	It consists of a president and two other members.	It consists of a president and four other members.
Who can be a President	A working or retired judge of District Court.	A working or retired judge of High Court.	A working or retired judge of Supreme Court.
Appointment of President	The President is appointed by the state government on the recommendation of the selection committee.	The president is appointed by the state government after consultation with the chief justice of the High Court.	The president is appointed by the Central government after consultation with the chief justice of India.
Jurisdiction	In 1986, it had jusidiction to entertain complaints where the value of goods	In 1986, it had jusidiction to entertain complaints when the value of goods	In 1986, it had jusidiction to entertain complaints where the value of goods

	or services does not exceed Rs. 5,00,000 but not the limit is raised to 20 lakh.	or services exceed Rs. 5,00,000 and does not exceed Rs. 20 lakh but now it is raised to more than 20 lakh and upto 1 crore.	or services exceed Rs. 20 lakh but now the limit is raised and it entertains the complaints of goods or services where the value exceed Rs. 1 crore.
Appeal against orders	Any person who is aggrieved by the order of District Forum can appeal against such order to State Commission within 30 days and by depositing Rs. 25,000 or 50% of the penalty amount whichever is less.	Any person who is aggrieved by the order of State Commission can appeal against such order to National Commission within 30 days and by depositing Rs. 35,000 or 50% of penalty amount whichever is less.	Any person who is aggrieved by the order of the National Commission can appeal against such order to Supreme Court within 30 days and by depositing 50% of penalty amount but only cases where value goods or services exceed Rs. 1 Crore can flue appeal in Supreme court.

☞ **Role of Consumer Organisations and NGO's**

In India there are about 500 consumer organsiations working in the field of consumer protection. The most popular are: Consumer Guidance Society of India (Mumbai), Citizen Action Group (Mumbai), Consumer Education and Research Centre (CERC) Ahemdabad, Common Cause (New Delhi) etc. Consumer Unity and Trust Society (CUTS). These associations are performing following functions:

(i)   Bringing out brochures, journals etc.

(ii)   Spreading consumer awareness.

(iii)   Collecting data of different products and testing them.

(iv)   Arrange seminar, conferences for the purpose of focussing on the problems of consumers.

(v)   Encouraging the consumers to boycott the goods of bad quality or harmful contents for example, CERC spread awareness among general public regarding pesticide contents in cola drinks and encourage the consumers to boycott the use of cold drinks.

(vi)   Filing suits or complaints on behalf of customers.

(vii)   Educating the consumers to help themselves.

(viii) Running voluntary complaint counters for consumer guidance and counselling.

(ix)   Helping government agencies to resolve cases of consumer exploitation and to carry on consumer awareness programs.

(x)   Educating women regarding consumerism.

(xi)   Motivating people to ask for quality marks such as ISI mark, Agmark etc.

☞ **Role of the Press**

Newspapers and magazines have been contributing for the needs of consumers much before the enactment of Consumer Protection Act. Various articles and columns dealing with consumer complaints and harassment are published. The Indian Express was the first newspaper to start a consumer complaint column and in many cases these complaints were referred to redressal forum by newspaper agencies and the result of redressal was also referred was also published. The success and popularity of column. Now almost all the leading newspapers are including this column and even some of the regional language newspapers have also started this column.

Along with print media, visual media is also playing an important role to spread awareness about consumer protection as many advertisements are shown with message of Jago Grahak and a special programme on right to consumer is shown i.e., Apne Adhikar. Various &lows are arranged in Vigyan Bhawan.

☞ **Role of Universities/Schools**

The schools and colleges can play a very important role by making students aware of consumerism. Indira Gandhi National Open University (IGNOU) has developed a complete syllabus which provides the basic framework for other universities to chalk out the curriculum of consumer education.

The "Kakitaya University" in Warrangal, Andhra Pradesh, is already running a one year post-graduation course in Consumer law. Maharasthra University has also started a course in Consumer Education in Pune. The CBSE has included consumer protection in syllabus of Class X and XII. CBSE has also published a teacher's manual on consumer education with live examples of consumer exploitation and activities of redressal forums.

EXERCISE – 1

Q.1   Ahmed wants to buy an iron. As an unware customer, how can he be sure about the quality of iron ?

Q.2   Mohit filed a case against Domestic coolings Ltd.' in the 'District Forum' but he was not satisfied with the order of the District Forum. Where can he appeal further against the decisions of District Forum?

Q.3   Rita wants to buy a packet of juice. As an ware customer, how can she be sure about the quality of juice she plans to buy?

Q.4   Amrit filed a case against Volvo Ltd.' in the State Commission'. But he was not satisfied with the order of the 'State commission'. Name the authority to which he can appeal against the decision of 'State commission'.

Q.5   Anjana wants to buy a gold ring. As an aware consumer, how can she be sure about the quality of gold ring she is going to buy?

Q.6   Amita filed a case against' Mahindra Ltd in the' National Commission'. But she was not satisfied with the orders of the 'National Commission'. Name the authority where she can appeal against the decisions of the' National Commission.

Q.7   Why is consumer protection necessary?

Q.8   Mention when as a consumer you are not in a position to resolve your grievances under Consumer Protection Act.

Q.9   Explain the 'Right to Safety'.

Q.10   Explain the concept of 'consumer protection'.

Q.11   Who can file a complaint on behalf of a deceased consumer?

Q.12. Which Act of Consumer protection provides for the formation of Consumer protection Councils' in every district and the state of the country?

Q.13.   Why Consumer protection is important for consumers? Give any one reason

Q.14.   Why should a consumer look for ISI mark on electrical goods?

Q15   Why consumer protection is important for a businessman ? Give any on reason

Q.16   Which Act of consumer protection provides safety to consumers against deficient services?

Q.17   Which kind of cases can be filed in the state commission under the Consumer Protection Act 1986 ?

Q.18   As a responsible consumer, how will you ensure about the quality of a juice packet purchased by you?

Q.19   Which cases can be filed in the National Commission under Consumer Protection Act. 1986?

Q.20   Name any two Non-Governmental Organisation (NGOs) which are working in India to protect and promote the consumer interests

Q.21   State, what is to be informed to the consumer under 'Right to be informed'.

Q.22   When can a consumer get more than on relief for a complaint?

EXERCISE – 2

Q.1   Explain the following as ways and means of consumer protection
         (i)   Consumer awareness
         (ii)   Government.

Q.2   Explain the following rights of a consumer.
         (i)   Right to choose
         (ii)   Right to seek red ressal

Q.3   Explain the following right of a consumer;
         (i)   Right to choose
         (ii)   Right to be informed

Q.   4 Explain the following rights of a consumer;
         (i)   Right to safety
         (ii)   Right to consumer education.

Q.5   Explain the following right of a consumer
         (i)   Right to be heard
         (ii)   Right to seek redressal

Q.6   What precautions should a consumer take while buying a product or service?

Q.7   Explain the following:
         (i)   Right of consumers': (Right to safety),
         (ii)   Right to choose

Q.8   Define consumer protection and state any three points of importance of consumer protection from the point of view of business.

Q.9   Anita purchased a book form 'Satish Book Stores'. While reading the book she found that ten page were missing. She approached the seller of the book and complained about the missing page. The seller promised that if the publisher was ready to change the book he would change the same. After a week the seller informed Anita that the publisher had refused to change the book.

Where can Anita file a complaint against the seller of book ? Give reason in support of your answer. Also, explain who is a 'consumer'.

EXERCISE – 3

Q.1   State any six functions of consumer organisation and NGOs for protecting and promoting the interests of consumers.

Q.2   Explain the following right of a consumer to safeguard his interests
(i)   Right to be informed
(ii)   Right to consumer education
(iii)   Right to safety

Q.3   Reena purchased on litre of pure Deshi Ghee from a shopkeeper. After using it she had a doubt that it is adulterated. She sent it for a laboratory test which confirmed that the Ghee is adulterated. State any six reliefs available to reena, if she complains and the consumer court is satisfied about the genuineness of the complaint.

Q.4   Prabhakar purchased an IS mark electric iron from 'Bharat Electricals'. While using he found seller satisfies Prabhakar by saying that he will ask the manufacture to replace this iron. The manufacturer refused to replace and Bharat Electricals decided to file a complaint in the consumer court. Can 'Bharat Electrical' do this? Why? Also explain' who is a consumer' as per consumer protection Act 1986

Part C
Project Work

CLASS XII: GUIDELINES FOR TEACHERS

Students are supposed to select one unit out of four and are required to make only ONE project from the selected unit. (Consist of one project of 20 marks)

1. Help students to select any ONE Topic for the entire year.
2. The topic should be assigned after discussion with the students in the class and should then be discussed at every stage of the submission of the project.

   The teacher should play the role of a facilitator and should closely supervise the process of project completion. The teachers must ensure that the project work assigned to the students whether individually or in group are discussed at different stages right from assignment to drafts review and finalization. Students should be facilitated in terms of providing relevant materials or suggesting websites, or obtaining required permissions from business houses, malls etc for their project. The periods assigned to the Project Work should be suitably spaced throughout the academic session. The teachers MUST ensure that the student actually go through the rigors and enjoy the process of doing the project rather than depending on any readymade material available outside.

3. The students must make a presentation of the project before the class.
4. The teachers must ensure that the student's self-esteem and creativity is enhanced and both the teacher and the student enjoy this process.
5. The teachers should feel pride in the fact that they have explored the different dimensions of the project in an innovative way and their students have put in genuine work.

I. Project One: Elements of Business Environment
The teachers should help the students in selecting any one element of the following:

1. Changes witnessed over the last few years on mode of packaging and its economic impact. The teacher may guide the students to identify the following changes:
a) The changes in transportation of fruits and vegetables such as cardboard crates being used in place of wooden crates, etc. Reasons for above changes.

b) Milk being supplied in glass bottles, later in plastic bags and now in tetra-pack and through vending machines.
c) Plastic furniture [doors and stools] gaining preference over wooden furniture.
d) The origin of cardboard and the various stages of changes and growth.
e) Brown paper bags packing to recycled paper bags to plastic bags and cloth bags.
f) Re use of packaging [bottles, jars and tins] to attract customers for their products.
g) The concept of pyramid packaging for milk.
h) Cost being borne by the consumer/manufacturer.
i) Packaging used as means of advertisements.

2. The reasons behind changes in the following:
Coca – Cola and Fanta in the seventies to Thums up and Campa Cola in the eighties to Pepsi and Coke in nineties.
The teacher may guide the students to the times when India sold Coca Cola and Fanta which were being manufactured in India by the foreign companies.

The students may be asked to enquire about

a) Reasons of stopping the manufacturing of the above mentioned drinks in India THEN.

b) The introduction of Thums up and Campa cola range.

c) Re entry of Coke and introduction of Pepsi in the Indian market.

d) Factors responsible for the change.

e) Other linkages with the above.

f) Leading brands and the company having the highest market share.

g) Different local brands venturing in the Indian market.

h) The rating of the above brands in the market.

i) The survival and reasons of failure in competition with the international brands.

j) Other observations made by the students

The teacher may develop the following on the above lines

3. Changing role of the women in the past 25 years relating to joint families, nuclear families, women as a bread earner of the family, changes in the requirement trend of mixers, washing machines, micro wave and standard of living.

4. The changes in the pattern of import and export of different Products.

5. The trend in the changing interest rates and their effect on savings.

6. A study on child labour laws, its implementation and consequences.

7. The state of 'anti plastic campaign,' the law, its effects and implementation.

8. The laws of mining /setting up of industries, rules and regulations, licences required for running that business.

9. Social factors affecting acceptance and rejection of an identified product. (Dish washer, Atta maker, etc)

10. What has the effect of change in environment on the types of goods and services? The students can take examples like:

a) Washing machines, micro waves, mixers and grinder.

b) Need for crèche, day care centre for young and old.

c) Ready to eat food, eating food outside, and tiffin centres.

11. Change in the man-machine ratio with technological advances resulting in change of cost structure.

12. Effect of changes in technological environment on the behaviour of employee.

II. Project Two: Principles of Management

The students are required to visit any one of the following:

1. A departmental store.

2. An Industrial unit.

3. A fast food outlet.

4. Any other organisation approved by the teacher.

They are required to observe the application of the general Principles of management advocated by Fayol.

Fayol's principles

1. Division of work.

2. Unity of command.

3. Unity of direction.

4. Scalar chain

5. Espirit de corps

6. Fair remuneration to all.

7. Order.

8. Equity.

9. Discipline

10. Subordination of individual interest to general interest.
11. Initiative.
12. Centralisation and decentralisation.
13. Stability of tenure.

OR

They may enquire into the application of scientific management techniques by F.W. Taylor in the unit visited.

Scientific techniques of management.
1. Functional foremanship.
2. Standardisation and simplification of work.
3. Method study.
4. Motion Study.
5. Time Study.
6. Fatigue Study
7. Differential piece rate plan.

Tips to teacher
(i) The teacher may organize this visit.
(ii) The teacher should facilitate the students to identify any unit of their choice and guide them to identify the principles that are being followed.
(iii) Similarly they should guide the students to identify the techniques of scientific management implemented in the organisation.
(iv) It may be done as a group activity.
(v) The observations could be on the basis of
□ The different stages of division of work resulting to specialisation.
□ Following instructions and accountability of subordinates to higher authorities.
□ Visibility of order and equity in the unit.
□ Balance of authority and responsibility.
□ Communication levels and pattern in the organisation.

□ Methods and techniques followed by the organisation for unity of direction and coordination amongst all.
□ Methods of wage payments followed.The arrangements of fatigue study.
□ Derivation of time study.
□ Derivation and advantages of method study.
□ Organisational chart of functional foremanship.
□ Any other identified in the organisation
vi. It is advised that students should be motivated to pick up different areas of visit. As presentations of different areas in the class would help in better understanding to the other students.
vii. The students may be encouraged to develop worksheets. Teachers should help students to prepare observation tools to be used for undertaking the project.
Examples; worksheets, questionnaire, interviews and organisational chart etc.

III. Project Three: Stock Exchange
The purpose of this project is to teach school students the values of investing and utilising the stock market. This project also teaches important lessons about the economy, mathematics and financial responsibility.

The basis of this project is to learn about the stock market while investing a specified amount of fake money in certain stocks. Students then study the results and buy and sell as they see fit.

This project will also guide the students and provide them with the supplies necessary to successfully monitor stock market trends and will teach students how to calculate profit and loss on stock.

The project work will enable the students to:
- understand the topics like sources of business finance and capital market
- understand the concepts used in stock exchange
- inculcate the habit of watching business channels, reading business journals/newspapers and seeking information from their elders.

The students are expected to:
a) Develop a brief report on History of Stock Exchanges in India. (your country)
b) Prepare a list of at least 25 companies listed on a Stock Exchange.
c) To make an imaginary portfolio totalling a sum of Rs. 50,000 equally in any of the 5 companies of their choice listed above over a period of twenty working days.

The students may be required to report the prices of the stocks on daily basis and present it diagrammatically on the graph paper.
- They will understand the weekly holidays and the holidays under the Negotiable Instruments Act.
They will also come across with terms like closing prices, opening prices, etc.
- During this period of recording students are supposed to distinctively record the daily and starting and closing prices of the week other days under the negotiable instrument act so that they acquire knowledge about closing and opening prices.
- The students may conclude by identifying the causes in the fluctuations of prices. Normally it would be related to the front page news of the a business journal, for example,

- Change of seasons.
- Festivals.
- Spread of epidemic.
- Strikes and accidents
- Natural and human disasters.
- Political environment.
- Lack of faith in the government policies.
- Impact of changes in government policies for specific industry.
- International events.
- Contract and treaties at the international scene.
- Relations with the neighbouring countries.
- Crisis in developed countries, etc.

The students are expected to find the value of their investments and accordingly rearrange their portfolio. The project work should cover the following aspects;
1. Graphical presentation of the share prices of different companies on different dates.
2. Change in market value of shares due to change of seasons, festivals, natural and human disasters.
3. Change in market value of shares due to change in political environment/ policies of various countries/crisis in developed countries or any other reasons
4. Identify the top ten companies out of the 25 selected on the basis of their market

IV. Project Four: Marketing

1. Adhesives
2. Air conditioners
3. Baby diapers
4. Bathing Soap
5. Bathroom cleaner
6. Bike
7. Blanket
8. Body Spray
9. Bread
10. Breakfast cereal
11. Butter
12. Camera
13. Car
14. Cheese spreads
15. Chocolate
16. Coffee
17. Cosmetology product
18. Crayons
19. Crockery
20. Cutlery
21. Cycle
22. DTH
23. Eraser
24. e-wash
25. Fairness cream
26. Fans
27. Suitcase/ airbag
28. Sunglasses
29. Tea
30. Tiffin Wallah
31. Toothpaste
32. Wallet
33. Water bottle
34. Water storage tank
35. Wipes
36. Washing machine
37. Fruit candy
38. Furniture
39. Hair Dye
40. Hair Oil
41. Infant dress
42. Inverter
43. Jams
44. Jeans
45. Jewellery
46. Kurti
47. Ladies bag
48. Ladies footwear
49. Learning Toys
50. Lipstick
51. Microwave oven
52. Mixers
53. Mobile
54. Moisturizer
55. Music player
56. Nail polish
57. Newspaper
58. Noodles
59. Pen
60. Pen drive
61. Pencil
62. Pickles
63. Razor
64. Ready Soups
65. Refrigerator
66. RO system
67. Roasted snacks
68. Salt
69. Sarees
70. Sauces/ Ketchup
71. Shampoo
72. Shaving cream
73. Shoe polish
74. Shoes
75. Squashes Washing powder
76. Washing detergent

Any more as suggested by the teacher.

The teacher must ensure that the identified product should not be items whose consumption/use is discouraged by the society and government like alcohol products/pan masala and tobacco products, etc.

Identify one product/service from the above which the students may like to manufacture/provide [pre-assumption].

Now the students are required to make a project on the identified product/service keeping in mind the following:
1. Why have they selected this product/service?
2. Find out '5' competitive brands that exist in the market.
3. What permission and licences would be required to make the product?
4. What are your competitors Unique Selling Proposition.[U.S.P.]?
5. Does your product have any range give details?
6. What is the name of your product?
7. Enlist its features.
8. Draw the 'Label' of your product.
9. Draw a logo for your product.
10. Draft a tag line.
11. What is the selling price of your competitor's product?
(i) Selling price to consumer
(ii) Selling price to retailer
(iii) Selling price to wholesaler

What is the profit margin in percentage to the
   ☐ Manufacturer.
   ☐ Wholesaler.
   ☐ Retailer.
12. How will your product be packaged?
13. Which channel of distribution are you going to use? Give reasons for selection?
14. Decisions related to warehousing, state reasons.
15. What is going to be your selling price?
   (i) To consumer
   (ii) To retailer
   (iii) To wholesaler

16. List 5 ways of promoting your product.
17. Any schemes for
   (i) The wholesaler
   (ii) The retailer
   (iii) The consumer
18. What is going to be your 'U.S.P?
19. What means of transport you will use and why?
20. Draft a social message for your label.
21. What cost effective techniques will you follow for your product.
22. What cost effective techniques will you follow for your promotion plan.

At this stage the students will realise the importance of the concept of marketing mix and the necessary decision regarding the four P's of marketing.

☐ Product

☐ Place

☐ Price

☐ Promotion

On the basis of the work done by the students the project report should include the following:

1. Type of product /service identified and the (consumer/industries) process involve there in.

2. Brand name and the product.

3. Range of the product.

4. Identification mark or logo.

5. Tagline.

6. Labeling and packaging.

7. Price of the product and basis of price fixation.

8. Selected channels of distribution and reasons thereof.

9. Decisions related to transportation and warehousing. State reasons.

10. Promotional techniques used and starting reasons for deciding the particular technique.

11. Grading and standardization.

Presentation and Submission of Project Report

At the end of the stipulated term, each student will prepare and submit his/her project report.

Following essentials are required to be fulfilled for its preparation and submission.

1. The total length of the project will be of 25 to 30 pages.

2. The project should be handwritten.

3. The project should be presented in a neat folder.

4. The project report should be developed in the following sequence-

☐ Cover page should include the title of the Project, student information, school and year.

☐ List of contents.

☐ Acknowledgements and preface (acknowledging the institution, the places visited and the persons who have helped).

☐ Introduction.

☐ Topic with suitable heading.

☐ Planning and activities done during the project, if any.

☐ Observations and findings of the visit.

☐ Conclusions (summarized suggestions or findings, future scope of study).

☐ Photographs (if any).

☐ Appendix

☐ Teacher's observation.

☐ Signatures of the teachers.

☐ At the completion of the evaluation of the project, it should be punched in the centre so that the report may not be reused but is available for reference only.

☐ The project will be returned after evaluation. The school may keep the best projects.

ASSESSMENT

Allocation of Marks = 20 Marks

The marks will be allocated under the following heads:

1	Initiative, cooperativeness and participation	2 Mark
2	Creativity in presentation	2 Mark
3	Content, observation and research work	4 Marks
4	Analysis of situations	4 Marks
5	Viva	8 Marks
	Total	**20 Marks**

Part-D:
EXAMINATION ZONE

CBSE

Class XII Business Studies

Time: 3 hrs   Max. Marks: 80

General Instructions:

i.   Marks for questions are indicated against each question.

ii.   Question Nos. 1–20 are objective type/MCQ questions carrying 1 mark each.

iii.   Question Nos. 21-25 are short answer I questions carrying 3 marks each.

iv.   Question Nos. 26–28 are short answer II questions carrying 4 marks each.

v.   Question Nos. 29–31 are long answer I questions carrying 5 marks each.

vi.   Question Nos. 32–34 are long answer II questions carrying 6 marks each.

SECTION A

1   "This Act defines the various relief alternatives in case the goods or services purchased by a consumer are not as per implied conditions or warranties" Which of the following Acts passed by the Government of India is being referred in the above statement? (Choose the correct alternative)

   (a)   The Contract Act, 1982

   (b)   The Competition Act, 2002

   (c)   The Sale of Goods Act, 1930

   (d)   The Essential Commodities Act, 1955

2   'This function of management involves setting standards of performance and accordingly comparing the present performance with the set standards.' Name the function of management being described in the given statement?

3   An employee can delegate his/her accountability in an organisation to some extent. (True/False)

4   According to the functional foremanship technique, there would be a _____ under the production in charge who would supervise the quality of work done.

   (a)   Inspector

   (b)   Workman

   (c)   Gang boss

   (d)   Disciplinarian

5   Which of the following statements is not true with respect to business environment?

   (a)   Business environment keeps changing.

   (b)   It is very difficult to predict business environment.

   (c)   Business environment remains the same across regions.

(d)   Various parts of a business are interrelated.

6   _____is a process which helps in increasing participation of subordinates in the organisation and grants them autonomy.

(a)   Organising

(b)   Decentralisation

(c)   Centralisation

(d)   None of these

7   In case an aggrieved party is not satisfied with the judgment of the National Commission, an appeal can be filed in the   .

(a)   State court

(b)   District court

(c)   Supreme court

(d)   None of the above

8   Which of the following statements is not true with regard to planning?

(a)   Planning is done for an infinite time.

(b)   Planning is done by managers at all levels.

(c)   Planning is concerned with setting objectives.

(d)   Planning defines the course of action to be followed

9   Name the marketing management philosophy which believes customer satisfaction to be the key to success.

10   The process of selection starts with .

(a)   Tests

(b)   Screening

(c)   Personal interview

(d)   Background checks

11   Debt financing is suitable when the organisation has a weak cash flow.

12   Which of the following alternatives is correct with regard to the given statements?

Statement 1: Controlling identifies the deviation from pre- defined standards.

Statement 2: An effort must be made to control everything in the organisation.

(a)   Only Statement 1 is correct.

(b)   Only Statement 2 is correct.

(c)   Both statements are correct.

(d)   Both statements are incorrect.

13   Radheshyam manufactures Ayurvedic medicines which help to reduce hair loss. He sells these medicines from his house. After researching a lot about ways to increase his sale, he decided to go to public places like railway stations, gardens etc. and gather a crowd to explain about the benefits of this medicine. He thought that this would help him to convey the features of this medicine to a lot of people and thereby increase his sales. Identify the tool of promotion reflected in the given case.

14   A form of communication in which information flows in all directions is called   communication.

(a)   Lateral

(b)   Vertical

(c)   Grapevine

(d)   Horizontal

15   Consumer protection is only important for the consumers. (True/False)

16   All trade in securities must be settled within days of the trade date.

(a)   3

(b)   5

(c)   2

(d)   10

17   ABC Ltd. is ready to take a financial risk but does not want to dilute control of its management? Which of the following sources of finance should it opt for?

(a)   Debentures

(b)   Equity finance

(c)   Preference share capital

(d)   None of the above

18   Who of the following can file a complaint in the consumer court?

(a)   Consumer

(b)   Central and state government

(c)   Registered consumer association

(d)   All of the above

19   Capital structure is optimal when the ratio of debt and_____ is such that the value of increases.

(a)   Equity, debt

(b)   Equity, equity share

(c)   Retained earnings, debt

    (d)   Retained earnings, equity share

20   Which of the following financial instruments is not traded in the capital market?

    (a)   Bonds

    (b)   Equity

    (c)   Debentures

    (d)   Commercial paper

SECTION B

21   Define planning. Why does planning precede all other functions of management?

22   AB Ltd. opened a new division in the organisation which deals with women's apparel. For this, it has identified and estimated the requirements of human resource. It now plans to hire competent and skilled personnel for the same.

    a)   Identify the function of management reflected in the question.

    b)   State two points highlighting the importance of the function

            identified above.

23   Explain the any three principles of directing.

                  OR

State any three differences between a manager and a leader.

24   PK Ltd. wants funds for opening a new factory. It finalised two sources for the same. First, it identified a group of investors to which it sold its securities. Second, it offered its existing shareholders new shares which would be a proportion of the shares already held by them.

Identify and explain the methods of floatation reflected in the above example.

25   Kalpana Ltd. manufactures laptops, mobile phones and tablets. Which type of organisational structure should be adopted by them? Give reason. Write two advantages of the identified structure.

SECTION C

26   Explain any four characteristics of management.

27   The business environment is constantly changing. It can be observed that increased awareness of healthcare has increased the demand for many health products and services such as Diet Coke, fat-free cooking oil and health resorts. Further, there are also continuous changes in fashion and tastes of consumers and technological improvements.

Identify and explain the features of business environment highlighted in above paragraph. Also, quote the lines from the paragraph.

28   Explain the importance of consumer protection from the point of view of a business. (Any 2 points)

                  OR

Explain in detail any two rights of a consumer.

SECTION D

29   "Although planning is essential for an organisation, it is not always possible for the organisation to adhere to the plans and the planning may fail." In light of the above statement, explain in detail any five limitations of planning.

OR

Enumerate any five features of planning.

30   Shreya works as an accountant in AI Ltd. Although her salary is at par with industry standards,   she feels that her designation is not according to her skills, knowledge and work experience.

a)   Identify the incentive which would be best suitable in the given situation.

b)   Explain four other such incentives.

OR

Explain the importance of motivation in an organisation.

31   Explain the modern techniques of controlling.

SECTION E

32   Explain any three scientific principles of management given by Taylor?

OR

Discuss the points explaining the importance of principles of management.

33   What is financial planning? What are its objectives? State any three points highlighting the importance of financial planning.

34   According to the governing rules for food items, it is mandatory to specify the ingredients and contents of the product on the package of the product.

a)   Identify the aspect of product reflected in the above question.

b)   What are the functions performed by the aspect identified above?

OR

Explain the role of marketing in a firm and in the economy.

CBSE

Class XII Business Studies

Time: 3 hrs   Max. Marks: 80

General Instructions:

i.   Marks for questions are indicated against each question.

ii.   Question Nos. 1–20 are objective type/MCQ questions carrying 1 mark each.

iii.   Question Nos. 21-25 are short answer I questions carrying 3 marks each.

iv.   Question Nos. 26–28 are short answer II questions carrying 4 marks each.

v.   Question Nos. 29–31 are long answer I questions carrying 5 marks each.

vi.   Question Nos. 32–34 are long answer II questions carrying 6 marks each.

Section – A

1   Management is a.
     A Science;
     b. An Art;
     c. both science and art;
     d. Neither.

2   The purchase, production and sales managers at Sharda Ltd, a firm manufacturing readymade garments are generally at a conflict, as they have their own objectives. Usually each thinks that only they are qualified to evaluate, judge and decide on any matter, according to their professional criteria. Name the concept which will be required by the CEO Mr. Raman, to reconcile the differences in approach interest or opinion in the organisation.

3   Principles of management are NOT:

     a. Applicable only in large firms;

     b. Formed by practice and experience of managers;

     c. Flexible;

     d. Contingent

4   _____ is considered a major element of the political environment:

     a. The extent and nature of government intervention in business;

     b. planned outlay in public and private sectors;

     c. Expectations from the work force;

     d. Administrative order issued by government authorities.

5   Name the step in the process of planning which is considered the "real point of

     decision making".

6   _____gives shape to the organisation structure.

    a) Extent of delegation;

    b) Span of Management;

    ;c) No of employees;

    d) Planning

7   Astra Builders has to deliver the flats to its buyers on time. Due to this there is a sudden rush of work. Therefore, the company needs to arrange workers to work at the sites at a short notice. The source of recruitment which may be used by the company to tap the casual vacancy is:

    a. Direct recruitment;

    b. Advertisement;

    c.Recommendation of employees;

    d. Employment Exchange.

8   SCT services CEO RajanGopinath's compensation includes salary, commission and other allowances. The company also pays for his insurance and vacations. Identify one indirect payment being made by the company to the CEO.

    a.Employer paid Insurance;

    b. Salary;

    c. Commission;

    d. Allowances.

9   At Support.com, there is no reward or appreciation for a good suggestion. Thus, the subordinates are not willing to offer any useful suggestions to their superiors. Identify the type of barrier to communication that has been created in the firm due to this.

    a. Semantic barrier;

    b. Personal barrier;

    c. Organisational barrier;

    d. Psychological barrier

10   M.R.Sarthi, the Ex-chairman of Swadesh Ltd, built up his successor before retiring. Following the norms set up by himself, he handed over the reins of the company to the co-founder Mr. Shravan, who had the potential to bring about change in the behaviour of others. Name the concept of management which was the reason why Mr. Sarthi chose Mr. Shravan to be his successor.

    a. Motivation;

    b. Leadership;

    c.Communication;

    d. Staffing.

11 An important project at AMB consultants is running behind schedule by a month. This has upset their clients and might affect the reputation of the company in the long run. No managerial action like assigning more workers, equipment or giving overtime has been able to solve the problem. What managerial action may now be taken by the company to avoid such a situation from arising in the future?

a. Revise the schedule;

b. Assigning additional workers and equipment to the project;

c. Get permission for further overtime work;

d. Both B&C.

12 A decision to acquire a new & modern plant to upgrade an old one is known as decision.

a) Financing decision;

(b) working capital decision;

(c) Investment decision;

(d) Dividend decision.

13 ABC Ltd. has Debt Equity ratio of 3:1 whereas XYZ Ltd. has Debt Equity ratio of 1:1. Name the advantage ABC Ltd will have over XYZ Ltd, when the rate of interest is lower than the rate of return on investment of the company.

(a) Trading on equity;

(b) Low risk;

(c) Low cost of equity ;

(d) Greater flexibility.

14 Vikrant joins his father's business of Organic masalas, near Kotgarh in Himachal after completing his MBA. In order to capture a major share of the market, he decided to sell the product in small attractive packages by using the latest packaging technology. His father suggested that they hire financial consultants to estimate the amount of funds that would be required for the purpose & timings when it would be required. The concept being discussed by Vikrant's father, links which financial decision with the investment decision.?

a.)Dividend decision ;

(b) Financial Planning;

(C) capital structure decision;

(d)Financing decision.

15 Raghav's friend Raman works as a Chartered Accountant in Solutions Ltd. Raman in a meeting with the Board of Directors of the Company came to know that the firm would soon be declaring a Bonus issue which would result in increase in the price of shares. Considering this, Raman advised Raghav to purchase the shares of Solutions Ltd., who acted on his advice and bought the shares before time. Which function of SEBI can control such malpractices?

(a) Protective functions;

(b) Regulatory functions;

(c) Development functions;

(d) All the above.

16   Large scale production done to reduce the average cost of production is the essence of   concept of Marketing management.

a) Product;

b) Selling;

c) Production;

d) Marketing

17   Saumya decided to start a business of selling dress material from her house. She did various online surveys to find out about the preferences of prospective customers. Based on this, she prepared a detailed analysis of the business. She then made important decisions including deciding about the features, quality, packaging, labelling and branding of the dress material. Identify the element of Marketing Mix discussed above.

(a) Promotion;

(b) Market;

(c) Product;

(d) Place.

18   Tomato Ltd., a food delivery service app has recently faced criticism for the tampering of their product, by their delivery boys. Tomato Ltd. decided to put a hologram seal on the food packets in order to protect the contents from spoilage, leakage, pilferage, damage, along with a tag with a safety warning for the consumers to check the seal. Which concept of marketing discussed above is performing the important function of communicating with the potential buyer and promoting the sale.

(a) Branding;

(b) Product designing and development;

(c) labelling;

(d) packaging.

19   Asserting oneself to ensure that one gets a fair deal, is the right of a consumer. (True/False)

20   Sheela went to a free eye camp & got her eyes operated for cataract. The surgery was not done properly, due to which she lost her vision. Where can she file a complaint under consumer protection act?

(a) At District forum

(b) State commission

(c) National Commission

(d) None of above

Section – B

21   List any three tasks that Mr. Armstrong needs to do, as a production manager, in his firm, to carry out the plans laid down by the top managers.

Or

Enumerate the three economic objectives of management.

22   "Delegation of authority, undoubtedly empowers an employee to act for his superior, but the superior would still be accountable for the outcome. Explain the elements of delegation of authority discussed above.

23   Banwari Lal is a cloth merchant in Karol Bagh. His grandsons are requesting him to let them diversify the business into bridal wear. Banwari Lal has agreed but on the condition that they will follow the function of management he has always followed, which helps an organisation in keeping track of the progress of activities and ensures that the activities conform to the standards set in advance so that the organisational goals are achieved. Name the function of management which Banwari Lal is asking his grandsons to follow. List any two reasons why it is considered an indispensable function of management.

24   The Research & Development department of Healthy Production Ltd. has decided to diversify from manufacturing health drinks to cereals made from millets. They are well aware of the fact that the company will have to communicate to the people the benefits of eating millets. For this purpose, they plan to sponsor various events like marathons and encourage people to switch to healthy eating through newsletters.

a) Identify and briefly explain the promotional tool being discussed above.

b) Also explain any two other promotional tool that can be used by the company, apart from the one discussed above.

25   Rita Sharma who works as a guard in a school, purchased two shirts for ₹460 each for her son. When she went back home, she realised that the shirt was small in size for her son. She decided to ask for return of money or exchange of the shirt with an appropriate size

.But the store owner refused to return the money or exchange the shirt. Rita Sharma was disheartened. Her friend advised her to go to 'Seva Sadan', anautonomous voluntary organisation working for the protection of consumer welfare.

The organisation helped her by explaining to her the legal procedure, as well as educated her about her rights as a consumer and helped her in filing the complaint and getting relief. With the help of the organisation Rita was able to get her money back from the store. Enumerate the rights of a consumer which Rita Sharma was able to exercise with the help of the voluntary organisation.

Section - C

26   The Government is considering a pioneer proposal to launch a single debit-cum- credit card to increase the ease and usage for the consumers. The card which will be called the "National Mobility Card" will have unique advantages for making payments in metro, buses, parking and making transactions during visits abroad. After hearing this news, Mega Bank decided to launch a "Mega Mobility Card" on similar lines , so that they could be the first to exploit the opportunity, arising due to the increasing trend of digitization. In order to improve their performance, they laid down a plan to hire more people in their marketing department and prepared guidelines to train their sales force to market the new card facility being launched by the bank. By quoting the lines, identify and explain any two points of importance of understanding Business Environment discussed above.

27   Infocom has diversified itself into several product lines: Telecommunications, Engineering, financial services. Each subsidiary is self-sufficient with their-own administrative functions, propagating the belief that people can assume the responsibility for the effective implementation of their decisions and should be given autonomy. This has reduced the need for direct supervision by superiors, has promoted flexibility, initiative and faster decision making. The orders of customers are never delayed, as a result of good policy decisions of top management.

(a).   Identify and explain any two points of importance of the concept being discussed above.

(b).   Name and briefly explain a suitable framework for the company within which

the managerial and operating task are to be performed.

28   State any four factors which affect the determination of the price of the product.

OR

State the four components of physical distribution?

Section – D

29   Name and explain with a suitable example the technique of Scientific Management given by Taylor, with the objective of determining the number of workers to be employed for a task.

OR

Name and explain with a suitable example the technique of Scientific Management given by Taylor to differentiate between the efficient and the inefficient workers.

30   An Auto Company, Win ltd is facing a problem of declining market share due to increased competition from other new and existing players in the market. Its competitors are introducing lower priced models for mass consumers who are price sensitive. The Board of Directors of the Company announced a meeting to discuss the decisions regarding pricing and launching a new range of models, in order to increase the market share of the company. Attending the meeting was not a discretion for the directors and a penalty was announced for not attending the meeting. The following decisions were taken in the meeting:

a) to define the desired future position of the company, as acquiring a dominant position in the market by increasing the market share to 10% in 1 year.

b) to change the criteria for choosing vendors for procuring supplies;

c) to invest in development of the human resources of the organisation by providing training to higher levels by holding seminars and providing on the job training for the supervisory management.

What are standing plans and single use plans? Briefly explain the plans discussed above, which can be classified as standing plans, by quoting the lines.

31   What is meant by Capital Budgeting? State any four factors affecting fixed capital requirement of a firm.

OR

Enumerate any five points of importance of financial planning.

Section - E

32 Ali Mohammad the CEO of Super Ltd believes that human resource is the most important asset of the firm. He believes that no organisation can be successful unless it can fill and keep filled the various positions provided for in the structure with the right kind of people. Identify the function of management being discussed above and state the benefits to the organisation that its proper application in the

firm will ensure.

33 What is the meaning of Directing? State any four points of importance of Directing as a function of management.

OR

What is the meaning of motivation? State the features of motivation as an element of Directing.

34 Kynaa, a beauty products e-commerce company, is diversifying into men's grooming. It is also tapping the demand for beauty products in the fashion industry and amid professionals such as make-up artists. As it diversifies its online presence, Kynaa is also expanding its physical presence. They have 41 outlets across 18 cities presently and plan to expand to 180 outlets. Each store requires a capital expenditure of 60-80 lakh rupees. The company has decided to raise funds by issuing equity shares but not directly to the public, rather by offering them for sale through brokers. Identify and briefly explain the method of floatation followed by the company. Also name & explain the other methods of floatation that can be used by the company for raising funds from the public, in the primary market.

OR

Radhika got 10, 00,000 rupees after selling her parental property which she had got as a gift from her grandmother. Her friend advised her to invest in securities in the stock market. Radhika was unaware of the procedure for the same. Her friend introduced her to a stock broker, who was registered with the National Stock Exchange. Radhika approached the broker. The broker guided her to open a DEMAT account with a Depository, as well as a Bank account. Radhika opened a Bank account & DEMAT account with Exin Bank.

(a) Identify the steps in the trading procedure for buying and selling of securities which have been discussed above.

(b) State the next four steps of the trading procedure.

Printed in Great Britain
by Amazon

69076614R00140